Great Pianists of Our Time

Great Pianists
of Our Time

JOACHIM KAISER

TRANSLATED FROM THE GERMAN
BY DAVID WOOLDRIDGE AND GEORGE UNWIN

DISCOGRAPHY ADAPTED AND EXPANDED
BY F. F. CLOUGH

HERDER AND HERDER

1971
HERDER AND HERDER NEW YORK
232 Madison Avenue, New York 10016

This translation © George Allen & Unwin Ltd 1971

German Edition © Rütten & Loening Verlag GmbH, Munich 1965

Library of Congress Catalog Card Number: 77-168547

Printed in Great Britain

To the Professor
who was usually listening too

PREFACE

How do they in fact play – all the great pianists, the veterans, the established figures in their middle years, and the brilliant young ones, who currently appear on the concert platform and issue their recordings? This seems at first sight a delightful, inexhaustible subject for debate for music-lovers and the late hours. In a world that all-too-often confronts us with more calamitous subjects, and hence unfortunately more 'important' ones, we may reflect on non-political matters of art, compare non-belligerent heroes with each other, and talk about sonatas and variations. Yet, on second thoughts, it seems that the question which sounds so harmless – who are the great pianists of our time and how do they play? – is itself somewhat rash.

For every pianist who plays Bach or Schönberg or Beethoven – well or badly, wilfully or with restraint, in a dashing or pedestrian manner – gives an answer, whether he wants to or not, to the challenge that lies locked up in the great works of our piano literature. No composition is ever a secure possession. Each concert is an audible answer, sometimes quiet, but sometimes loud, to how we are coping with the 'great heritage', whether it continues to live. This answer comes not only from the pianist, but also from the audience. According to whom they acclaim, whom they reject, what they are pleased to like, and what not to like, they help to decide. It is often only a matter of tiny impulses, but these in their entirety signify a part of our culture.

Our stock-taking will be devoted to what is happening today, not to the past or to what may be desirable. We will attempt to characterize and assess in detail only those pianists who are living in our decade, giving concerts or making recordings.

For one cannot seriously pretend to speak in the same tone about Franz Liszt and Vladimir Horowitz, or d'Albert and Solomon, or W. A. Mozart as pianist and Friedrich Gulda. This is ruled out not only because the dead Lazarus must always occupy a more exalted position than the living Dives, but because there exists no basis for comparison. Of all the great ones in the history of the piano there are no recordings – or at least only a few, very indistinct 'historical' ones which tell us nothing. The almost incalculable influence which d'Albert had upon his own generation – described so vividly by Harold

Schonberg in his book *The Great Pianists from Mozart to the Present*
(Simon & Schuster, New York, 1963) – cannot with the best will in
the world be divined from those recordings which d'Albert has left
us. It seems likely that he was no longer at the height of his powers
when he made them, and he perhaps took no trouble for a medium
which was then still relatively unimportant. At any rate, only a highly
trained and sympathetic ear could deduce from such remarkably
clumsy and unrhythmical playing that a great artist was here at work –
an artist who has been described in terms of utmost reverence by all
who heard him. But if most of us today can no longer appreciate
d'Albert's artistry – as can those still alive who remember his playing –
then how much more helpless must we be in the case of Sophie
Menter, Carl Tausig or Clara Schumann, where we have no recordings and only the mute evidence of letters, reviews and eyewitness
accounts to guide us? In simply attributing to the imitators of Liszt
and the pupils of the great Viennese pedagogue Theodor Leschetitsky
all those more or less unconscious habits, wayward tempi and exaggerations of style which every generation owes to its time, we are
probably being unjust.

There can never be a definitive answer to the question whether
Vladimir Horowitz plays the Liszt B minor Sonata better or worse
than Liszt himself played it. Nowadays many musicians are inclined
to assume that music-making 'then' did not have the precision and
the finish that it has now. We know that Clara Schumann apparently
found the Brahms–Handel Variations unplayable, while pieces which
are today regarded as essential for the diploma examinations of every
conservatory were, in their time, thought to be impossible. But when
one considers the monstrous technical difficulties which Franz Liszt
piles up in his compositions, hardly in the conviction that nobody
would be able to perform them after a fashion, one wonders afresh
whether Tausig could not perhaps have done more than Cherkassky
can.

We propose to consider both public concerts and performances for
recording purposes. All the artists discussed here are appearing –
with very few exceptions – on the concert platforms of Europe and
America. The recorded 'translation' of the artistic achievement will
thus be checked against the original impression of the live concert.
Today it is certainly no longer permissible to ignore gramophone

8

records while surveying the concert world. Yet most recordings can only be truly assessed and understood when one has had the opportunity of hearing the pianist in question in the flesh, and experienced his public sense of pianistic address.

Records are often misleading. Edwin Fischer's playing was much more captivating and beautiful than his recordings suggest. The mature Backhaus on the concert platform has a gentle animation, a masculine warmth, hardly any of which comes through in his recordings.[1] Van Cliburn's effect is more forceful and brilliant in his records than in public. Alfred Brendel and Paul Badura-Skoda appear to be more collected, concentrated and committed to their playing on records than on those evenings – perhaps just 'off nights' – when I heard them. Even the mature Wilhelm Kempff sounds purer and more intimate on his records than in the concert-hall. With Sviatoslav Richter, on the other hand, his concert-hall impression surpasses that of his recordings.

The influence which the concert tradition and records have on each other will be discussed in the first chapter. The reader will be continually referred to recordings which many record-shops will maintain simply do not exist. The big firms are in the habit of deleting from their current catalogues all the records that are not selling well, or which might stand in the way of an established favourite. It is virtually impossible for the uninformed buyer to acquire records which for one reason or another have been deleted from the catalogue or not even appeared in it at all.[2] Since many remarkably good recordings are discussed in this book, and their reference numbers given in the discography, interested readers will at least have the chance to follow their inclinations.

I have constantly asked myself whether such a book about pianists may not consolidate fleeting, spontaneous impressions unjustly, and draw false conclusions from the fact that Mr X played the Appassionata particularly slowly on Friday the 13th because he had taken it much too fast at his previous recital on Wednesday the 11th, and reached the limits of his technique, of which fact Friday's listener, however, knows nothing. Such an objection is unavoidable. Nor is there any

---

[1] This is now, sad to say, in the past tense. Wilhelm Backhaus died in July 1969 (ed.).

[2] Apart from the lists of the many dealers in Deleted and Used records (ed.).

doubt that the mature Rubinstein has little to do with the 'early' Rubinstein, or that it is precisely the first-rate, adventurous pianist who is more likely to have a bad night occasionally than those who always play safe and never go astray – and so hardly ever reach a worth-while goal.

Indeed, whoever strikes this inevitable chance moment and hopes to avoid the risk of fixing young talent falsely is quarrelling, in our special case of the pianist, with imperfections that beset any attempt to capture something living, revocable and growing in permanent written form. Two biographies meet when a thirty-seven-year-old critical music-lover listens to the fifty-year-old Sviatoslav Richter playing the Brahms B flat concerto. Richter has changed, and next time, too, he will play somewhat differently – and in twenty years' time the listener may in turn have other insights and aspirations. But what does this mean? No more than that in the realm of art truth without an element of subjectivity and without a specific situation is hardly conceivable.

As soon as it is a matter of actors, conductors or pianists, as soon as people are to be characterized and not just works, which float free to suffer their own destiny – then the Moment is understood as a symbol. No one can change this or avoid it. (And even concerning works, little that is 'objective' can be said, once the sphere of aesthetic judgement is reached and that of the measurable left behind.) All the same, chance must surely be denied too sharp a victory if one hears an artist continually over the years, and if one compares concert impressions, which may be deceptive, with recordings, which the artist has made and released and so at least reveal what he will, if not what he can. And finally, a concert does represent more than a sum-total of right and wrong notes: behind it is a human being true to himself, the identity of an artistic personality which even at its extremes cannot run counter to its own laws, even if it wanted to.

All this may sound extravagant, but it can in fact be given concrete technical form. Even a first-class pianist, for instance, can have a Stygian black night, when his playing will be hair-raisingly inaccurate and unmusical. Yet even then the rhythmic tension will still be there. The left hand will perhaps accompany abominably, but not amateurishly. And the right will perhaps be harsh or dead or thoughtless in phrasing – but never cheap, never trivial. The type remains true to

10

itself, despite all temptations. (And now I await examples to the contrary . . .)

Felix Mendelssohn remarked that music is by no means always less clear than the defining word, but that it sometimes speaks of states of the soul with far finer distinctions than words can convey. There are half-tones for which no adjective is adequate.

Whoever writes about music and musicians may either try to achieve the impossible with words, or he may hope that while no single sentence can capture the unsayable, a multitude of sentences may perhaps encompass it. The second way seems to me more practicable. For one can slip all too easily into artificial, over-subtle language, drunk with nuances, if one tries to devise a fresh vocabulary for every situation. The burden rests, not on individual observations, phrases of praise or blame, but on the coherence of the whole. Some things, of course, are common to some of the best living pianists of our time – sovereignty, the tendency to neutrality or mannerism. These should not be concealed simply because they are true also of the next man. Someone writing a book about surgeons will hardly refrain from alluding to the fact that A *and* B have sure hands; someone giving an account of the saints must say whether they were pious and truth-loving people. To the writer it may be more profitable and amusing if they were not. But as a rule they are.

So one should not be surprised if great pianists also have much in common. Naturally we propose to keep our eyes more closely fixed on the differences than on the common features. But I believe it would be dishonest if in the name of over-precise analysis one were to conceal what links the best – or that there are more kinds of pianissimo than adjectives to name them.

This book is based on a series of talks commissioned by the West German Radio. Without the support of Karl O. Koch and the kind suggestions and advice of Dr Kruttge and Manfred Gräter, it would have been impossible to procure the 'listening-material', often by no means easy to come by. I hope we may all – readers, helpers, well-disposed publishers and author – be able to sit for many years at the feet of the pianists whose talents we are about to survey.

J.K.

CONTENTS

ILLUSTRATIONS

THE CONCERT TRADITION AND THE GRAMO-
PHONE RECORD

It is no surprise to come across a piano in Central Europe, in the school-room, the village hall, the local inn, on board a river steamer, or in a middle-class living-room. It is impossible to pick up a radio programme or study a concert leaflet without becoming involved in pianists and piano playing. The day when the piano lesson was as indispensable as the dancing class to the young lady of good family has vanished with the young lady herself, but its influence has persisted. Although our three-room civilization has made both serious practice and idle strumming almost intolerable to family and neighbour alike, the piano still retains its enthusiastic following. Piano teachers are not starving, youngsters are still thrust on to the concert platform by adoring parents, piano music and piano recordings enjoy large sales, and it is nothing unusual to find the local paper devoting a lengthy review to the latest performance of the Wanderer fantasy.[1]

Night after night in the small towns of our cultural area, and even more in the large ones, smartly dressed people come together in concert halls to hear a pianist – not so many as to a football match, but still, on occasion, 2,000 or more. It is true, dressing up for a concert comes more naturally to Central-Europeans than to the British, say – although a public concert tradition was already established in Britain at the beginning of the eighteenth century, whereas in Germany and Austria it was not until the middle of the century that regular concert performances became customary.

The tradition of public concerts is therefore over 200 years old. Thus it is that today, in Vienna or Munich, half a dozen or more serviceable recital halls are available, whereas in Athens, for instance, which is after all the cradle of western civilization, even the most illustrious pianist has to play in a cinema. Nothing can be taken for granted where there is no concert tradition such as we take for granted. I once heard the admirable Rena Kyriakou play Beethoven's sonata Op. 111 in an Athens cinema. Technically it was faultless, but the artist clearly had not the slightest idea just what it was she had put her hand to. The progressions of the opening Maestoso, its ecstatic

[1] Perhaps truer in Germany than elsewhere (ed.).

accents and long breath-pauses – of all this the lady's hard-working fingers said nothing. Yet the handful of listeners in the stalls of the cinema (only the front rows were occupied, mostly by foreigners and members of the diplomatic corps, with a few local people dotted about at the back) seemed to find nothing amiss. In the thirty-second-note variation of the Arietta the artist took fire, her black hair flew, her technique shone, and a well-prepared pianist became an Athena Promachos, a conquering Mediterranean goddess. It is disturbing to think that we may fail the classic Greek tragedies in just the same way.

Let us return from this Athenian modulation to our theme: the European concert tradition, which has now spread to a large part of the globe. This tradition is no gift; it has to be won, preserved, defended. For it sometimes seems as if the noble, convivial delight in the piano and its lone mode of expression belongs to a vanishing era. And one need not recall those audiences, which always seem particularly exalted and anachronistic, at Chopin recitals, for instance, where exquisite toilets, rhetorical red hair and burning, ravaged eyes suggest decadence to the aesthete, but more likely laudanum to the doctor. One might well suspect that in an age of home music-making which is indeed widespread, but threatened, of record-culture and the mass media, the necessary interest in octaves a shade too slack or grace notes a shade too nicely conceived is on the decline and to some extent the hobby of a dying class. For the concert itself represents a much-loved, but necessarily anachronistic form of public art. This form may be preserved, so long as Bach's fugues, Beethoven's sonatas, Chopin's études and Brahms's intermezzi are still a part of our musical existence and call forth spontaneous, personal interpretations.

While division of labour in its widest form, the principle of teamwork, is invading not only technology but also the arts, the pianist – like the conductor – has remained the great individualist. Whenever a solitary interpreter at the grand piano confronts a work, an orchestra and an audience, he is always surrounded therefore by an aura – just as a conductor often enough has a touch of the conjuring witch-doctor. This is no accident. In what other branch of musical reproduction does everything still depend so much on the individual, on his ability to perceive, shape and dispose, as in piano playing? Even the solo violin, even the prima donna, generally needs an accompanist or an accompanying orchestra. Conductors, too, solitary and great though they sometimes like to appear, would be dead without the response of a live orchestra. Only the pianist – and of course the organist, in a quite different way, far less visible, individual, or con-cerned with concert-recitals – is completely on his own, and offers in the age of team-work, of division of labour and the security of num-bers, the image of the great, self-reliant subject. He has something of the lone hero, of the gladiator. As long as this 'subject' can still arouse interest, as long as people still want to hear his joy and secret tears (audible to the back row), for so long will there be piano recitals.

This lone independence of the piano may be linked with the fact that keyboard instruments have since the days of Johann Sebastian Bach represented the intimate realm of many great composers. Mozart, Beethoven, Schubert, Schumann, Chopin, Liszt, Brahms and Reger appeared as concert pianists. So they all wrote 'for themselves', and turned the pianoforte into a place for their personal experiments. Beethoven on the piano was, as it were, one jump ahead of his com-posing; thus he tried out certain formal and dynamic areas of the Pathétique, the Moonlight Sonata and the D minor Sonata, Op. 31, No. 2, first on the piano. The overwhelming innovations connected with these piano discoveries, in symphonic expression or in string-quartet polyphony, always came later. Nor was it any different with Brahms. Since Chopin, Liszt, d'Albert and Rachmaninoff, moreover, the great and intelligent composer and virtuoso has existed as a type. It was highly logical that the most famous of all pianists, i.e. Franz Liszt, also introduced the solo recital, when previously miscellaneous programmes had been preferred, in which singers, orchestra and instrumental solos were permitted to succeed each other. The piano recital, let alone one devoted to a single composer, had to be 'fought' for. Today an all-too-worthy sense of style sometimes turns a concert programme into an exercise. Variety need not always mean a loss of style. At any rate, in 1835 it was still possible for Liszt, in presenting Beethoven's Moonlight Sonata to Parisians for the first time, to play only the second and third movements on the piano. The introductory Adagio, to which the C sharp minor sonata presumably owes its name, was performed on that occasion by an orchestra. The age of Liszt has vanished. When one considers the great role the piano played for composers and virtuosi of the nineteenth century, it is striking how decisively composers of the twentieth century have

19

turned away from it. Mahler, Stravinsky, Richard Strauss, Webern and Berg have left few piano works behind. Often, especially with Stravinsky, the meagre piano works assume the character of duty-pieces. With Hindemith, too, the keyboard plays no central role, nor does it with Schönberg. Only Prokofiev and Bartók – who in any case belong more among the 'moderate' moderns – wrote numerous effective sonatas, shorter pieces and concertos for their favourite instrument.

For many modern composers, the tone of the piano has too much of the 'salon' clinging to it, perhaps, too much late-romantic Titanism. The preference for orchestras or small wind or string ensembles may also be connected with the fact that even gifted amateurs nowadays are not in a position to play piano compositions of the twentieth century as they should be – if they are by Schönberg, Křenek or Boulez. Contemporary piano music can thus no longer count on that support from talented and interested laymen which must have been taken for granted by Bach or Brahms. The incentive to compose piano music with the aim of achieving 'popularity' (in the way that Chopin's E flat Nocturne, Op. 9, once became a hit) no longer exists. Only Hindemith's sonatas and a few works by Debussy, Ravel and Bartók have penetrated very far beyond professional circles.

So one must take the following as given: the public concert tradition, which seems at times anachronistic, offers in our presence, now as ever, the dialogue between the great 'individual' and the enormous bulk of transmitted piano music. Modern composers are taken into the programme of the average, middling piano recital only exceptionally. The renown of a pianist depends on how he masters the eighteenth, and above all, the nineteenth century. For the moderns there are a few pre-eminent specialists. Apart from the works that have been written with a manifestly pedagogic tendency, the piano music of the twentieth century does not belong to the permanent stock of home music. This could change. Yet, since readiness to devote much time and energy to music at home is more likely to diminish, it is questionable whether the difficult pieces of recent decades will ever be assimilated.

But however 'willing' all concerned with the concert tradition may be, however sophisticated the pedagogic tricks, however subtle the

20

techniques of splicing and manipulating tapes, however favourable the general conditions, the whole music business has a vacant place, to which all eyes are turned. This is the optimal interpretative performance achieved by an individual at a specific time. Nothing can take the place of this individual, or disguise his mistakes.

The virtuosi, the great interpretative virtuosi of our time, fill precisely this vacant place. Amongst refined art-lovers it is customary to speak contemptuously of 'virtuosi', as if indeed even one of those who by their playing are able to set the tone for a decade or more could be reproached with being nothing but a 'pure virtuoso'. In fact, along with an agreeable exterior or an anecdotal quality, the great ones who were not just swept up by a passing fashion possess interpretative originality. Every audience is indeed at the same time naïve in its readiness to enthuse and naïve in its cruelty. It tends as much to mechanical admiration as to wanton treachery. 'X hasn't fulfilled his early promise', 'Y used to play more brilliantly', 'Z has become sterile'. Beneath such remarks lurks an often unconscious wish to destroy. Steady fame is consolidated only if this wish is survived. The gladiators have not only to play; they must also fight. They put themselves at risk, which is the will of the predatory public.

The virtuosi fulfil an elemental need. In them, sensitivity must be combined with the constitution of an ox. They travel the continents and must offer a hundred times a year or more, and keep it up for decades – both the objective state of interpretative art at its highest and, over and above that, something wholly personal, not to be confused with anyone else. What a life! They can all speak several languages, know the managers, the great, the hotels and the good restaurants, and are accustomed to admiration. Rubinstein has confessed that he begins to get bored if he has to stay in one place too long – he clearly needs the variety of audiences that are continually fresh (fresh for conquest). Arrau, who within a space of a few weeks gave concerts in Japan, where there is supposed to be such a good audience for Beethoven, America, London, Munich and then London again, finds that only constant changes of air are refreshing; they keep him physically resilient and healthy. Of course, the world-famous cannot count on blind enthusiasm. But they can assume in their audience a readiness to be enthused. They must stake their all on this, absolutely. There is no more discreet, less blatant way of putting it. Even

21

'devotion' sounds too passive. Rubinstein has said that if a pianist did not shed a few drops of blood and lose a few pounds, then the concert was no good. This is scarcely an exaggeration. I remember how Walter Gieseking injured himself in Frankfurt right at the beginning of the Tchaikovsky B flat minor concerto, and finished this fortissimo piece on gradually reddening keys. The aged Cortot could no longer stand up to such exertions. In London, in Chopin's F minor concerto (which he had played a thousand times) he lost the thread; an impasse was reached. But Cortot indicated with magnanimous gestures that he was to blame, that it was not the musicians in the accompanying orchestra who had broken down, but he himself.

Their nerves have to be of steel. Many cannot stand it, or see it through. When Arturo Benedetti Michelangeli, perhaps the most talented pianist of his generation, is to play, the managers are in despair. However careful the preparations may be, however expensive the tickets, he will still call it off, so that many organizers are delighted if he declines at once and matters fail to get even as far as the extensive preliminaries. The phenomenal Vladimir Horowitz finally appeared in public again after a break of several years of depression. The New Yorkers stood all night for tickets for a piano recital! It was a sensation – hardly anyone had reckoned to hear Horowitz again. Byron Janis, Horowitz's one prominent pupil, inquires nervously for the weather forecast before concerts which he is to give. In rainy conditions the grand piano loses brilliancy and sounds dull. The young Glenn Gould is incredibly eccentric, plagued by maladies and marked by preoccupations and circulation deficiencies; he plays seldom and clearly no longer very gladly. Even so calm, apparently unassailable a man as Wilhelm Backhaus threatened, after foolish fans had stolen his piano-stool from the concert hall in Hamburg, that he would never play there again – and perhaps nowhere at all any more. Fortunately, he did not put these threats into effect.

We have no wish to adduce evidence here that all artists of importance are cranks. But this list may well suggest what a tense, dangerous and burdensome profession it is to be a virtuoso. One must stand in awe of these heroes, often physically weak and seemingly delicate, who are possessed by the arduous passion and task in life to expose themselves to the master-works and the demands of a public presence and of a 'world-audience' as importunate as it is intangible.

Our concert tradition, not only with regard to the historical circumstances of its origin, but also by its nature and its claim, can be called middle-class. It has existed for about 200 years – since musicians ceased to feel they belonged inevitably to an ancient guild system, in which fees were tightly regulated, but tended towards private enterprise, with free competition and free opportunities for reward; since the public had free access, on payment of an entrance fee, not only to the at first semi-private house-recitals and club performances, but also to public concerts. During these two hundred years there has probably been no greater musico-sociological turning-point than that represented by the spread of the radio and records. Interpretative performances are now omnipresent: if one likes, democratized. The change can be expressed in numbers – yet the quantity has far-reaching qualitative effects. The concert tradition no longer stands alone. At the same time, because the listening situation and listening awareness could not remain unaffected, it has changed.

First, one must bear in mind that even in Germany – where anyone who gives his profession as 'musician', who describes himself as a clarinettist, say, in an orchestra, is just as naturally esteemed and accepted as anyone who in France calls himself a 'writer', which in Germany probably still tends to evoke associations of the starving and unreliable literary world (one would rather marry one's daughter to a viola player than to a 'writer') – a visit to a symphony concert was for long the more or less natural privilege of the educated middle class. About fifty years ago Paul Bekker described with class-conscious pathos the disadvantages of this state of affairs: 'The true public, capable of creative co-operation,' he maintained, 'is still outside, before the doors. It must either let itself be fobbed off with popular concerts or it will remain indifferently to one side, powerless to gain from this sort of musical activity any incentive to join in.'

We should not be too sure that the gulf which Bekker described has yet been closed. In Britain for instance, even today, a class-conscious proletarian will still tend to avoid concerts or solo recitals: he does not belong there.

Such sociologizing imputations are always rather vague in effect and prompt examples to the contrary. But are we not forgetting too quickly, intoxicated by the idol of free access, to what a high degree an evening at the concert seems ritualized? One has to be 'initiated' in order to feel at home there. A lot must be taken for granted and as given. One must know, for instance, how one should dress for a night at the opera or for a church concert, when to clap, what a cadenza is in an instrumental concerto. One must be accustomed to not smoking right through a Bruckner symphony, and understand a general pause as an event, and not as nothing. One must know what an 'encore' is, and why the soloist, when she takes her applause, shakes hands not only with the conductor, but also with one of the violinists and one of the 'cellists (i.e. the leader and principal). Naturally, there is no *must* about it. One can get along without. But anyone who does not know, who is not initiated into these rites, might well feel a little as though he were watching and listening to a game whose rules were unknown to him. Is there much pleasure in that? Will the tyro really long for a repetition of such an evening?

Music-lovers usually have no idea how much they take for granted. When John F. Kennedy invited the 'cellist Pablo Casals, the pianist Mieczyslav Horszowski and the violinist Alexander Schneider to give a concert at the White House, which took place on November 13, 1961, before an illustrious audience, there was clapping after each of the four movements of Mendelssohn's piano trio in D minor, even after the slow one. Yet those who applauded clearly had a justified feeling that something was not quite right. For at the close, the applause sounded freer than the hesitant manifestations of natural sympathy during the piece.

But what has changed since the radio and the gramophone record have thrust their way into musical life? (In Western Germany alone, 5·7 million long-playing records of 'serious, classical' music were sold in 1962.) The answer is radical: in our relationship to musical interpretation nothing has remained unaffected. This change has touched the passive, non-practising, but merely listening music-lover just as much as the performing amateur, those professionally concerned (managers, organizers, teachers, music-writers, critics) and the artist himself.

There exists today an astonishingly large, though elusive class of interested people whose connection with music is made only through the gramophone record. In the country and in small towns, where concerts are few and not so attractive, live well-informed record-lovers and collectors (often equipped with tape-recorders to pick up

24

radio programmes worth repeating), for whom 'listening to records' is the rule and concerts the exception – if they still go to concerts at all. Even in the big cities, there are many who avoid the inconvenience of concert-going, who confine themselves, on grounds of health, finance or aesthetics, to the private enjoyment of so-called 'canned' music. The more accustomed they grow to listening to records, the harder it often becomes for them to adapt whenever they do for once essay the concert experience and its imperfections. Their neighbours cough, the man in front keeps moving, the artist plays badly, the work is encumbered with applause, poor acoustics and an endless journey there and back. They prefer to carry on in their pure, imaginary museum of tapes, records and radio concerts. This large group did not exist, of course, before the emergence of the gramophone and the radio.

But even those music-lovers who are still – and increasingly – fascinated by the festive 'here and now' of a concert, who feel how little the full sound, especially of an orchestra, with its rich overtones, can be reproduced in a living-room or studio that is much too small, however refined the apparatus: even they, influenced by the experience of recordings, now listen differently at a concert. And the artists play in the knowledge that they will be judged against the records of their competitors and be compared with their own recordings.

These remarks seem to amount to something rather obvious: audiences accustomed to records are more enlightened. They all have a clearer idea of what is possible than formerly: the finest performances are available at will. Now, even in remote provincial towns, the 'leading' lady piano-teacher or the ruling bandmaster can no longer lay down the law unchallenged about what is to be regarded as good and correct, as was formerly so often the case. As a result of this record-enlightenment, 'fame' can be won no longer only through personal appearances. Several artists have acquired their public through records. In many towns they have had full houses even at their debuts (e.g. Fischer-Dieskau, Van Cliburn, Herbert von Karajan). Yet one should not over-estimate this echo-effect of the record. Even today, the first and most important verdict on the calibre and quality of an artist is still likely to be given in public, in the presence of the public at a concert-hall. If a reputation gained through personal appearance in centres of music or capital cities is then extended and multiplied through records, something will be added, but nothing material will have been changed. Liszt and Paganini too, on their tours of Germany could count on full houses even in places where they were appearing for the first time. Seen thus, record-fame is only a fresh nuance of the 'advance reputation' that was once prepared in the same way by advertising, critics and rumour. Except that a record is no rumour, but a document.

Is it possible to adopt a naïve attitude and simply ignore the difference between the artificially manipulated record-impression and the direct concert-impression? There are many music-lovers who listen to a record as to a concert. They adapt. Round their awareness of the record they create the frame of the concert and let the differences go at that. This attitude can be practised. For it is possible, after all, to watch a film shown on television involuntarily as a film; in spite of the television format, one can imagine the size of the familiar film-screen and so trick oneself into forgetting that television drama and film drama are two different things. In just the same way it is possible to view a photographed stage-show on television as a theatrical performance, in that one supplies the theatre ambience. One then detaches the television impression as it were from the apparatus and transposes it on to an imaginary stage.

This probably never quite succeeds. With a bit of practice – and assuming one is equally concerned with the two media being interchanged – it may almost be possible.

Yet wherein do the changes lie in the listening habits of even those musicians and music-lovers who say that for them records represent only an extra, necessary to the decisive concert-impression because they provide the opportunity for informative, careful study? On the point that the acoustics are not the same as in the concert-hall, that they may be technically 'fixed' or wangled or even false, unanimity can soon be reached. Unanimity can also be had over the fact that the repeatability of a record changes something in the character of the listening experience.

But paradoxically, there is also a change in an element that appears nevertheless to remain demonstrably constant: namely, time. Record-playing time and concert time are just as distinct as physical time and time experienced – though not in the sense that one experiences a record, say, less 'intensely'. Wherein lies the difference? Furtwängler and Fischer, after all, require the same 38 minutes 25 seconds for Beethoven's E flat concerto both on the platform as well as on records (especially if the record is made from a concert). As to the problem that many interpreters do in fact choose other tempi (usually faster!) when they play slow movements for recordings, we will disregard this. For the difference exists even when the actual performances are of the same length.

Let us begin with a quite simple experience: a concert which one has attended between 8 and 10.30 in the evening becomes amazingly shortened when one plays over the same programme on records at home afterwards. In one evening, diligent record enthusiasts can get through the programme of three or four piano recitals without any trouble. The complete works of Anton von Webern, whom many regard as the most significant composer of the twentieth century, fit on to three long-playing records. One can begin after supper with Op. 1 and well before midnight one is 'through' with the audible essence of a long musical life. We are not concerned now with the supposedly greater listening-intensity at a concert. One can also listen attentively to a record, without the annoyance of late-arriving neighbours hung about with jingling chains, rings and gold coins, and yawning callously. Who knows whether one does not listen more closely at home, more incorruptibly, because one can follow the score and even go back if one loses the thread.

The contrast between concert-time and record-time cannot be reduced to contrasts between concentration and distraction, capacity for experience and fickleness. But how about the 'isolation' and 'significance' of the actual hearing impression? One can ask music-lovers who often go to concerts and like listening to records about their greatest musical experiences. They will probably speak only of live concert-impressions; it will probably never occur to them to mention recordings. For the time of music heard in the knowledge that it is unrepeatable, the uniqueness of the moment, is for us mortals clearly a prerequisite for depth of experience (just as it is for tragic destiny). The knowledge that I can have all this again, just the same, does not impair concentration, pleasure or devotion – but it does the significance, the (rightly) so-called 'uniqueness' of the impression. In his essay on 'the work of art in the age of technical reproduction' Walter Benjamin coined the term 'aura' for every-

27

thing that is taken away from a technically reproduced work. At the time Benjamin was not concerned about the possibility of adaptation, about the new immediacy that can arise when one and the same person tries to play the Moonlight Sonata, when he goes to a concert in order to hear it – and is ready to listen to it on records.

The 'uniqueness' of the concert impression has more to it, however, than just the awareness that it cannot be repeated. Namely, the endorsement of being public, the feeling of involvement, in which, in one way or another, by being elevated, enthusiastic, enthusing, or even protesting – one is there, responding. Publicity and presence are necessary for a judgement to be formed which is no longer a judgement of taste by one private listener, however cultivated.

All this, the minutes taken up by applause, the preliminaries, the beginnings of a collective reaction, and by the interested and expectant conversations in the intervals, falls away at home. That is why matters go so much faster within one's own four walls. To escape from this solitariness, many record-lovers have an irresistible urge to display. They are never tired of proudly presenting their records. They behave as though they had not only discovered them, but also performed them. In fact, they are looking for testimony to their joy. They suspect that endorsement by someone else, or several others, though it may not improve the record, may yet lend justice and solidity to their own impression. Thus it is that record-owners are sometimes like anecdote-collectors. Each wants to have his say; not to listen to the other, but to display. To parade what they own, as though it were a part of themselves, something that cost a couple of pounds.

'Realistic' music-lovers – there are such, though the contradiction in terms is hard to ignore – will reject such speculations about 'time' and 'presence' as being just that, 'speculations'. The existence of light-bulbs makes no difference to the sun, they will say. Unimpressed they will ask to what extent one listens to a concert differently than before. That records accustom one to perfection says nothing. Wrong notes have been wrong notes since the days of Orpheus. That a musically educated middle class has also learnt to recognize wrong notes today does not in any way affect the rightness or the wrongness.

To this the following might be said: the availability of records, and the great consumption of records (to say nothing of the many thousands of hours of recordings sent out by the radio, of tapes and repeats), have in the meantime reversed the relationship between 'canned' and 'natural' – the terms are used here with no value-implications. Whoever takes any part at all in record-culture most probably hears far more from records than from the platform. Even in a big city many years must elapse before an interested music-lover will have heard the Eroica as many as five times. If he collects records, one winter would be enough, indeed even a month or a week, according to inclination and mood. Whoever has a good radio-set can probably hear the symphony on some programme or other every evening. Is Erwin Stein right, then, when he sees in this avail-ability a dangerous preconditioning of the listener? Stein writes: 'Students and listeners of tomorrow are bound to be confused by the varying interpretations which, let us say, Toscanini, Weingartner and Furtwängler permit a Beethoven symphony to be given. . . . I would not in any way underestimate the examples of great interpreters. Talented students can learn much from them, but along with their merits they often acquire their faults at the same time' (Erwin Stein, *Musik, Form und Darstellung*, Munich 1964, p. 14).

The danger does exist. Records with which one has grown up can take the place of the thing itself. For instance, I can hardly imagine the variation movement from Mozart's sonata in A any more except as played by Wilhelm Kempff decades ago on a record. Again, for the great development section from the first movement of the Brahms violin concerto, Ginette Neveu opened my ears once and for all – or in fact preconditioned me. Who knows whether such formative (not informative) experiences do not make the listener unjust to other efforts. Yet this applies after all not merely to the experience of records, but even more to many concert experiences, to teachers, friends, childhood memories, etc. So it is not clear how Erwin Stein can combine the reproach of fixation with that of confusion. It is, indeed, only the often grotesque differences between several interpre-tations that can resolve fixations and turn the impression of musical father-figures into a relative one.

It has often been wondered whether the synthetically bred per-fection of the record has not accustomed the public to a standard which makes the life of the virtuoso, not in an impossibly demanding way, like walking a tight-rope. Clearly, anyone who, like Jürgen

Meyer-Josten, compares intelligently no less than twenty-two renderings of the piano concerto in A minor by Schumann (*Fono Forum*, March 1964, p. 99 ff.) has got himself into a situation that is in the pejorative sense 'artificial'. For prior to the invention of the gramophone record, a chain of circumstances such that someone could hear, or have to hear, the same piece twenty-two times by different interpreters within quite a short space of time was simply inconceivable. Today the record magazines are full of it. (A pianist who is studying the concerto will certainly play it even more than twenty-two times, but he is then like a sculptor with his chisel, not an onlooker continually staring.) Of course, in the end, in spite of Gieseking, Lipatti, Richter, Rubinstein, Cortot and many others, Meyer-Josten can no longer decide about anything. He begins his report: '22 × (op.) 54 = 0, so I must unfortunately confirm; for the artistic equation did not come out, the result is disappointing . . . a reproduction of the Schumann piano concerto which to me would be ideal in every respect, I have still not heard on records. Nor up to now, for that matter, in the concert-hall.'

The critic then characterizes all twenty-two recordings and comes to a conclusion which shows where the free availability in time and space, the ubiquity, of record-listening can lead. 'What a pity,' says Meyer-Josten, 'that there is no recording of the Schumann concerto with Wilhelm Furtwängler, Edwin Fischer (from his best period) and the Berlin Philharmonic. Perhaps this would have been the ideal version.' These remarks of a professional listener to records denote, of course, an extreme. Yet the extreme is where the consequences become most clearly visible. Let us suppose that someone like Meyer-Josten – i.e. an equally passionate, critical, widely experienced listener to records – goes to a concert performance of the piece. How will he stand with regard to what is offered?

No wrong note will escape him – any more than it would a pianist who had mastered the piece by heart. Perhaps, however, he will take the 'perfection', i.e. the lack of wrong notes, too much for granted. He has not practised the work. He does not know how hard it was to learn the right ones – and yet how easily something can happen.

To put it another way: the record-collector will be just a little too casual about what is 'right' – and with regard to the wrong notes, just a little too fastidious.

But the result is paradoxical: manual virtuosity becomes not over-valued, but undervalued. One is so very accustomed to what is 'right' that one hardly realizes it any more. A case in point is the difference, which hardly appears any more to the record-listener, between the average and the quite good. Even a weak pianist today no longer allows any record to go out which bears too many misleading errors – and a moderately good pianist can also do little more than play the same concerto with respect for the music and care for technique. Records permit the energy that went into the overcoming of tech-nical difficulties to disappear. This is also why manual diversions, such as pieces for the left hand only, are quite ineffective on records (unless they are musically effective!). One cannot see the limitation, of course, any more than one can appreciate the effort that led to its being over-come. But the result is undreamt-of by those who are scornful of records. Virtuosity, which at a concert often enough (rightly) evokes admiration as a pure *tour de force*, on records remains immaterial, unless it expresses something beyond this: unless it answers for a compelling temperament, a radiant feeling for life, or an imperious exertion of the soul. Horowitz on records plays no more right notes than Byron Janis, nor does he play them any faster. In spite of this, one listens to him with greater enchantment, for his 'rightness' is backed by the truth of an unfettered pianistic temperament. As against this, the fact that Byron Janis or Van Cliburn also make no mistakes counts, on records, for less! Thus records tend to lead away from virtuosity. They allow it, as a prerequisite, to disappear. Yet, in the sense of the purely musical, it had to be the keeper of the grail.

Even the most refined manipulations, however, cannot turn a technically weak pianist into a very good one. It is true, there are recordings which nobody has in fact ever played. Variation after variation was repeated until enough right notes were obtained to cobble up a version free of mistakes. Luckily, the recording industry is seldom prodigal enough with time to make such manipulated versions also in hard cases. To the replacement of an unsuccessful passage there is, of course, little objection, though the spliced version almost always lacks the tension that a homogeneous version can have. In addition, for orchestral concertos, recording time is far too expensive for it to be possible to allow a bad pianist the necessary weeks of trial and error. The outcome of all this sounds reassuring: bad pianists,

31

even on records, are worse than good ones. Beckmessers of every time and place can readily be caught out, not only on old shellac records, which had to be made, of course, at one go, but also on the manipulated modern ones, in countless mistakes, inaccuracies and weaknesses of articulation. So even on the piano, there is no short cut to truth.

In a very sharp attack on the records of Sergei Rachmaninoff, the intelligent pianist Alfred Brendel (though in tearing apart Rachmaninoff's recording of Chopin's Funeral March Sonata he spared himself any precise justification for the first two movements, in spite of an assurance to the contrary) re-endorses the weaknesses of many electro-acoustically forced piano-recordings: 'I am still waiting for the expert who can explain to me why the piano tone of Cortot or Edwin Fischer on the "historical" records of the thirties was more faithfully reproduced than on all post-war recordings. One has the impression of sitting in a good seat in a good hall. One can distinguish the personal timbre. When listening to numerous hi-fi piano-recordings, on the other hand, one is sitting unexpectedly inside the grand piano, or on top of it, or even hanging somewhere below the ceiling' (*Phono*, Vienna, Vol. 8, No. 6, p. 117 ff.). In this criticism of recordings which place every possible refinement of electro-acoustical advance at the 'service' of the matter, and yet only achieve a record-grand-piano that sounds like no earthly grand, Brendel is clearly right. Nevertheless, it belongs to the patina of the 'historical' recordings to reflect, in a broken way, the individuality of the piano tone of Rachmaninoff or Cortot or Schnabel. These records did not pretend to be a substitute for the real sound. Therein lay their imperfection, but also an advantage. One was never tempted to identify record-music and concert-music with each other. Karl Kraus in quite a different connection – namely in 1908, when he was lamenting Alexander Girardi's decision to leave Vienna for Berlin – extolled this as it were 'alienating' quality of records. Of 'the dear man Alexander Girardi', he wrote, 'all we Viennese have left are a few gramophone records. He was enough of a patriot to sing something for us to record before his removal. I sometimes play over the old songs, for although they always sound like a farewell to departing glory, the bustle of life enslaved to the machine now gives them a horribly moving tone.'

But are not the true mourners of the record-evolution really those artists who worry too much about records – and their effects on the awareness and listening habits of the public? Anyone who, like Claudio Arrau or Rubinstein, is continually, and with vigour and delight, giving concerts, making records, and even recording the same works several times, completely differently, may feel tape- and record-culture to be a welcome and heightening enrichment of the concert tradition.

Yet not all artists can do that. For many recording virtuosi there really is a ghost that stands between them and their audience when they step out on to the platform: the record. They dread this ghost; they cannot escape it. For the ghost is themselves. If it is bad enough to come forward with one's own performance and individuality against the record-perfection or interpretation of a colleague, how much worse must it be to start playing against one's own record in the ears of the audience! Many have already confessed with groans that this is almost more than human strength can bear. Records create precise expectations. Whoever has heard Wolfgang Schneiderhan's recording of Beethoven's violin concerto a dozen, or even several dozen times, knows probably note for note – so great may be the power of solitary record-listening – how Schneiderhan played the work. And now it follows that Schneiderhan will play it at a concert in exactly the same way, at least no less beautifully, no less purely, no less 'perfectly'. The expectation may be unconscious, but it is there. Every deviation, every lapse, every impurity – such as are unavoidable at a concert, owing to conditions created not for perfection alone – will be felt as an impairment. Records are then a prison for virtuosi, making them uncertain and embarrassed and tempting them into copying themselves – hence into simply becoming a living record of themselves, which spells the death of all artistic freedom. How suggestive the power of a record-preconditioning can be may be judged by the fact that, with often-heard records, one never fails to recognize at a concert the spot where the record has to be turned over. But, surprisingly enough, the living artists go on playing, even so. . . .

Only naturalness can lay this ghost. Wilhelm Furtwängler, whose struggles with recording equipment gave rise to many anecdotes, clearly did not possess it. He did not have the capacity or the desire to go into technical matters (other than musical ones, of course). It is through these that records hold out the possibility of being able to express musical matters more beautifully and more correctly than ever at a concert or at the opera. Karl Böhm once emphasized that in every opera-performance of *Elektra*, the singer of the title role 'is tired at the end, and the orchestra, of course, loud'. At a recording, however, one can not only turn 'up' the microphone over Elektra so strongly that the singer's voice remains audible without effort, and intelligible, too, even above the roaring of the orchestra – but one is also free, of course, to record the difficult final passages while the singer is fresh. Such a suggestion, to which thousands of similar ones could naturally be added, illustrates how greatly records can serve interpretational clarity and truth. On the horizon of these possibilities a specific record culture will then emerge, which will no longer want to *substitute*, but, in its own way, to *interpret*. The sound engineer will become the sound director – and a record will no longer offer a would-be *copy* of a concert, but an electro-acoustical *interpretation* of the score to which no 'reality' will be able to correspond any more.

The record will then stand as far beyond the bare document as the 'patina-tone' of the historical recordings fell short of it. It will also then no longer be just an adjunct for the 'audience-shy', who at a concert can never give their all, owing to self-consciousness and agitation – but a means of interpretation in its own way. Since it is already beginning to fulfil all these functions today, a look at the current state of interpretation would be not only incomplete but downright unjust, if it did not also take into account the care which has been, and is being, devoted to records, and if it disregarded performances and experiences which are represented on records – and nowhere else. Naturally, every artist devotes to the record nowadays a different proportion of his energy, his art, and his seriousness. Yet in the second half of the twentieth century, a career as pianist without recordings no longer exists. At the moment there is a fruitful tension between concert tradition and record. It would be a sign of deafness to stifle records.

34

Artur Rubinstein

The older an interpreter becomes, the more wisdom, experience and tricks he stores up to withstand the impositions of being a virtuoso, to keep pace with the physical and psychological demands, the greater is the danger of his becoming set, hardened, cramped. It was not, for instance, the aged Cortot's mistakes that disappointed – mistakes which, to adapt Brahms, 'any fool could hear' – but rather his mechanical ritardandi. One felt, sadly, that when Cortot employed a rubato he had originally conceived perhaps twenty-five years before, he was now only playing like that because he had always done so. This, it is true, was followed often enough by unique nuances which prompted a younger pianist, a Cortot fan, to remark with justice: 'I would rather have Cortot's wrong notes than my own right ones.'

Rubinstein has an inner freedom, an interest in the piano and the immediacy of the music so much greater than in any of his own previous conceptions, that he surmounts all these dangers of becoming set in a manner that is almost inconceivable. He can convert an outstanding concert experience into spontaneity. Now in his eighties – he was born in 1889 – and still giving frequent recitals, Artur Rubinstein's playing is a miracle. Miraculous, astonishing, inconceivable, however, are not only his technical lucidity, the heart-stirring nobility of his phrasing in slow movements, and his tumultuous outbursts of temperament. All this counts for much, has to be conquered, preserved and kept alive; yet there are, throughout the world, a few pianists who can compete with Rubinstein the virtuoso or be compared with Rubinstein the poet. The miracle, on the other hand, is that Rubinstein can make all this his own, master it with magnificent understanding – and at the same time spread spontaneous happiness. For Rubinstein, who says of himself that he remains at heart a gipsy, to whom music is in the blood – for Rubinstein, piano-playing seems to be a form of breathing, of well-being. He is an old-fashioned pianist, the last of the Titans from the nineteenth century. His tone – delicate, full and sweet – knows nothing of self-doubt. Even when Rubinstein wants to evoke half-lights and secrets, he evokes at the same time the fullness of an unbroken personality. Great though his fame and popularity may be with the public all over the world, if one has heard him often and collected his records, one becomes quite convinced that this eternally fresh musician has no wish in spite of everything to set a style as *praeceptor musicae*, oppressing and inhibiting the rising generation. Out of his playing blows the breeze of joy and freedom; his tone is his own – nowhere does he make the schoolmasterly demand that everyone ought to follow his example. Untrammelled self-expression of the highest order does not turn into sectarianism as with Horowitz, for instance, whom many young American virtuosi try to imitate. Rubinstein is a 'burden' to no one.

Rubinstein was born in Lodz, Poland, in 1889 (not 1886, as has often been stated), grew up in Germany, and was an infant prodigy and the protégé of Joseph Joachim. Suddenly he had had enough of Berlin and the Berlin Music Academy, and fled to Paris. There he went to the dogs. Paul Dukas saved him, as Rubinstein admits. 'Amuse yourself as much as you like,' Dukas said to him, 'but don't squander yourself. Paris is not for you. Go back to Poland, look after yourself so that you get well again, physically and morally; drink milk, ride, and go to bed early; in short, become an honest man.' This was – so Rubinstein goes on in his lively confessions – 'sound advice, and the best of it was – I followed it'.

But, to begin with, he did not follow it very thoroughly. He lacked the patience to perfect himself technically. He relied on his immense talent and prodigious memory. Not only can he play by heart all the main works in the literature of the piano, chamber music and the symphony, but in Paris in 1907 – he relates – he played Salome from memory, and once performed the second act of Carmen for some friends, note for note, singing all the arias as he went. In Spain and South America, impetuosity and frivolity were overlooked – but not in England and the U.S.A. Germany he avoids, on account of a vow from the time of the First World War. At the age of forty-seven he was still not a great pianist. Then he became one.

Rubinstein can stand as a hope and model for all those who at first go astray in their lives. He was always talented – but just as interested in good food, pictures, great wines and women, as in close study of the piano. At the age of forty-three Rubinstein married Aniela Mlynarski, the daughter of a conductor under whom he had played many years earlier in Warsaw. Now matters became serious. As a Jew, marriage for him was somewhat different than for a Hollywood film star. Rubinstein began to practise with passion and scrupulous accuracy. Then, on November 21, 1937 – after he had already given numerous but never wholly successful concerts in America – he experienced his great come-back, his real début in New York. Since that time he has been regarded by many music-lovers as the foremost pianist of the world. When he heard a young pianist at some competition or other in New York, he said to the quaking youth characteristically: 'You are really musical, but you can't afford to be as lazy as I was at your age. How I hated practising! Actually, I never practised properly until I came to America. . . . Here they expect us pianists not to overlook the slightest note. It's terrifying.'

All this sounds jovial, typical, like fermenting must, and ripe wine – and the way everyone likes the phrases to sound about a life that began in anarchy and grew to such fulfilment. A large head on a small body, piano-playing as a spontaneous triumph of fluency and ease – that is the Rubinstein concert today. Yet behind it lies much passion and doggedness, and a courage for the greatest risks. When Horowitz conquered Paris, 'tore it from my hands', Rubinstein was nearly in despair. 'I saw in him another Liszt,' he relates, 'capable of dominating his time. I wanted to throw everything aside. Before I die I want to show what I can do – I said to myself. I clenched my fists, which, however, as a professional pianist, I could not do for long; I opened them again, and began to work hard. I had a revenge to take – not on Horowitz, but on myself.'

What is it now that makes Rubinstein's playing so incomparable? Is it just the calm, full, blissful tone, which belongs to him alone? This would already be much, for on the piano the touch is to some extent the man. Yet this harmonious tone often becomes a prison. Sometimes, especially in Beethoven, it sounds almost too beautiful, too uncluttered, too sure. But Rubinstein has at his disposal not only this tone, but experience, growing wonderfully and turning into wisdom.

37

The man who found such pensive words in Beethoven over the sad pauses in the Adagio of the Hammerklavier Sonata, Op. 106, now possesses a calmness of articulation, of mastered polyphony, of breathing advance and delay. He is the Orpheus of the piano. Anyone who has not wearied of a long life as a great artist, who has seen, heard and experienced much, who has not tied himself to routine and tricks and mannerisms, but has always remained frank and open, to him in the end comes abundance. When Rubinstein now gives gentle voice to the Andante of Brahms's F minor sonata, a disposing intelligence prevails, a maturity, which grips even a hardened listener who hears its nuances as does scarcely any other concert-hall experience. Rubinstein, no doubt aware of the living reaction of his audience, creates in a discreet manner a plain for his espressivo. In the slow movements of Beethoven and Brahms, his tone is so captivating that he has no need to employ sentimentally dragging tempi in order to be intimate and expressive. This liveliness, which has nothing superficial or banal about it, gives him, however, the opportunity for compelling ritardandi and caesurae, though these are nevertheless not gross or affected, precisely because slow is not turned into too-slow, but movement into expressive restraint. Rubinstein has no need to sacrifice tempo to gesture. He has no need to create surprises through trickery, by inserting more indifferent moments before them for the sake of contrast. His immense musicality adds the enrichment without any previous poverty. When in the demure Chorale of the coda to Brahms's F minor sonata he stops briefly and then plays with soft, melancholy dedication, there is, as far as the piano is concerned, nothing more sublime.

But we should not want to make a hero of Artur Rubinstein and forget the exuberance and passionate extroversion of his nature. He loves not only cigars, but also individual characteristics. Earlier he used to rise from the piano-stool at every concert – one used to wait for it – at the powerful parts in order to give more weight to his attack. A Friedrich Gulda would never do that. And at his piano recitals in recent years it has been his habit to introduce some minor, innocuous but incredibly virtuoso little piece by Villa-Lobos which, after the great works of Brahms and Chopin, always sounds like light music. But he enjoys it for this very reason, and it is guaranteed to arouse enthusiasm. Those who perhaps take exception to Rubinstein because he stands up for witty, attractive and dazzling music have not understood what it is to be an old virtuoso of the old school, or what he can do. The gulf between priest and clown is lightly bridged by violinists and pianists of the blood; they love the perfect, the vital and the attractive for their own sake. If they are great, they will not fail for all that, when matters become serious.

Belonging to the heights of what Rubinstein can do are his interpretations of the two Brahms concertos. To the second – in B flat major – he gives deep, dark colours, and a powerful fullness. The first, on the other hand, in D minor, a child of sorrow in the Brahmsian muse, he plays with greater, often archaizing, harshness. He declines to subdue the inferno of the octave trills, the symbol of misfortune in this piano-drama. He takes the second subject, which is reminiscent of the Larghetto from Beethoven's second symphony, not indeed in a robust forte, but in that soft and brooding piano which is so difficult to wrest from the thickness of Brahms's piano textures. From the triplets of the closing section of the first movement he evokes a lonely Brahmsian drowsiness which is far removed from the happy dreams of Schumann. This turns into floating, etherialized folk-song.

Yet Rubinstein's imagination can only be fully appreciated if one has ever felt how, in the hymn-like Adagio – regarded as thankless – of this first piano concerto of Brahms, he adds to the wide-ranging melody of the second movement a vagrant element, boundless, rapturous, wild, without however at once turning every fresh note into a drama. Rubinstein enriches the passage, but without exaggerating it. Freedom does not lead to instability or expressive distortion.

The young Brahms has written here a completely unconventional cantilena – seventh, tritone, ninth, all done in syncopation and set freely against an unobtrusive bass-line and filling-in harmonies (Example 1).

Unlike Claudio Arrau, whose heavy breathing is audible even on his recording, Rubinstein does not play the passage as a sudden outburst. His right hand is free to lose itself as it were, to enter the hurly-burly. Everything is not aimed at the cadence, through which this wild, swelling melody is in any case tamed sooner or later. The pianist ventures out into the no-longer-controllable. In spite of this the passage does not disintegrate. His touch is so clear, his non-legato so masculine, and the dynamic independence of his hands from each

39

Example 1

From: Brahms, Piano Concerto in D minor, Op. 15, second movement, Adagio.

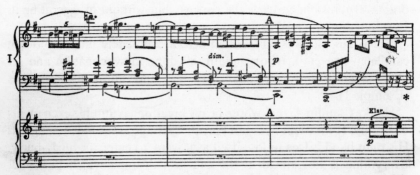

Rubinstein plays this wide-ranging melody with a sonorous tone, powerful and fresh. The great leaps, especially in bars 6 and 7 of our example, reveal an almost wild abandon. Prevailing here is the freedom of an improvisation, yet no denaturing rubato nuance or inappropriate touch of Chopin comes into the interpretation.

40

other so great that Rubinstein can make a whole of it in spite of every liberty, and has no need to force any note or step. He plays it a shade more relaxedly and imaginatively than Arrau. Imagination and a flowing style are convincingly combined.

Sometimes, however, the beautiful round tone, so sure of itself, is also a limitation, a *conditio sine qua non*. Then one feels how Rubinstein's wisdom, his almost harsh clarity and his pianistic sensuality come together in an exciting, delightful state of tension.

When Rubinstein plays Beethoven's Pathétique, everything sounds clearer, more measured, rounder and more flowing than say with Edwin Fischer – whose recording, incidentally, is a mere shadow of Edwin Fischer's art. With Rubinstein, Beethoven's sullen wrath is missing. He takes the second subject of the first movement in a curiously mannered way as to rhythm, as though he wanted to point the duet between soprano and bass – Romain Rolland called it 'operatic' – even more extremely. But otherwise Rubinstein interprets the early Beethoven sonatas and concertos – especially the healthy world of their sublime slow movements – with unsurpassable insight. No supposed 'Beethoven specialist' is his superior. It is true that in the Appassionata, which Rubinstein plays with stormy impetus, with wild violent tempi, too little happens, in spite of the ecstatic close. There should be, say in the recapitulation of the first movement, even more reverberation as the aftermath of something tremendous; the finale ought not to be rounded off as it were by the stretto. Rubinstein's art sometimes allows the abrupt, the rough and the ragged to disappear involuntarily.

If further evidence were needed of the unique quality of the 'Rubinstein tone', the recording of Beethoven's Spring sonata by Rubinstein and Szeryng would suffice. One can hear how a grand piano can 'sing' more beautifully than the violin. The great pianist almost outplays the violinist, self-assured and sovereign though he is indeed. No sooner has Henryk Szeryng's violin sung the melody of the Spring Sonata than the piano comes in with an enchanting vibrance, though never forced – and takes charge of the violin. Very uneasily Szeryng then wanders with Rubinstein's help through the land of Beethoven's sonata.

Not everything fixed on records, however, is the last word in wisdom. Rubinstein, as he once said, becomes bored with the achieved.

41

Only a few years ago, in Lucerne, he rediscovered Beethoven's third piano concerto – not only for himself, but for everyone. There is a famous recording of this concerto under no less a person than Toscanini, with Rubinstein – a few decades younger – as soloist; but it is somewhat superficial, too fast and smooth. The passages light up like rockets.

But the C minor concerto by Beethoven is indeed neither a virtuoso piece nor a mixture of the fifth symphony and the Pathétique – although it is in C minor and begins with a gloomy triad theme. The 'mature' Rubinstein has finally restored this piece to its dignity. He has taken it out of the sphere of commonplace drama into the realm of youthful feeling. The concerto begins to live. One suddenly grasps what even Rubinstein had previously missed: the rapturous Werther-mood of this music. The youthful melancholy in which the piano becomes absorbed immediately after the pithy main theme is typical and characteristic of this work, which only begins to breathe and live when the soloist plays it, in an unforced way, with sweet, rapturous, but never heavy pathos. Rubinstein subjugates all passages to this keynote – after he had made the work express, with Toscanini, a somewhat frivolous virtuosity. Now the melancholy-sweet E major larghetto fits into the piece quite organically and the minor humour of the last movement is no longer a falling-away, but a sentimental-ironic answer to the pounding feeling of the opening. Rubinstein has thus conceived Beethoven's C minor concerto in two highly contrasting ways: the first animated by Toscanini's brio, the second contained by Vladimir Golschmann's restraint.

This freedom of Rubinstein's, this mixture of spontaneity and sweetness, makes him *the* player of Chopin. The first movement of the piano concerto in E minor, Op. 11, in Rubinstein's interpretation is one of the most beautiful records in existence. Rubinstein's majestic grasp and delicacy are overwhelming. In spite of all the sweetness, the interpretation never becomes cloying; for Rubinstein emphasizes the rhythmic and dynamic aspects, the springy and the dangerous. He discovered the trilling motion at the end of the movement, and plays it with the boldness and mastery of – here the word can be risked for once – genius.

Rubinstein plays a proud Chopin, a virile Chopin, not that kindly, sentimental *émigré* who listens wistfully to the old tunes of his home-

Example 2

From: Chopin, Piano Concerto in E minor, first movement.

Here most pianists have already begun to flag. Not Rubinstein. Out of the menacing trills in the left hand and the passage-work in the right, he obtains a climax rich in contrasts.

land. Rubinstein knows Chopin's manic component, that no longer by any means so friendly, quiet Pole, who, as George Sand had reason to know, 'was terrible in his anger', who occasionally threw heavy articles at his piano pupils. (In his book on Chopin, Alfred Cortot describes Chopin's pride and contempt for mankind.) If Chopin had in fact been so charmingly effeminate as all those Polish countesses in whose arms he died would have us believe – and as Liszt himself portrayed him – then the wild outbursts of *fff* which occur in most of Chopin's major compositions would be quite incapable of correct interpretation. They would be incredible. Rubinstein makes them credible. He has an infallible instinct for Chopin's wild, dynamic thrust, pointing beyond the mere beauty-filled moment. Whether Rubinstein begins the E major Scherzo, Op. 54, like an elf-dance by Mendelssohn, and then raises it into the heroic ballade of some Polish Liszt; whether he sometimes so exaggerates the nuances of the nocturnes that they are no longer mere pleasing nuances; or whether he suddenly creates a polyphonic bacchanale of trills and arpeggios from an otherwise not-very-well-understood passage in this E minor concerto – Chopin's music always acquires the by no means calm authenticity of the self-evident. With regard to formal structure too, these agitato bars – we print an extract here – offer something surprising. In the recapitulation they follow the second subject. In the exposition, they were not present! Since Chopin in the sonata-form often so proceeds that he leads on from the development straight into the second subject, this dynamic outburst has the effect of a mixture of still reverberating momentum from the development and covert coda. It is a high point (Example 2).

Naturally it is immaterial whether Rubinstein intended to emphasize all this consciously or not. The irresistibility, the power of his conception reveals so much about such a passage that we listeners are fully entitled to trace the paths of a great interpreter and chart with pedantic precision the landscape which he has revealed to us (whether he had 'proceeded' instinctively or consciously).

Writing in the *New York Times* to celebrate the 150th anniversary of Chopin's birth, Rubinstein expressed the conviction that Chopin behaved more like a 'classical' composer than a 'romantic' one; that Mozart and Bach had been his models. In an interview, Rubinstein went even further. He said (according to the Zurich *Weltwoche*,

June 8, 1962): 'Chopin is not romantic at all. It's a great mistake to think that! He is called a Romantic only because he is always seen in the context of the 1830s. People who were born in those years or made any kind of contribution to that era are usually disposed of as romantic. . . . In my view Beethoven is the greatest Romantic, because he had sufficient confidence to break the strict classicism of a Haydn or Mozart. . . .'

Stravinsky, Prokofiev, Villa-Lobos, Szymanowski – numerous composers of a folkloristic modernism, if one may say that, are or were friends of Rubinstein, and their names find a frequent and welcome place on his programmes. With the Viennese atonalists, let alone the serial school which has arisen since 1945, he appears, in public, hardly ever to have concerned himself. He gladly leaves that to Glenn Gould.

He obviously feels at home musically among the late-Romantics – how he can shade César Franck, set the stretto from the finale of the Grieg concerto in springy movement, and pay homage to Rachmaninoff and Tchaikovsky, but also to Schumann or Schubert. How Rubinstein copes with Brahms, one of the corner-stones of his art, we have already appreciated. We know that he is regarded as the world's foremost player of Chopin. Let us now follow the final step in his 'development'. How does Rubinstein play Mozart?

There is no public utterance of Rubinstein's from recent years in which he has not got around to saying that today he values Mozart 'above all'. Although Rubinstein puts Mozart's concertos into his programmes comparatively rarely, he has now recorded some of them: the great C major (K 467), the famous A major (K 488), and the C minor (K 491). Rubinstein plays a Mozart as if on velvet. Naturally the passages ripple, glow and breathe: that goes without saying. For all that, one can say that Rubinstein's interpretation of Mozart is old-fashioned, sentimental, that there is a trace of Ludwig Spohr mixed in, just a grain of Chopin – and not the slightest concession is made to rococo silver. Here tastes must differ: to me it seems that Rubinstein offers a Mozart who is indeed eloquent, often downright declamatory, but not without style, not distorted. He gives the notes weight, without ever exaggerating their loudness. When one hears on a record the beginning from Mozart's late A minor rondo for piano, then a record has captured the immediacy of the Rubinsteinian improvisation. That is roughly what it sounds like at a concert, when Rubinstein strays cautiously through the spiritual landscape of an adagio. The pianist's hands, which here conjure up the note of sweet discouragement, must have tremendous strength; otherwise they could not be so even, so controlled, so eloquently soft.

Perhaps Rubinstein sometimes plays the outer movements of the Mozart concertos a little too powerfully, too inflexibly. The finale, say, of the A major concerto, or the variation movement of the C minor: they could certainly not be more transparent, more rippling or harmonious; but they could be more graceful, more winged. How serious Rubinstein was when he confessed, 'I value Mozart above all: he has the whole of my great and profound veneration', is illustrated beyond even such words of veneration by his performance of the slow movement of the A major concerto (K 488). It is an ineffably sad pastorale in F sharp minor, which even in Mozart's production was a great moment. Its theme is famous and familiar. Alfred Einstein declares in his biography of Mozart that it is an andante, and that Mozart had superscribed it adagio 'by mistake' (Example 3).

In his recording, Rubinstein plays the movement as an andante, and needs 49 seconds for the twelve bars of the theme. Wilhelm Kempff plays it as an adagio, hence in fact slower, but requires only 39 seconds for the same twelve bars. Physicists and lovers of precision instruments can see from this that in matters of musical interpretation nothing can be relied upon. The same bars with Kempff in adagio-time are shorter than with Rubinstein in andante. . . .

Yet that is hardly the sum-total of the differences. Rubinstein takes the theme more darkly, more weightily, less nervously than Kempff. For Rubinstein gives a sustained sonority to the rhythm of the left hand. A despairing but regular heart-beat pulses to the melody, whereas the same accompanying chords with Kempff are much more incidental, less important, flatter, indeed are sometimes almost left out (bar 8, second chord). But because Rubinstein's left hand performs its desperately sad measure so calmly and with such beautiful feeling, his right – and this corresponds indeed with Mozart's suggestion on the difference between the two hands! – can articulate more freely and with greater expression. The great melancholy sixteenth-note passage in the seventh bar, which Kempff still conceives in a sharp rococo way, has with Rubinstein a sad fullness. Kempff avoids

46

Example 3

From: Mozart, Piano Concerto in A major, K 488, second movement.

How self-evident everything seems in these ineffably beautiful bars of Mozart – and how hard it is to catch! The left hand keeps up its pastorale rhythm almost unperturbed; the right is of differentiated variety, pensive seriousness, subdued staccato. Artur Rubinstein and Wilhelm Kempff interpret the theme as differently as might be; especially in bars 2, 7 and 8, the differences are downright programmatic. (See our comparison, pp. 46–8.)

47

any expressive, let alone tragic elucidation. He declines to draw breath before the fifth bar, but almost plays across the important rest (two eighth-notes). Instead, he emphasizes in the second bar the surprise staccato G sharp in the right hand, which makes the bar brittle and restless. With Rubinstein, on the other hand, the E sharp in the left hand becomes a great and important event. Indeed, because this note falls on a strong beat, more calm is involuntarily created. The two grace-notes in the fifth bar are also played differently by the two pianists. Rubinstein lets them emerge from the rhythm of the left hand; the first grace-note coincides with the third chord of the accompaniment. Kempff concentrates on the melody, so that with him the highest note, F sharp, falls with the accompanying chord.

Thus two great pianists demonstrate a difference that goes as far as details: one, Rubinstein, allows himself a great and magnificent expression on the solid ground of a rhythm sustained with tragic calm; the other, Kempff, is really more reticent, yet his playing seems more decorative and nervous (and, for my taste, not nearly so compelling here), because he has to try to achieve by original and sharp articulation in the right hand, and in spite of a great dread of romantic sentimentality, what fell to the polyphonic calm of Rubinstein as though of its own accord.

Freedom from routine and towards himself, easy, frivolous happiness, and the talent to grow old productively: these three characteristics form Rubinstein's musical physiognomy. If there could be a 'first' among pianists, it would be he, so long as strength and imagination continue to live in him.

1. Artur Rubinstein

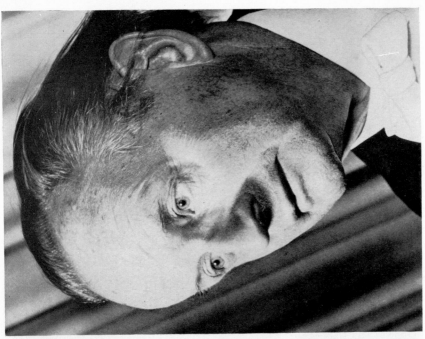

3.   Wilhelm Kempff

2.   Wilhelm Backhaus

Wilhelm Backhaus[1]

Compared with Artur Rubinstein, Wilhelm Backhaus, the other grand old man of the piano, seems almost easy-going, almost insensitive. Backhaus is no original genius, yet by now all criticism of him easily wears an air of silly dogmatism, of superfluity. This is not because Backhaus – born in 1884! – has for many years been in the 'close' time of life, which is the well-earned right of all artists who have been true to their muse throughout their lives, and who in old age pay for the decline of their physical and manual powers with spirituality, wisdom and wrong notes. The aged Backhaus laughs at such indulgence (as does his only contemporary, the aged Rubinstein). In the scherzo of Brahms's B flat major concerto, he can afford to ask the conductor for a faster tempo in rehearsal – for the cost of this tempo in the form of crazy pianissimo octaves he pays, now as ever, in his spare time as it were. His playing bears out what he once demanded of the great pianist: Liszt's Campanella should be available, even if it is not on the programme – in reserve, so to speak. The sovereign calm with which Backhaus plays Beethoven thus has in addition a quite simple technical basis. The most extreme difficulties are still far from requiring anything extreme from him.

In the *Golden Book of Music*, which appeared long before the First World War, there is a picture of the young Backhaus. It reveals the thick, flowing locks of an artist, a gaze enterprising but cool, awareness of his own abilities, and the great realism of a Saxon musician. Liszt at that time might not have been only a technical reserve. (Nor is he completely so even today, moreover: Schubert-Liszt transcriptions, of which younger musicians unfortunately want to know nothing at all, were still being played by Backhaus after the Second World War.)

[1] Died July 1969 (ed.).

We are only too readily inclined to see Backhaus in the light of what his later style, his understanding above all of the great lyricism of the last Beethoven sonatas, means to us. At an age when other pianists have to retire, there came with Backhaus, suddenly and increasingly, an added element of sweetness, of gentle movement and soft magic.

In his early and middle years Backhaus was in no way regarded as a great Beethoven player. Nobody would have thought of putting his interpretations on the same level as those of Artur Schnabel, Frederic Lamond, Eugène d'Albert or Edwin Fischer. At that time it was Backhaus's magnificent sobriety and technical infallibility that made him famous. When today he 'does' Mendelssohn's Rondo Capriccioso Op. 14, one can get an idea of how he may have played as a young man – with precision, with expressive feeling, with not exactly phenomenal brilliance, except in the sense of greater accuracy. Backhaus dodged none of the virtuoso difficulties, but he mastered them with sureness only, without Rubinstein's joy in succeeding.

So shrewd and keen an observer as Walter Niemann wrote of Backhaus in 1921:

'Where neo-classicism is leading, through intellectual and spiritual indifference and technique raised to the highest degree, the Leipzig-born Wilhelm Backhaus is an instructive example. For the virtuoso Backhaus, who, like Dohnányi, received his ordination as a pianist through Eugène d'Albert, there are no technical difficulties. Backhaus offers us the universally valid content of a work of art as a polished surface, perfect in form and technically crystal-clear. Backhaus the virtuoso and technician became popular early on in England and North America. Which is very significant, understandable and characteristic, since Anglo-Saxon feeling for art sets the highest value on this music-making, irreproachably perfect in technique, graphically clear and sharp, and academically formal. At any rate, the Anglo-Saxons at once correctly discerned the brilliant musical 'championship' [sic] of Backhaus the great virtuoso and marvellous technician. As such, Backhaus was already a phenomenon in his youth. The accomplishment of his enormous technique, which allows even very hectic preludes, sonata and concerto movements to be 'taken' with absolute technical clarity at the most furious tempo of a study; the evenness of his touch; the energetic modelling of his wonderful, great and compact piano-tone, which suffices for every degree of the decorative, the heroic; his capability and fullness; the strength, endurance and accuracy of his playing; the absolute reliability of his prodigious memory – all this is complete mastery, which one can thoroughly enjoy again and again, with honest wonder and admiration. But, however generous and natural all this may be, however sound and sure the rhythmic instinct with which the artist shapes, articulates and phrases, however remarkable the great sweeps of melodic line he spans, his capacity to shade his piano tone remains limited; as a result, the 'neutral' middle colours predominate to a tiring degree, and his piano is cold. The intellect, which abounded in these precious gifts received from Nature, neglects the soul, which makes the sound the echo of an interior richly and imaginatively stirred. Backhaus is and remains the academic technician. His sense of style and art of individual characterization is scarcely developed. Thus he plays, not only tonally but also spiritually, Bach like Liszt, Brahms like Rubinstein, Schumann like Debussy, Beethoven like Chopin. The intellectual-spiritual gulf yawns widest where more is required than, first and foremost, brilliant external playing for the masses . . .' (Walter Niemann, *Meister des Klaviers*, Schuster and Loeffler, Berlin, 1921, pp. 48 ff.)

This lengthy quotation is instructive not only with regard to Backhaus and his development. Walter Niemann, composer, pianist and writer on music, lived in Leipzig for decades. Although it may be possible to detect in his characterization the slight animosity, often to be noticed, of one Saxon towards another, this article reveals in addition something of the German contempt at that time for Anglo-Saxon taste in music. Paradoxically, the academicism which Niemann attributes to Backhaus, and thinks of as something for export to England and America, is regarded rather in America today as typical of German pianists, whose playing is often said there to be solid and tediously correct – which understandably inspires more respect than affection.

Thus times and prejudices change. All the same, Backhaus, whom Niemann describes and disposes of as the type of pure, tasteful virtuoso, no doubt did grow only slowly into the great Beethoven player. Walter Niemann died in Leipzig in 1953 – so he could still have witnessed the transformation in Backhaus. Yet Backhaus would certainly not have let himself be troubled by such a judgement in the past, any more than he would by enthusiastic words of praise. Impassive and reticent, like his playing sometimes, he went on his way as a pianist as though he suspected that at some later date he would be granted a magnificent fulfilment. Oddly enough, the successful careers of Backhaus and Rubinstein, the grand old pianists of our epoch, although made easier by phenomenal technical command, have not in other respects been by any means straightforward and free from set-backs. Only late in life did they become what they are. Yet such late enlightenment would not have been possible without the previous decades of long, sometimes mistaken endeavour. Born in Leipzig in 1884, helped on by Nikisch and d'Albert, and made known through the Paris Rubinstein prize, Backhaus has thus been playing the piano now for over seventy years. Since he quickly became famous, he could afford to give teaching activity a wide berth.

Concerning Backhaus's encounter with the B flat concerto, Op. 83, by Johannes Brahms, what it really is can be stated quite explicitly: pianistic experience. It takes an effort to realize that Backhaus played the Brahms B flat major concerto, certainly the most difficult and weighty work in the classical-romantic tradition, for the first time in public in 1903. He was then not yet twenty. As conductor and adviser he had Hans Richter to help him, the famous conductor of Wagner and Brahms who during Brahms's own lifetime directed so many first performances of Brahms. And in 1903, Brahms had only been dead six years. Is there an actor who can play Hamlet or King Lear or Faust for sixty years (and on top of that, who studied his role in the shadow of its author)? In the realm of music it is possible.

The B flat concerto begins with a horn motif: three quarter-notes, and an eighth-note triplet, and then a third, beckoning as it were in the distance. Backhaus rejects an opening tempo that strides away too briskly; he likes to see the tempo of the motif as evolved from the lyrical diversions that surround it at the end of the development. And he likes to rule out the temptation of the ritardando from the start. 'The older one becomes,' he says, 'the more ridiculous every ritardando becomes.' The music must speak for itself; only second-class compositions need the support of added ritardandi and accelerandi. The triplet figure in the horn should be taken in complete calm; any touch of emotion would weaken the effect.

Naturally, if one renounces sentimental effects, then one has to listen all the more carefully, and in detail, to the heartbeat of the theme, of the music. Such considerations also include Backhaus's request to the orchestra not to develop too powerful a fortissimo in the first great middle movement; it ought not to sound like a Bruckner forte, otherwise everyone will forget that there is a piano playing too. In the expressive second subject (forte expressivo), one should never forget to play out the second eighth-note, 'otherwise it becomes trivial'. Such considerations may seem to many laymen harmless and insignificant; they might perhaps have expected something more than workaday tips from a tradition extending from Brahms, through Hans Richter, to Backhaus. But Backhaus considered: 'Ought I to let my chord sound here into the horn entry?' Or: 'In the fortissimo of the coda, no accelerando – rather the opposite. It must sound great, completely and utterly great.' Or: 'Tranquillo does not mean slow, but calm. . . .' Here there are almost unplayable octaves for which pianissimo is prescribed. Conductors are happy to take this trio movement much more slowly, although it is marked only largamente ('with breadth'). For this reason Backhaus encourages a relatively smart pace, whose cost the pianist must bear. Not everybody can do this. All the same, the pace of the Scherzo ought not to be so smart that the syncopated rests at the end would no longer emerge. The Andante with the 'cello cantilena (often a little treacly) should be taken almost as an adagio. 'The simpler the more beautiful.' One of the subsidiary subjects in the last movement is supposed to have been copied from a barrel-organ in the Vienna Prater. At a really unplayable spot, the conductor has to grant 'mercy before justice', as Hubermann put it. Concerning the theme of the Rondo, which Backhaus knows how to point delightfully, everything depends above all on taking the transitional octave sixteenth-notes in the fourth, sixth and eighth bars very precisely in time. The violins, too, should do this in the repetition of the theme. Only then can transparency begin, which is superior to any showy virtuosity.

Naturally, not every pianist has to play the B flat concerto like Backhaus. He confronts this late work of Brahms with a sober austerity of expression. Sviatoslav Richter plays the concerto with whole-hearted élan, youthful and urgent – this too is possible. Horowitz manages to draw a Verdiesque brio from the late fire of Brahms.

This may not be stylistically permissible, but when the conductor is Toscanini it soon turns out that even this characteristic can be won from the work. Rubinstein, finally, converts all that Brahms secreted bitterly in this concerto back into pianistic euphony. Yet the ill-humour, the melancholy ponderousness, the introversion of late Brahms: these are in Backhaus.

Because the first movement might be thought too quiet, Brahms put a lively Scherzo in the second position, which is unusual in piano concertos. Backhaus plays the Scherzo with dogged severity. He is insistent, but abstains from sentimental shading. Oddly enough, one notices on the record more than in the concert-hall that the pianissimo octaves do in fact give him trouble.

Despite his interpretations of Brahms and Schubert, Wilhelm Backhaus is regarded today simply as a Beethoven player. In contrast to Rubinstein, Backhaus seems little suited to the early Beethoven sonatas. He needs vast brooding opposition: the joy-in-playing of the early sonatas perhaps no longer concerns him so much. Graf Kalck-reuth described this as follows: 'When Beethoven has little to say (Op. 10, No. 2), then Backhaus too has little to say. But if the former raises his esoteric voice, astonishment knows no end. . . .' The Moonlight sonata can also be played with more differentiation and power than by Backhaus. Backhaus pushes the first movement relatively compactly into a near-ballade akin to Brahms. He takes a comparatively speedy tempo, emphasizes the bass, puts in accents and perhaps overdoes his avoidance of fine articulation, sensitivity and decadence. Then in the Allegretto it is apparent that Backhaus breaks certain crucial chords without realizing it. The final Presto Backhaus plays speedily, with concentration, seriously, and without any virtuoso conceit, though also not exactly exuberantly. Backhaus takes the Adagio with distinguished, masculine composure, but perhaps nevertheless a little too robustly – in the way that a healthy, vigorous old gentleman can no longer really enter into the sentimental woes of young people.

Vladimir Horowitz, whom everyone charges with the heresy of being a technician, needs two minutes longer for this Adagio. By the third bar one already notices how a new tone-colour has come into the playing. Horowitz plays the first movement of the Moonlight Sonata with greater sensitivity and more nervous power of expression.

While Backhaus makes the bass lines and the correspondences in the middle section abundantly clear, Horowitz creates a sensitive poem from the rising eighth-note triplets. With Horowitz, it is true, the danger arises that the piece will fall apart into mere beautiful passages. At the same time, he by no means exaggerates the rubato, but plays the slow accompanying figure with that unflagging regularity that only a great pianist can achieve. Slowness and tranquillity can be immensely difficult, as is notorious. One knows indeed that it is precisely for the Adagio on points that the ballerina needs feet of iron. Thus the first movement demonstrates the difference between tremendous, almost balladesque robustness in Backhaus and a romanticizing, though in no way capricious fragility in Vladimir Horowitz.

But how does Wilhelm Backhaus play the Presto agitato in comparison with Horowitz? Horowitz certainly holds on to the tempo, but not to his own temperament. Before the long trill, for instance, there are wild passages in A major. With Backhaus a section like this has gravity and weight. With Horowitz, on the other hand, one feels it no longer has anything to do with Beethoven, but with an exploding sewing-machine. What emerges here baldly is sheer pianistic accomplishment; the cohesion of the sonata appears to be burst; the matchless clarity has the effect that certain Alberti basses become audible at a speed which is so to speak trans-musical. Backhaus, who was not aiming at exaggerated clarity, is here more appropriate to the piece. He lets himself be driven on by the spirit of Beethoven, and plays the crackling eighth-notes not harmlessly, plainly or euphoniously, but at least with due weight. Although some things lose their clarity for him, he is able to stay the course of the Presto. It is precisely not of details that Backhaus's interpretations of Beethoven consist. Indeed, with him one sometimes cannot help feeling that greater differentiation and variability would be conceivable; yet when the work is over, one is aware that Backhaus has given a whole. One has heard Beethoven. One has not been cheated. The details do not stand in each other's way, the great lines are there, nothing has become sentimental or loaded with all-too-personal espressivo. A masculine, intelligent and great art allows the work to emerge as if of its own accord. Thus in the Hammerklavier Sonata in B flat, Op. 106, Backhaus plays the majestic introduction slowly, then draws the tempo to a great climax,

Example 4

From: Beethoven, Hammerklavier Sonata, Op. 106, in B flat, first movement.

The abundance of expression and wealth of inner connections, which ought not to be suppressed, can lead, precisely in late Beethoven, to the loss of the great, simple relations. When he interprets the Hammerklavier Sonata, Backhaus draws attention at this spot to a connection that is simple, compelling and unmissable – once one has only recognized it! He stresses the fourth-interval in the bass octaves (bar 3 of our example). This fourth recurs (bars 9 and 11, and so on), and leads to a magnificent, quite unforced climax.

56

and takes the passages in a very measured way. In this gigantic work Backhaus is ready to emphasize, with unforced stress, the contrasts between the musical features rather than what links them. In spite of this, a stirring, delightful and yet imperturbable calm prevails 'o'er all the mountain tops'. With Backhaus – and this marks a striking difference from Rubinstein, Kempff or Horowitz – it is almost misleading if one concentrates too much on details. To do so is to miss the intention of his playing. If any particular nuance in it can be recognized and described as a nuance, then – in the sense of the best Backhaus interpretation – this would to some extent already be too much. For Backhaus is possessed, in a way that is hard to describe, by the (naturally not otherwise than musically expressible, non-conceptual) concept of the whole. Not because he appears to want to realize any precise conception of the whole, but because an almost instinctive architectonic understanding grows in his playing: it sounds not pre-arranged or well-ordered, but self-evident and tremendously natural.

When Backhaus plays Mozart concertos or Haydn sonatas, he brings the contrasts of speed and feature almost too close to each other. His Chopin, of masculine composure, his sonorous playing of Schumann, but also his performance of the Beethoven concertos, ever calmer and expressively 'neutral': all this sometimes appears too reticent. The idea of the whole triumphs almost too much over the details. Sometimes, when Backhaus concedes a Schubert impromptu, when he has some great, pensive sonata behind him and is on holiday as it were from his objectivizing self, charm pervades his playing. This charm is the outcome of pianistic severity. With such an incorruptible and calm musician as Backhaus, small, intimate nuances are so much the more touching. When an imperturbable person, so Backhaus's charm might suggest, decides on a gesture from the heart, then this gesture will have a greater effect than the threadbare declarations of a cheerful extrovert.

With regard to the late Beethoven sonatas, yet another function may fall to the reticence of the mature Backhaus: with him the greatness of this music is not encumbered with the sentimental. When it speaks through Backhaus, Beethoven's transcendental subject can speak powerfully and solitarily about matters that hardly resemble earthly sorrows any more. Sometimes, it is true, the music sets itself in motion, 'as if of its own accord', to roaring, glorious articulation.

When Backhaus, in the first movement of the Hammerklavier Sonata, almost imperceptibly dramatizes the course of the music with his left hand, when the bass octaves import energy into the musical events here (which Backhaus achieves by an acceleration and accentuation, so slight as to be hardly expressible, of the ever more urgent octaves of his left hand), then indeed an effect is attained which as a 'detail', for copying say, is by no means striking – but certainly helps to determine the total impression (Example 4).

When Backhaus performs the Hammerklavier Sonata in the concert-hall, it has a magnificent self-evidence, as though it were written for him. He owes it nothing, neither the ethereal transparency of the passages, nor the force of the chords or the on-driving power of the harmonic tension. The Adagio sounds as though summoned from the depths, anticipating Brahms and Chopin as it were into the bargain. The fugue Backhaus can play even in the concert-hall with astonishing power and speed. And again the miracle takes place: in spite of technical perfection, which so often distracts from the expression, in spite of cool composure, which is so often devoid of 'expression', Backhaus brings it off, so that one thinks of Goethe: 'This stern heart, so gentle and tender in feeling.' He is probably the only great pianist of the present day who has the gift of letting the whole be understood in its entirety, beyond all details, in such a way that its great effect only sets in long after the artist has taken his hands from the keys.

Vladimir Horowitz

'Piano-playing consists of intelligence, heart and technique. All should be equally developed. Without intelligence you will be a fiasco, without technique an amateur, and without heart a machine. The profession has its perils.'

These remarks might be thrown out by any conservative piano teacher to a gifted but endangered pupil. They come, however, not from the mouth of some well-meaning and unimperilled pedagogue but from Vladimir Horowitz. But they are thereby already a subject of pianistic politics. Some see the hectically applauded, fashionably imitated, excessively brilliant, and hysterically shy Vladimir Horowitz as an anti-musical wizard and perverter of pianistic youth, which follows, thundering mechanically, in his footsteps. These will say that the warning was the outcome of defensiveness, that it was at bottom a self-accusation, an alibi to create concord. For in no great pianist of our time is the difference between technical, pianistic power and musical, interpretative innocuousness, indeed, insipidity, supposed to be greater than in that unhappy phenomenon Vladimir Horowitz. The Horowitz-party will thereupon insist that he is quite definitely not a mere keyboard acrobat, but that he is able to captivate as no other pianist, that he penetrates the pieces with intelligence and passion – that he has a burning concern for their musical content. Indeed, without musical commitment, Horowitz would not, for instance, have recorded Chopin's B flat minor Sonata, Op. 35, twice within a relatively short time. Although the first recording was pianistically an enviable success, Horowitz seemed dissatisfied. To him the recording did not sound sufficiently stirring or cohesive. So in 1962 he tried once more to combine the rhapsodical element and the stringency of this B flat minor sonata. If one compares the two recordings, the second does in fact sound more stirring, more collected, drier, stricter. It is not quite so ecstatic as the mannered first version, but it now exaggerates the architectonic cohesion and in this way becomes indeed highly dramatic, yet somewhat too massive.

Vladimir Horowitz, Emil Gilels, Sviatoslav Richter, David and Igor Oistrakh, Nathan Milstein, Jascha Heifetz, Leonid Kogan and Msitislav Rostropovich, i.e. that dozen or so world-class instrumentalists, all come from Russia, and today – whether they have become American citizens or whether they are politico-cultural parade-horses for the U.S.S.R. – they dominate the concert platforms of the world as no other comparable group of artists. If we let them pass before our inner ear, the question at once presents itself of the connection between interpretative culture, nationality and virtuosity. It is tempting to dispose of the Russian school of instrumentalists as indeed a specific 'school'. It is said to have been almost customary a few decades ago in Kiev, say, to train the children of middle-class Jewish families, if it was at all possible, into world stars. (In this way the young virtuoso escaped from anti-Semitic resentment and an oppressive existence.) And because some of these had chosen a career with success, there came from many a window in Kiev the sound of industrious piano or violin playing. Naturally, there will always be a good rising generation wherever there are good artists, models and above all teachers. Nothing is so fruitful – or so difficult to create – as a climate for musical development. Without pedagogues like Seidl-hofer in Vienna or Neuhaus, who died in Moscow in 1964, the piano world would wear a different look. It is well-known, moreover, how carefully the younger generation is fostered precisely in Russia. When once the young pianist or violinist has won a few competitions, the state does everything possible for his education, takes care of his maintenance and procures him the best teachers and examples. This is, of course, still no guarantee of success, and it can even lead in certain circumstances to a dreary levelling; but with regard to the good average so necessary for all art and culture, such care does pay.

Great talents who can do it alone – and only alone – are rare. Most interpretative artists thrive better with careful cultivation. And the higher the average level the more certainly can even the exceptional artist be recognized. The brilliant young Russian pianist Vladimir Ashkenazy, who now lives in England, has described the Soviet

educational system (the *Observer*, April, 1963). It is enviably thorough and commits a young talent to hard work, but it also gives
him great opportunities and remarkable liberties. To the Russians, it
seems, their pianists are worth something.

The class of a violinist is determined by the nobility of his playing,
the seriousness of his 'conception', but above all by the power, sweetness and fullness of his tone. It is in their tone, which is not produced
merely technically, but results from the tense unity of instrument and
body, that violinists differ. Among 'experts', after even a short
hearing, there is hardly any doubt about the calibre as violinist of a
young Milstein or Oistrakh – however differently the nuances of the
performance might be judged.

The class of a pianist is harder to define. Of course 'touch' has certainly nothing to do with the purely mechanical production of
sound: a miracle such as the tone of Artur Rubinstein, Emil Gilels or
even the very specific touch of the early Alfred Cortot, belongs to the
individuality of the artist. Yet 'touch' does not differentiate the
great pianists so categorically as tone does the violinists. With the
piano, which has indeed a good deal of the percussion instrument
about it, what counts mainly, besides questions of clarity, shading
and beautiful fullness, is whether a person can obtain from the
demure instrument true sonority of sound, breathing, speaking
tone-lines. But here differentiating already becomes difficult. A
violinist quite without gipsy temperament, quite without mettle,
could hardly become a violinist of class. Pianists, however, can be as
different as Eduard Erdmann and Simon Barere, Clara Haskil and
Vladimir Horowitz. With regard to the endlessly different demands of
the vast literature of the piano, there are numerous criteria of quality.

What part does virtuosity play? If one wants to do justice in particular to the great artists of the Russian piano school, one must
clarify this somewhat pedantic preliminary question. What is virtuosity on the piano, and what ends does it serve? The most obvious
and immediate answer is this: virtuoso technique ought never to be
an end in itself. Virtuosity has to subordinate itself to purely musical
requirements; otherwise music is turned into a mere artistic effect.

This is the answer always given whenever for some reason or other
the so-called 'mechanical' element in piano playing claims interest;
but is it really true? Must virtuosity subordinate itself in service to the

music, because it otherwise turns into a striving for effect? The pro-
position is true only in so far as it cannot be inverted: the meaning of
virtuosity never lies in itself. If it appears as a principle set above the
musical situation, then indeed there is nothing but 'empty virtuosity'.
The diligently practised mechanical overcoming of manual difficulties
cannot be the Alpha and Omega of a piano recital – and still less the
sole quality of a gramophone record.

Yet how are virtuosity and piano playing related to one another?
When it is a matter of the nature and possibilities of a grand piano,
can one distinguish at all between absolute music and virtuoso
wizardry?

The early Robert Schumann wrote brilliant piano music of virtuoso
demands – the Toccata Op. 7, say, or the Symphonic Studios, Op. 13.
Grown older, he wanted to produce pure, self-sufficient music: but his
compositions were not only non-virtuoso, but weaker, feebler, poorer
in nuance, less differentiated. In middle-Beethoven, in Schubert
(Wanderer fantasy), in Chopin, Brahms, indeed even in the Mozart of
the great concertos and in the Bach of the Goldberg Variations, the
display of bravura is never in conflict with the purity or depth of the
musical expression. On the contrary, the pianistically animated, virtuoso, bravura, temperamental-executant component possibly belongs (N.B. with the piano) also to the musical matter itself. Whoever
would eliminate the virtuoso element, or merely deflect it into a means
to an end, has not properly understood the piano, the strengths and
weaknesses of the keyboard instrument. He wants a great pianist to
produce from a Steinway the effects of a string quartet: those wonderful ethereal effects which arise when a quartet with feeling performs
the slow movement of Beethoven's Harp Quartet, say, or some pieces
from the Art of the Fugue. With typical piano music, however, the
contrast evoked again and again between spiritual permeation and
technical accomplishment is a distorted, not of course absolutely
false, but also not appropriate auxiliary device of the lazy-minded
critic. It must be stated differently: great piano music has a technical-
virtuoso dimension. Sometimes the technical-virtuoso dimension is an
aid to musical understanding. It can even be a way to get at the idea of
the work (more suitable, of course, is to approach the whole via
musical abstraction or submersion). The technical dimension can also
shrink to carefree, musically-neutral performing sport. Such per-

forming sport sounds quite gay now and then, but after a time it does become boring to listeners. That is why a virtuoso like the industrious Shura Cherkassky, say, can certainly call forth amazement and ovations from innocent listeners – but to the question of how the piano is being played here and now, or of how the current state of interpretation stands with reference to the great literature of the piano, Cherkassky's deft industry hardly provides an answer.

The playing of Vladimir Horowitz or Emil Gilels stands high above musically-neutral wizardry. To give a picture of how distinguished are the artistic claims of Vladimir Horowitz as interpreter, a sacrifice must be made here. The name of the victim is Julian von Karolyi – and of course our intention is not to play off the admirable virtuoso Karolyi against the greater Horowitz, but to compare their interpretations of the famous G minor ballade by Chopin. 'Karolyi belongs' – so the Deutsche Grammophon-Gesellschaft informs us – 'to the élite of living pianists. He is regarded not only as an authoritative interpreter of the masters of piano music, but in particular as a definite specialist in Chopin and Liszt.' Thus far and thus rhetorically ('not only authoritative . . . in particular, definite') the Deutsche Grammophon. When one hears how Karolyi plays the beginning of the G minor ballade, the question certainly never arises whether Julian von Karolyi is technically up to the piece. On the contrary: the calm theme of the ballade flows along fluently, the first great passage is brilliantly taken, with a yearning, picturesque ritardando, and then the eighth-notes tear over the piano.

When Horowitz performs the same piece, the beginning, so innocent with Karolyi, turns into a sober, ceremonial opening. Horowitz, the Russian virtuoso, understands the G minor ballade far more poetically. This mournful beginning, sadly singing away to itself, he, the reputed mere virtuoso, takes far more slowly than his Hungarian colleague. Horowitz not only emphasizes the top notes of the measured eighth-note groups, but turns what is with Karolyi a fairly neutral motion into a song. The work gains manifold dimensions and relations. The bass sounds different, the middle voices come to life – the melody dreams its sad dream. Then, when the first great sixteenth-note passage arrives, so typical of Chopin, Horowitz keeps rigidly in time. For this reason he can then afford to play out the following figure with slow grandeur and a slow climax. So, although Horowitz may

63

be regarded as an unthinking virtuoso, he begins the G minor ballade far more calmly, poetically and thoughtfully than Karolyi. Infinitely more happens even in the first minutes. That Horowitz then intensifies the ballade, to the extent that the piano statement becomes richer; that he plays out dramatically the pride and burning sorrow with which the music sings here, 'Poland is lost indeed' – this one may still chalk up against him as exaggerated, too tightly-packed virtuoso playing: it remains nevertheless beyond all dispute that Horowitz plays the G minor ballade, even purely musico-dramatically, far more thoughtfully and reflectively than Julian von Karolyi, so well-known and everywhere so rightly praised.

Vladimir Horowitz was born in Kiev in 1904. The matchless virtuosity of this pianist, which has a demonic effect on many listeners, has been bitterly bought: after a sensational career, Horowitz has had to retire almost completely since February 25, 1953. Nervous afflictions, shyness, the fear of being inadequate to his own fame, private cares and entanglements: all this brought it about that for many years the greatest pianist of an epoch only made recordings; that he announced concerts time and again, and called them off – until at last, in 1965, he had a sensationally successful public comeback. Clearly, Vladimir Horowitz lacks the naïve naturalness of those virtuosi for whom self-exhibition and the pleasure of brilliant display are enough. After an operation, which brought him to an enforced standstill, Horowitz decided that one does not, after all, go through life in order to play octaves – though he knew how to play them, indeed, in a way for which many pianists would be prepared to go through life.

Horowitz's career began in the twenties. He himself was surprised that his conquests were not made through the capital cities of the countries. 'In Russia it was Leningrad, not Moscow, in Germany Hamburg instead of Berlin, in America not New York but Chicago. The capitals only came later.' Horowitz playfully maintains that he may have owed his career to an accident. After an unnoticed and financially unrewarding concert in Hamburg, he came back to his hotel towards evening a few days later, cold and hungry from a walk through the Zoological Gardens. There the manager was waiting: Horowitz was to take the place of a lady pianist who had suddenly been taken ill, and who had intended playing the Tchaikovsky

Example 5

From: Franz Liszt, Piano Sonata in B minor.

In these prestissimo octaves (from bar 10 of our example), the highest virtuosity turns into unfettered expression. This is where the class of a Liszt player is decided. Here only Gilels comes near Horowitz.

concerto under Eugen Pabst. Horowitz asked for a glass of milk, shaved, and hurried to the concert-hall, where the symphony had just finished and Pabst had no idea at all whether a soloist would appear. Pabst came into the artist's room, hardly looked at the young pianist, said in a few words what tempi he would be taking, and ended with the hint: 'Just watch my stick, and everything will be all right.'

After the first few chords, the conductor was staring at the young unknown; at the end he rushed to the piano. The concerto was a hysterical success. The critics declared that not since Caruso's appearance had Hamburg witnessed such a triumph. Another concert was arranged at once, and two hours after it was announced 3,000 tickets had been sold.

Such stories are part of the life of every virtuoso. A fairy-tale moment of cinema and high drama is in keeping with an artist's life. Virtuosos are indeed no bureaucrats – a real debut has to be like a fairy's kiss, which suddenly changes the whole of life. With Tchaikovsky, Rachmaninoff and Liszt, Horowitz then played his way to victory. We can judge what he was like at that time if we study the recording he made in 1932 of Liszt's great B minor sonata. Virtuosity turns into mad tension. If one hears the piece, the famous fugato, the re-entry of the main subject, the brilliantly embroidered second subject, as played by Vladimir Horowitz, one must marvel at the wonderfully intelligent, cleverly ascending structure that Horowitz gives the work, which never loses itself in detail and yet pervades every nuance. Piano playing like this is not 'playing'. In the notorious octave runs near the end, one no longer even notices how marvellously fast Horowitz can take the octaves, how cleanly, how powerfully; instead, one feels that in these octaves a hounded and magnificent Lisztian temperament is expressing itself, that it is a matter of life and death. Horowitz is one of the greatest pianists of our epoch because he can do this (Example 5).

Although most of the young pianists of the present day, but also so intimately musical an artist as Clifford Curzon, a Wilhelm Kempff or an Artur Rubinstein, refuse to share in the branding of Liszt as a heretic, and devote their skill time and again to Liszt's great *oeuvre*, Vladimir Horowitz is probably the greatest Liszt player of our time. Only Sviatoslav Richter and Emil Gilels can match the bravura of

Example 6

From: Liszt, Nineteenth Rhapsody for Piano.

It is not only tempo and virtuosity that counts, but grasp. Here, in bars 2, 3, 4 and 5 of our example, Horowitz plays with most emphasis, not by any means the rolling thirty-second notes, but the two sixteenth-notes which fall each time on the third beat of the bar. The rhythmic refinement with which he here at the same time builds up and holds back, points and forces, is something that cannot be learned.

67

Example 7

From: Chopin, Mazurka in C sharp minor, Op. 63, No. 3.

The last two bars – both of our example and of this mazurka – have to bring an extraordinary climax to a checked, balanced and decisive end. Horowitz can afford an extreme forte here, because he has taken the imitation-crescendo of the previous bars with a seriousness far beyond the bounds of the conventional. Chopin's mazurkas are regarded as short, almost innocuous little genre pieces which any exaggeration will damage. This is probably a mistake. For if the notes are taken literally, without following 'traditional' readings, there is nothing diminutive in this supposed miniature. By forcibly uniting brevity and extreme expression, Chopin anticipates a stylistic feature of musical expressionism.

Horowitz's Liszt interpretations, which tell not only of dexterity, but of a feeling for life that is at the same time original and magnificent. Horowitz has captured Liszt's second, sixth, fifteenth and nineteenth Hungarian rhapsodies on astonishing records – and also arranged them (made them more difficult, of course). The end of the sixth rhapsody, the beginning of the fifteenth, and the beginning of the nineteenth, so very strange harmonically, he plays with breath-taking fascination – although sometimes perhaps going beyond the bounds of the piano and so-called discretion. As almost always when Horowitz gives of his best, the effect arises less from breakneck speed than as the outcome of his predatory grasp, flexible, urgent and brilliantly thought-out. The sparkling dance measures from the Lassan of the nineteenth rhapsody are certainly not so difficult that a gifted amateur must despair at them (Example 6).

Yet when one has once heard how Horowitz during these Lassan measures can come to grips with the piano; how with fierce flexibility he sets a minute hesitation in the staccato sixteenth-notes against the hardly perceptible acceleration in the urgency of the rolling thirty-second notes; how he lets the piano speak, and how not one note escapes the control of his brilliant rhythmic instinct, then one understands again how little mere correctness means, even with a Liszt. With Scarlatti, Chopin, Liszt, Schumann, Brahms and Prokofiev, Horowitz creates a plane of pianistic data on which – to move his listeners as it were to complete capitulation – he then, and only then, allows his unsurpassable virtuosity to triumph. So it is also no accident that to the disappointment of his 'fans' he turns to the supposedly easy little pieces – Schumann's Träumerei, Schubert impromptus, or a Haydn sonata – with exactly the same scrupulous accuracy.

When one has heard an average Chopin interpretation, and then puts on Chopin's Mazurka in C sharp minor, Op. 63, No. 3, which lasts even less than two minutes, played by Horowitz, the difference bowls one over. No one else could risk playing the rhythm so flexibly and tautly, without the left hand becoming too obtrusive; no one could so ecstatically pile up the stretto, through which the late-Chopin shows how close Bach's polyphony was even to his thinking and composition; no one could play the last two bars with such iron hardness, without killing the mazurka as an expressive phantom-piece, distorted into the unrecognizable – or the recognizable? Yet

69

none of the spices, sometimes affectedly sharp, obtrudes with Horowitz. Everything is in balance (Example 7).

The comparative restraint which Horowitz imposes on himself in the smaller pieces sometimes falls prey, nevertheless, to senseless speed. It is incomprehensible why the man who can play the great Chopin Polonaise, Op. 22, with overwhelming discretion and irresistible, fantastic brio, should take the quiet, introductory Andante spianato, which Chopin indeed was quite especially fond of, unfeelingly at a killing speed. In a few of Chopin's large works too – not in those of Liszt – Horowitz occasionally lapses into thundering, into martellato, in a frenzied display of force. Then his virtuosity discloses nothing. Then it kills the intimacy of the Barcarole or the tender coquetry of the A flat ballade. And when Horowitz dashes away thoughtlessly, as in the finale of the F major sonata (K 332) by Mozart, there is not even any suspense. One knows nothing will happen to him; nothing at all will happen, and one lets matters take their rapid course.

Horowitz has not sinned often. The power with which he makes the close of Chopin's first and third scherzos into an only just conceivable peak of pianistic expression he owes to an almost unbearable, extreme vehemence. Each detail is presented with fantastic clarity, penetrating verve and a mysterious capacity for simultaneous expressiveness.

Let us dwell further on the revealing, the discerning virtuosity of Horowitz: on the verve with which Horowitz (with Toscanini's help) Italianized Brahms's second piano concerto; on the expression with which he rescued Rachmaninoff's third concerto, which collapses if it is taken moderately, discreetly and with restraint. Typical of Horowitz was his plan to present Brahms's D minor concerto as 'Brahms without beard', as the work indeed of a young composer. Clearly, the shadows that emanate from the person of the sour old bachelor should not fall on Opus 15.

All that has been said here suggests that Horowitz can sooner find notes even for Debussy or Poulenc or Scriabin than for Beethoven. And yet it is precisely for the Beethoven sonatas that the passionate care of this great pianist is of value. The Pathétique, the Moonlight, the Waldstein, the Appassionata, the C minor variations, and the E flat major concerto he has already recorded. Even the Hammer-

70

klavier has not been avoided. Now if technical problems no longer play any part at all, Beethoven's sonatas are more 'difficult' than his concertos to the extent that they impose on the pianist the whole burden of the shaping, the planning. In a piano concerto, an orchestra is there, which stimulates, answers, takes the lead and offers opposition. Can Horowitz, whose special characteristics are revealed when he plays Slavonic and late-Romantic works, when he has to overcome technical opposition intelligently, when he can bring finesse and sensitivity into his playing, can he become an interpreter of Beethoven? The answer which is given at least by most European music-lovers is an unconditional No. And even in America, there is no lack of criticism. Virgil Thompson called Horowitz a 'master of exaggeration and misrepresentation'. 'One should not gather from this that Horowitz's interpretations are absolutely wrong and indefensible,' Thompson went on with seeming mildness, 'some are, some are not.' But then Thompson, hardly seeming mild any more, lets fall his death sentence: 'Anyone who had never heard the works which Horowitz played last night might easily come to think that Bach was a musician of the Leopold Stokowski type, Brahms a sort of frivolous Gershwin employed by a first-class night-club, and Chopin but a gipsy violinist.'

Criticism like this, sure of its mark, flies from the pen. Everyone reads it with delight, for *Schadenfreude* unites the human race. But are such conclusions admissible when the sins have been committed, as it were, at the Horowitz level?

This level is to be observed, that is to say, even in Horowitz's piano-battle with Beethoven. Horowitz distorts hardly anything. In the E flat concerto, his playing is imperious, powerful, measured – but not without a feeling for style, not without taste. The wide-ranging parts of the work – the cadenzas right at the beginning, the Rondo – come with cast-iron assurance. The pure poetry of some of the transitions, the inner tension, the deep seriousness, which is somewhat different from the 'Emperor' grandezza so often read into this concerto – all this Edwin Fischer, considerably inferior to Horowitz pianistically, has caught better, it is true. But Fischer also had Furtwängler's Berlin Philharmonic at his side – and they were an incomparably more serious, more thoughtful partner than the musicians, sharp in style and rich in the upper register, of the R.C.A.

Victor Symphony Orchestra under Fritz Reiner. The danger to Horowitz's Beethoven playing comes not from excessive virtuosity, but from excessive sensuality! Where Horowitz becomes expressive, a late-Romantic twilight too readily comes into his playing, a heavy, dreamily pointed Tchaikovsky tone, a dash of 'Russian soul', as in the Largo of the Sonata, Op. 10, No. 3, for instance, or in the introduction of the Pathétique. Yet in all this, it is a matter not of breaches of style but only of 'colouring' – and who is to say that the German image of Beethoven is the only possible one? Sometimes Horowitz discovers, even in Beethoven, further opportunities for pianistic improvement. In the variation movement of the Appassionata, that is to say, Horowitz succeeds in introducing a two-part character that is clearly held throughout. Naturally, this two-part character is there, prescribed beyond doubt. From the outset, the bass line of the theme has not only significance as harmonic support, but at the same time the function of a passacaglia bass. The first variation then also holds this two-part character clearly throughout, and so does the second.

Everybody knows this, or could know it. But Horowitz manages to shade his left hand in the theme in such a way that, without any mannered disjointedness, it both supports the D flat major chords of the chorale-like melody and also – in the form of a meaningful bass line – exists clearly in its own right. Now the first variation no longer sounds as meaningless as in many interpretations of the Appassionata (Example 8).

With the chivalrous poetry of the early Schumann, Horowitz naturally has an easier time than with Beethoven. The Toccata, Op. 7, is one of his gems, the variations from Op. 14 blossom under his hands, the Presto Passionato has nobility, and even in the Scenes from Childhood he commits no crimes of virtuoso violation.

Sometimes he is too careful, rather. This was why he sought advice from the brilliant harpsichordist and Scarlatti interpreter Ralph Kirkpatrick, and even let himself be encouraged into this or that octave-doubling. His last Scarlatti record has become the intimate high-point of an almost mellow, gentle pianistic art.

Horowitz has hardly any pupils, but he has numerous imitators. There is in the life of every piano-mad youngster a time of absolute Horowitz-worship – unless this piano-mad youngster happens to live

Example 8

From: Beethoven, Piano Sonata in F minor, Op. 57, Appassionata, second movement.

This variation from the Andante of the Appassionata gives many interpreters trouble. For it only makes sense, apparently, if it carries on the two-part character that has already been set out in the theme. Here Beethoven has demonstrated the two-part character, which was at first contained within the simultaneity of the chords, by a shift of phase. The syncopations explain, as it were, what the initial chords concealed. Horowitz's technical resources are so great that he can use his artistry of touch here to interpret a complicated situation.

73

in Germany, where in many record-shops most Horowitz records are not even stocked.

Byron Janis is Horowitz's one prominent pupil. Horowitz offered the young man tuition, and Janis worked with Horowitz for three years. In the magazine *Musical America* (October 1962, pp. 32 ff.), Janis has given an account of what he learned from Horowitz. The 'Master' went so far as to write studies for the young pianist, which were to further the development of Janis's piano hand. In addition, Horowitz begged his pupil rather to make his own mistakes than copy the mistakes of others. Not without pride, Janis lets it be understood that he too, of course, was in danger of becoming a copy of Horowitz. Yet one only had to come to one's senses in time.

Jürgen Fehling once remarked that when a theatrical performance runs its course quite without an element of showmanship, in stylistically pure seriousness, the evening can become dry, sterile and refined in a dreadful way. A touch of trickery, of delight in expertise, belongs entirely to the notion of art, which would indeed betray the very idea of its 'sublimity' if it sought to be sublime the whole time. Mozart, Beethoven, Schubert, and all the other great ones were well aware of this. . . . Now Horowitz sometimes has this pure enjoyment of artistry, particularly in encores. Then he may play his own arrangement of Philip Sousa's march Stars and Stripes for Ever, or thunder out Mendelssohn's Wedding March in Liszt's arrangement, with added difficulties of his own composition, or sparkle with little salon pieces by Moszkowski; he has even played a mad Carmen Fantasy. Now there are no piano-lovers anywhere in the world who are not glad to succumb to such bravura pieces. Then later they say, shaking their heads: the pianist is not serious-minded. But because Horowitz performs such things to perfection, they tend in a curious way no longer to trust him in his classic or romantic interpretations. They feel he should indeed only do what he can do best: i.e. play popular attractions only. This wish may be an obvious one. It is destructive – and kill-joy. Does the fact that someone can overwhelm with certain trivial pieces have any significance whatsoever for his Schumann, Beethoven or Chopin interpretations?

Besides, Horowitz scorns well-trodden paths. He has revived Clementi sonatas and even discovered a charming, innocuous variation piece by Carl Czerny, so dreaded as a writer of studies. The trifle is called La Ricordanza. Its theme derives from a violinist named Rode. Horowitz plays it as though the dear Lord had turned pianist. But his most famous interpretation – although the records have acoustically appropriate defects – probably remains after all his performance of the B flat minor concerto by Tchaikovsky. Wild rumours circulate about it, of how many rehearsals Horowitz's inexorable father-in-law, Arturo Toscanini, demanded, and of how urgently the exhausted pianist had to seek the sheltering walls of a nerve clinic. Indeed, forty or more rehearsals of Tchaikovsky can ruin even a healthy man. This is why even average pianists and con-ductors, who might be in greater need of it than Horowitz and Tos-canini, spare themselves such rehearsal work. It will go all right, they reckon. But how it can go when a daemonic will and an unbridled temperament take up the Tchaikovsky concerto with intense concen-tration; of this, happily for them, they know nothing. And while those who despise Horowitz's art continue to amuse themselves over his supposed 'superficiality', Horowitz has long since also discovered for himself the intimate realm of refined piano playing. His gentle Scarlatti record has already made ears prick up. The recordings of his second début, which took place in New York after a twelve-year break, show that the thunderer can also sing. Since Alfred Cortot recorded a Bach aria beguilingly, hardly anyone has wrung from the piano such a cantilena as Horowitz in his interpretation of the A minor Adagio from Busoni's arrangement of Bach's Toccata, Adagio and Fugue in C major. Extreme refinement turns here into pure artlessness!

Wilhelm Kempff

It is striking that Wilhelm Kempff, the German pianist whom many today regard as one of the most remarkable interpreters of our time, appears to surpass the piano-playing élite of the world not indeed in thoughtfulness, 'dedication' and profundity, but rather in individuality, in an intelligence of phrasing which often extends to coquetry, and in sensitive charm. If one tries to imagine how English-speaking music-critics generally think of a German pianist, and what it is they are afraid of, one continually comes up against fear of dry-academic, brooding earnestness – and the expectation of austere thoughtfulness. This is not surprising. Pianists such as Eduard Erdmann or Edwin Fischer or Elly Ney, who in Germany are shown the great veneration to which they are entitled, have given the world the example of a somewhat unworldly and very German ideal type. They have cultivated what might be called an anti-virtuoso 'dramatic inwardness'. Often, since the days of Clara Schumann, with a touch of high priestliness, which attracts as much veneration as ridicule among colleagues.

And Wilhelm Kempff? Whether he is untouched or flattered by the fact that many of his friends and admirers make a 'prophet' of him (not only in Germany, moreover; French admiration for Kempff is no less strong), his playing contains no trace of titanic thundering, either cheap or high-minded. In reality it amounts by no means to blind endorsement of long-accepted cultural goods. For what counts is not what is written in emotional autobiographies, what is stammered out by breathless and inarticulate amateurs, but only the pianistic development, the acquired style. Heard thus, Kempff is still a 'decadent' rather than a 'thunderer'. His touch combines grace, transparency, irony and self-assurance. Perhaps for this reason, the effect of his touch is often a little brittle, sharp, fragile, 'unreliable'.

The fact that twenty-five years ago, during the time of Hitler, Kempff could say, 'However many swastikas the Nazis may paint in front of the Waldstein Sonata – they still can't play it', can still be heard today in his alert and supple playing. And a good deal more, too. Wilhelm Kempff, born in Jüterbog in 1895, comes, so it says in every biographical note, from an old family of musicians in Prussia. His grandfather was an organist, and so was his father; and when the ten-year-old grandson in short trousers could not only play preludes and fugues from The Well-tempered Clavier at an entrance examination, but also transpose them into any required key, astonishment knew no bounds. Why question too closely whether such a child-prodigy story is really wholly true. . . . It is enough that it could be true. For talent, intellect, ascendancy and a lofty spirit, emerging as they sometimes do in late-arrivals, belong completely to this pianist. Now it should not be concealed, however, that with Kempff, who for decades has been one of the most popular artists, at least in Europe, a necessity has been made of a virtue: for the cultivation of the personal and the individual against all dynamic temptations collapses only too easily into manual unreliability. It goes quite without saying that an artist even of the pianistic class of Kempff takes any such collapse in his stride. Yet when he interprets the two piano concertos by Liszt, for instance, it becomes obvious what a gulf exists between such playing and the technical standard of the world élite.

Certainly, Wilhelm Kempff is no Liszt player. Kempff's strength – his sense of values, his delight in intelligent sensitivity – remains powerless in face of the demands of a Liszt concerto, the stretto, say, of the A major concerto. When one hears Kempff's attempt to humanize this music tastefully, when it is really a matter of disclosing its manliness, its seriousness, its pride, one feels that Kempff trod on dangerous ground when he took up the struggle with Liszt and the great Liszt interpreters. If one applies the highest standards, Kempff is pianistically not up to the A major concerto.

With Liszt, however, the bravura belongs to the matter itself: Liszt's feeling for life was bravura – the delight in technical arrangement, in pianistic self-display, is here nothing superficial, no decoration, but of the essence. Kempff has neither power nor brilliance enough for Liszt.

77

Now it is well known, of course, that it was not indeed as a Liszt player that Kempff made a name. Anyone who compares Kempff's Liszt with that of Sviatoslav Richter, will not avoid the conclusion that Richter plays a more powerful, clearer Liszt, formulated more arrestingly and mastered with greater technical sovereignty. But many culture-proud music-lovers might actually consider it to Kempff's credit that he fails with Liszt. They will rightly draw attention to Kempff's Schumann playing. Kempff does not play Schumann like a ballade; he does not thunder out the Florestan pathos with the fury of a concerto; but neither does he sentimentalize Schumann for the cosy in their nooks. Kempff has grasped, rather, as hardly any other living pianist, the mixture of brokenness and happiness, of dream and intelligence, of longing and vision, which can be evoked into sound in Schumann's compositions, when a pianist strikes the magic word. Kempff's taut sensitivity teaches one to understand Schumann. Precisely because Kempff emphasizes not just one tendency in Schumann's compositions, but abandons himself to their multiplicity, which can often hardly be synthesized any more, Schumann's works gain dimensions and perspectives that reach beyond the purely musical. When one hears Kempff's Papillons, Humoresque, the Symphonic Studies, the piano concerto or the Kreisleriana – if the pianist has a good, inspired evening under no pressures – then miracles of refinement are at hand, which need fear no comparison with Cortot's greatest moments. As against these, the occasional technical irregularities, the obscurities of the pianistic formulation, are of no consequence.

Naturally, such moments of spontaneity are not easy to capture on records. To 'dream' them up alone in a recording studio is particularly difficult. Fortunately, there are nevertheless a few recordings which have caught Kempff's blissful, high-strung dream. Kempff's grasp of Schumann is shown by his recording of Kreisleriana, Op. 16. Robert Schumann dedicated his Kreisleriana to Chopin, who incidentally could make little of the work. To the form-conscious Pole, these fantasias inspired by E. T. A. Hoffmann were possibly too ragged, too eccentric, too entangled.

Now under Kempff's hands, no vagrant, imaginative nuance is lost. Yet through them all Kempff can demonstrate the Schumann unity, the compelling inner – one could almost say psychological –

onward movement. The last three pieces (Nos. 6, 7 and 8) Kempff interprets inimitably. He manages to incorporate the brittle and hectic elements, which so many music-lovers dislike in Schumann, into the cosmos there depicted and to make them enchanting. He by no means harps on the excitable, the yearning eclectic elements, if one may so put it. He makes of these tendencies, rather, a comprehensible, fulfilled expression of the Schumann spirit, necessary and aesthetically convincing. Suddenly the 'breaks' become a monument to delicately attested Romantic truth. Schumann appears as a forerunner of Gustav Mahler.

The sixth of the Kreisleriana fantasias is very slow and 'to be kept absolutely soft'. An almost rigidly calm beginning, profound and dark in tone, is interrupted by abrupt, scattered thirty-second notes, but remains nevertheless, unbanished, like a Romantic dream. Kempff plays with persistent sensitivity, as the dream then takes on a soaring motion, which rises to a promise of happiness – enclosed in its own magic, shy, unworldly, but indestructible. This certainty in fragility is evidence of concealed mastery. There is about the piece here – quite legitimately, in view of the title alone – something unmistakably literary. In the seventh fantasia, the interpretative tact of style with which Kempff at the same time fulfils and alienates the demands of Schumann's neo-baroque is perhaps even more tremendous. From our example it can be seen how closely Schumann stuck to J. S. Bach. The sixteenth notes could be a quotation from Bach's Organ Toccata in F major (Example 9).

But Kempff interprets Schumann's return to Bach in such a way that one feels that evocation of the past was for the Romantics no stylistic game, not the expression of a clever Alexandrianism, but – as with Novalis – the ever impossible attempt to recuperate from one's own discord in the grandeurs and delights of the past. Schumann, who admired and arranged Bach, composes in the style of a toccata: pithy, powerful, with a baroque flow.

Kempff – and this is why his playing grants such an overwhelming, verifying perspective – manages to let one hear the metaphorical, the strained, the delightfully overheated elements of Schumann's yearning baroque. By bringing out the weakness – more correctly, the element that cannot come off – in the stylistic imitation, he at the same time rescues Schumann's greatness. Instead of a meaningless

Example 9
From: Schumann, Kreisleriana, Op. 16, seventh movement, 'very fast.'

Kempff gives Schumann's neo-baroque a yearning rapture and creates a poetically broken, differentiated cosmos. After that, the dreamy half-light at the end is no longer mere contrast, but Romantic actuality.

eclecticism, one grasps the ardent longing, impossible of fulfilment, which lies in such a Quixotic turning to the past. Brokenness stands in for truth – and this is more than cheap imitation of baroque might. When Kempff plays them, the notes have not Bach's majesty, but Schumann's ardent excitability. They slip by, in Kempff's interpretation, like a ghost, like a blurred dream of knightly castles and vanished glory. The sweet and drowsing chords, ever-fading, of the 'somewhat slower' bring the dreamer back again, into the Romantic present. Kempff makes no virtuoso piano feast of it, but catches the eternity of dream-time, the moment of pure poetry. Two superscriptions from Scenes from Childhood are combined in Kempff's playing of Schumann: 'The poet speaks' and is 'almost too serious'.

Wilhelm Kempff has not only had a public for decades; he is at the same time a pianist for professionals. Some peculiarities and manual unreliabilities may occasionally tarnish the impression: yet Kempff's independence of mind is prepossessing. In nearly every piece, he discovers details overlooked by others, brings out transitions, draws attention to modulations. He is one of those pianists who 'hold on' passionately to whatever is individual to them, refusing to let it be thrust aside; who always give and dare their own expression – if necessary at the cost of technical perfection.

In this, of course, lies also a persistent coquetry, to which that very sharp-eared music critic Alexander Berrsche drew attention as early as 1927. Berrsche wrote at that time:

'Kempff has that charm of touch which seems like a convincing rehabilitation of the much mishandled and much-abused piano, and he is so conscious of this gift that one could often be in doubt whether he is more pleased with Beethoven or with the tonal magic of the instrument. I have already drawn attention to this conflict in earlier years, which became particularly clear in Kempff's playing of Bach: to his tendency to allow dynamics and tone-colour to be governed sometimes, not by the natural course and expression of the melos and the whole compositional situation, but by a delight in sound that is purely of the moment, in the primitive way of a strolling player. This time too, pleasure in the sweetness and fullness of his piano quite often led him astray, into turning a pronounced, indeed prescribed, crescendo tendency into a diminuendo.'

This criticism contains a great respect for Kempff's art, for Kempff's

passion in interpretative freedom and shading – but at the same time
it describes the dangers that can lie in any *hubris* over conception.
While with Sviatoslav Richter, say, it would be difficult for us to
determine a personal tone, with Kempff personality is triumphant.
His pleasure in dryness, suppleness, in an intelligent, slender piano
tone pared of all excess, in his typical pointing, is unceasing. If
Richter, with regard to pointing, has no style, then Kempff's playing
consists only of style; while Richter looks for pure directness of
expression and of temperament and of impetus, Kempff finds the
nuance, the between-tone, the brokenness. Kempff avoids riotous
sonority. When he plays the great Brahms concertos, or even the
Brahms-Handel variations, his tone is often a shade too decorative,
too finely wrought, too weak. But the unrest of a late-Brahms intermezzo, its gentle agitation, which wanders on without exultation,
intangible and yet irreparable – this Kempff catches with arresting sensitivity.

Want of violence combined with the grand manner, and a wayward
intelligence that can also draw attention to unobtrusive musical
relations: this is the picture of Kempff. Tchaikovsky would be
nothing for him. But very much in his line is the splendid manner, the
autocratic solitariness of intelligent expression. When he presents the
theme of the symphonic studies by Robert Schumann so sonorously –
there is no other word for it – one regrets all the more that he is
unable to master all the variations themselves with equal sovereignty.
Wherever the virtuoso, pianistic expression becomes the matter itself,
Kempff often falls short. If, however, he has the chance in some way
to 'subjectivize' difficulties, then his interpretative instinct is like a
divining-rod. He is even able to make his own the rushing thirty-
second notes of the F sharp major Impromptu, Op. 36, by Chopin
(there is also, it is true, an unfeelingly sketchy interpretation by
Kempff of Chopin's A flat Impromptu, Op. 29, in which the razor-
sharp pianist even fails to make the final point; the rests there are
really supposed to substitute exactly for the theme, which is offered
ever more fragmentarily, so that the listener has to make up ever
more for ever fewer notes).

Yet what is the outcome when so much sheer sensitivity, so much
wit, wayward intelligence and pensive brooding encounter Beethoven? It is not first and foremost the so-called 'confessional' sonatas

that stir Kempff, but the as it were more objective ones in major keys. Kempff has the freedom to point the Rondo theme in the Sonata, Op. 2, No. 2, which is repeated with terrible frequency, slightly differently each time it comes round, whereby he reduces all other pianists, who here repeat the same phrasing twenty times, to people who wind up musical boxes. For the Rondo from the early B flat major Concerto, Op. 19, for the clear charm of the G major Sonata, Op. 31, No. 1, and for the staccato Bacchanale of the E flat major Sonata, Op. 31, No. 3, he also finds a pleasing personal equivalent. The 'inner tension', which is so often missed here by the great virtuosi, is produced in Kempff without any titanic forcing. Kempff is an atmosphere-creating pianist. For this reason solo pieces (even out-of-the-way and innocuous ones, such as Beethoven's early Bagatelles or the whimsical Rage over a Lost Penny) are even more in accord with the natural bent of this pianist than the great piano concertos. For in playing with an orchestra the pianist indeed is relieved of much – by no means all! – of the work of shaping, of 'ordering', and is required instead to be so much more brilliant.

Certainly, in view of the empty, superficial skill and accuracy with which many young pianists play Beethoven's piano concertos, as though it were a matter of Czerny, Kempff's intellectuality, his feeling for relations and harmonies, is a tonic. The way in which, in the E flat concerto, he accentuates the development right at the beginning, goes for expression and shading in the G major concerto, and in the rondos of the early concertos offers rhythmic charm, not rhythmic stamping: this has masterly independence.

Yet in all this it is hard to ignore the fact that Kempff's tone lacks the greatness, the calm power, which one expects after all from a Beethoven concerto.

Astonishing, at any rate, is the mixture of the old-fashioned and the independent-minded. Thus Kempff – in contrast to most young pianists – is convinced that Beethoven's cadenzas have an 'unfinished quality'. Kempff associates himself explicitly with Franz Kullak's words, and so, in the first four piano concertos, instead of the available Beethoven cadenzas, he plays his own. (In the E flat concerto, Beethoven abolished the freedom of choice.) Now it would be perfectly understandable if a pianist, at the spot in a classic instrumental concerto open for his own improvising, really did want to make 'his own' statement – whether there were Beethoven cadenzas or not.

Yet the dispute cannot be settled with the argument that Beethoven has provided nothing usable. The great cadenza of Beethoven's for the first movement of the G major concerto is on the level of the Waldstein Sonata; and the cadenza to the first movement of the B flat concerto is more distinguished and more weighty than the whole piece (we shall have something further to say about this anachronistic masterpiece with reference to Glenn Gould and Friedrich Gulda). Oddly enough, many pianists who still derive from the nineteenth-century harbour an aversion to Beethoven's supposedly 'dry' cadenzas. Kempff is not alone in seeming to regard his own artless bits of cadenza-making as more 'finished' than the 'unfinished' ones of Beethoven. The brilliant Leschetitsky pupil, Benno Moiseiwitsch, has also expressed himself strongly, even as a seventy-two-year-old artist, against Beethoven's cadenzas. In the magazine *Musical America* (March, 1962), Moiseiwitsch is quoted as follows: 'I hate cadenzas. In Beethoven's first concerto I never play a cadenza, and neither did Rachmaninoff. I have something unique for Beethoven's fourth concerto. It is a cadenza by Sir Francis Tovey, only a page long, and it is composed as though Beethoven had stood behind him. I have the only copy. I rarely play the second concerto, and for the third I have an old-fashioned, simple cadenza by Reinecke. I don't like Beethoven's cadenzas.'

Kempff, who seems slightly better disposed towards cadenzas as such, can make equally little of those by Beethoven. And so he makes nothing at all.

This fearlessness towards the accepted is kindled fruitfully, on the other hand, by tiny things that leave Backhaus cold. When Kempff plays the little C minor Sonata, Op. 10, No. 1, for instance, he raises this piece, with which piano pupils are confronted right at the start of their studies, to the heights of a whimsical art. At the close of the Adagio, where a calm cantilena emerges from the A flat figurations like a gift, Kempff becomes not, say, particularly expressive, but in fact strikingly simple. Yet the effect of this simplicity is not naturally spontaneous. It is an extreme, rather, of nuancing – and at the same time more effective than any nuance, however refined its presentation. If one hears the introductory Adagio of the Moonlight Sonata from

Solomon and from Kempff, one is really forced to wonder whether both have played the same piece. Kempff sticks to the alla breve marking of the Adagio; he reads two quarter-notes as one unit and so plays the piece nearly twice as fast as Solomon, who gives each triplet its face value. With Backhaus too the Adagio is two minutes shorter (that is a lot!) than with Gulda or Horowitz. With Backhaus, the decision to take a firmly progressive tempo also signified at the same time the expression of an anti-sentimental tendency. Kempff, on the other hand, interprets the Adagio swiftly and yet with fragility, sensitively and yet with briskness. It is no wonder that the Waldstein Sonata, as symbol of classical animation, corresponds perhaps most of all to Kempff's talent. Its throbbing liveliness, the trinity of pure feeling for nature, latent piety, and eternally productive joy of life, is, with Kempff, neither emasculated into study runs, nor does he have to play the piece as if it were an Appassionata in a major key. The great minor-key sonatas open to his grasp less readily. While the Waldstein Sonata is mastered with similar art only by Friedrich Gulda, the Appassionata and the realm of the last sonatas, between Op. 101 and Op. 111, are not Kempff's domain to the same degree, well though he breaks up and differentiates the slow movement of the Hammerklavier Sonata. Under Kempff's hands the seemingly unmysterious surface of the classically reserved Beethoven acquires magic. Others may play it more austerely and compactly, with greater virtuosity and feeling of menace: he is close to the mystery because he can abandon himself to it with apparent relaxation.

Claudio Arrau

Compared with Artur Rubinstein, Wilhelm Backhaus, Vladimir Horowitz or Wilhelm Kempff, whose artistic physiognomy seems clear, indeed sometimes downright exaggerated, as though every artist has to have an individual label, the pianist Claudio Arrau is enveloped in an aura of apartness, of impenetrability, of mystery. The word 'mystery' should not be misconstrued as romantic. There is nothing daemonic, nothing Paganini-like in his playing. And if Paganini's contemporaries suspected that whenever this violinist appeared there was a faint whiff of sulphur, and that Paganini had made the G-string of his violin from the gut of a dear departed, similar suppositions with regard to Claudio Arrau and his grand piano would be completely misplaced. All the same, one can still speak of an 'Arrau mystery', even if there is really nothing mysterious about it. For just as it seems obvious to characterize certain modes of interpretation as 'typical Rubinstein', 'typical Kempff' or 'typical Horowitz', so is it hard to discern what is in fact 'typical' for Arrau. He is not engaged in any cult of individuality. He has a brilliant technique at his disposal, like a range of armament, which wards off any attack, any penetrating criticism – but he is still by no means like those young American perfectionists whose playing often enough emits the boring thunder or hum of a machine.

Arrau is not only one of the most famous virtuosi of the world, but also one of the most industrious. He gives concerts one after the other in Tokyo, New York, Munich, London and New York again; he believes that the constant changes of air keep him fresh and resilient; and he has at his disposal an extraordinarily large repertoire. The mystery is clearly connected with Arrau's universality. An example of how hard it is to characterize Arrau is offered by the book *Contemporary Concert Pianists* by Hans-Peter Range (Moritz

Schauenburg, Lahr), which appeared recently. Range writes of Claudio Arrau: 'When this distinguished artist plays an adagio in a Beethoven sonata, every listener believes himself transported into another world, for Arrau achieves the absolute maximum of solemnity and dignity. Full of depth and pearl-like precision are also his performances of Chopin's works, to which he often and gladly turns. The interpretation of the Schubert sonatas too,' so our informant continues to specify, undaunted, 'or of the rhapsodies of Liszt, are mastered by this supreme artist just as convincingly as the presentation of a fugue by Bach or the performance of a concerto by Mozart. In sovereign fashion this congenial interpreter,' Range maintains, 'performs all works, from Bach to Brahms and Ravel, with exemplary sense of style, profundity, precision and complete perfection. His interpretative style is distinguished above all by gentleness and deep sincerity, though he is also fully able to arouse enthusiasm with the virile strength of his touch.'

More one cannot ask with the best will in the world, at least, not from Arrau. Now it is certainly no accident that the lamentable Hans-Peter Range has hardly anything further to say about Arrau than: he can do everything very well. The Arrau phenomenon is also not in the least explained by the fact that the artist was born in Chile in 1903. It is true, South American composers occur in his programme occasionally, but no more often than with Rubinstein or Gieseking. Even if one were to imply that there is a typically South American way of playing, just as there is a 'Russian school', one would be on the wrong track with Arrau. Not only because this great pianist was educated in Berlin and only went to America shortly before the outbreak of the Second World War, but also because in his playing the difference between the so-called 'German' and let us say Latin interpretation of Beethoven is completely obliterated. Claudio Arrau does not make it as easy as that for those who seek to plumb the mystery of his particularity. Whenever Arrau appears, even the most hardened and snobbish concert-goer is startled afresh each time by the feeling, My God, how this man can play! Anyone who goes to concerts a lot becomes, indeed, not only more fastidious about the middling, but to the same degree more appreciative of the exceptional and the great. With Arrau one comprehends again the meaning of 'ability' in piano playing. The uncommonly clean chords, precisely struck, in which no other half-touched notes resonate to muddy them; the completely self-evident two-, three- and four-part character, which is so often neglected among the by no means unpolyphonic Romantics; the passages, played in full and not merely thumped out in a welter of pedal, in which nevertheless there is no obtrusive vanity; the physical and psychological ordering: all this belongs to great piano playing, and can be heard in Arrau.

Now a cleanly struck chord is not indeed just something self-evident that is prepared by good conduct at piano lessons, but a good deal more: the expression, namely, of great inner tension. A chord also contains, as it were, frozen polyphony. A parade horse of piano virtuosi ridden almost to death, the piano concerto by Edvard Grieg, takes on new life under Arrau's fingers. One suddenly hears the Norwegian components, not merely as folkloristic trimming, as nice, piquantly tuneful extras, but as essence, which is contained indeed not only in the handling of the melody and in the Spring-dance rhythms, but also in the specific structure of nearly every chord. Arrau brings this out clearly. Yet with him the discovery does not become mannered. Arrau plays with such control that the precision in no way turns into pedantry or an end in itself. When he begins the recapitulation of the first movement with the A minor theme, then knows how to give the cantilena continuation a singing tone, and finally wins from the majestic cadenza a Lisztian greatness – no wonder Franz Liszt once loved this concerto and to the shocked surprise of Edvard Grieg was able to play it at sight, complete with all orchestral parts – then one begins to see why for decades Arrau has been among the leading pianists of the world.

When Arrau plays the first big solo from the B flat concerto by Brahms, one can witness – shaking one's head in admiration and amazement – how this pianist does it. His attack is so pure, so infallible and vehement that the piano itself seems to speak. The metallic might of tone of a great Steinway blends as it were with what Brahms has to say, or with what Brahms puts into the hands of the soloist as answer to the orchestra's question. The chords are of iron, and yet not mechanical, electro-acoustic. Quivering within them is that inner tension which arises only when a temperament subdues technique. The hardness has nothing inhuman about it, but rather something artistic, purposive, living. This is what Arrau is able to do.

He accelerates when the feeling requires it; he groans with exertion when he concentrates (but not over wrong notes; there are none). And he becomes slow and expressive when that element of primitive obduracy makes itself felt in the music, terse and lapidary, which is part of late Brahms. Yet it is precisely Arrau's unique pianistic attack, full of temperament, that becomes a problem. From the outset, a degree of heat is created – also in the interpretation of Brahms's D minor concerto – which demands too much. Then, even an Arrau cannot keep up the tension, because he is too high-minded to devise sure-fire tricks for himself to get round over-fast tempi.

Anyone who has ever heard how Arrau performs Schumann's Carnaval will know that Arrau plays a sparkling, intimate and brilliant Schumann. Ever present is the radiant joy of the ballroom rout, the candle-light and the masquerade, but at the same time also the moist-eyed emotion, though never exaggerated. In order to come closer to Arrau's particular characteristics we will try to discern and analyse how he and other pianists conceive the ending of Robert Schumann's piano concerto. There is a series of famous interpretations of this concerto, rightly the most widely loved of musical Romanticism. Alfred Cortot, Walter Gieseking, Dinu Lipatti, Clara Haskil and Claudio Arrau have come to terms with it, as have Friedrich Gulda, Geza Anda, Solomon and Van Cliburn.

For our deliberations we choose, not the famous first movement, where Alfred Cortot explained and exploited the dialogue between clarinet and piano with matchless depth, and where Lipatti played the cadenza with magnificent, lively verve, but rather the coda of the finale. Here the piano comes in with a wide-ranging, rolling figure, interrupted by mordents, in an intimate conversational tone. The feeling intensifies, the main theme is repeated, far-flung passages run all over the piano, the rolling figure occurs once more, arpeggios play round the powerful orchestra, and with the utmost brilliance, prescribed by the composer, the concerto comes to an end. If one compares a few interpretations, one discovers in the first place something remarkable: it is not the young pianists, i.e. Gulda or Anda, who play the concerto fastest, but the old ones. The usual preconception, according to which Schumann in our day is rushed far too much by the young pianists, is not correct therefore, at least as regards objective, measurable time. The blue ribbon, though not the Blue

Flower of the Romantic movement, is chased by Walter Gieseking, who ripples the piece at the end as though it were exploded Mozart; but Clara Haskil also takes it relatively fast, as does Cortot, incidentally. Gulda and Anda play this ending much more calmly. By far the slowest interpretation is that of Claudio Arrau. One hardly needs to emphasize that such comparisons of time say nothing about the value or otherwise of an interpretation. But if one takes all other factors into account, it is nevertheless entirely symptomatic that Arrau should need half a minute more than Gieseking for the same bars.

Arrau does not let himself be led astray, like Gieseking, by delight in smooth virtuosity, which would also certainly be at his command. He takes the ending in a comparatively restrained manner. A tiny nuance, which shows how tremendously carefully Arrau interprets, is worth noting (Example 10). Hidden under the graceful passages – disguised as an innocent accompanying figure in the left hand – is a charming waltz-like melody. Other pianists, of course, might also have noticed this little melodic fragment; Arrau, however, not only notices it, but brings it to life. He reveals it as it actually is. And this is not done in the trifling manner of some Chopin players, who by arbitrarily accentuating particular notes in a richly-scored passage suddenly spell out quite new melodies, because wherever there are a hundred notes, it is naturally possible to pick out 'Baa-baa black sheep' or a national anthem. Arrau's discovery is not the outcome of an intense passion for originality, but the result rather of curiosity, of desire for change, and of an inner poise that allows him to concentrate on the particular because he can in any case be sure of the obvious. The nuance does not turn into a caprice. The listener is suddenly aware, however, of one more charming fragment of melody in Schumann's A minor concerto. If another pianist now overlooks or disregards this fragment, the person concerned will be obliged to explain why he conceives the passage differently. Perhaps because to him the melody part is more important, the whirling tempo more essential, the clarity of the sound pattern more crucial. If, however, one of Arrau's competitors lets these notes fall mutely under the piano, without offering some kind of compensation, then one's thoughts will go back to Arrau. Even in the realm of interpretation there are models, standards, perceptions, below which no great and

90

Example 10

From: Schumann, Piano Concerto in A minor, Op. 54, last movement.

In this brilliantly animated passage from the finale of Schumann's piano concerto, Arrau brings out the upper part of the left hand in a waltz-like manner. (From bar 4 of our example onwards.) In doing so, he neither allows the right hand to be neglected, nor does he point his 'find' too much. But he shows that a great pianist, even in a work regarded as fully understood, can give reality to things which other pianists might indeed have recognized but dare not play because otherwise confusion would ensue. Arrau's lucidity easily copes with problems of this kind.

conscious performance ought to fall. Even in the realm of art the conservation-of-energy law ought to apply.

Thus a great pianist, even in so well-known a work as the piano concerto by Robert Schumann, can still discern new features and bring them to life. Yet the consciousness and the discipline which Arrau imposes on himself have their price. How high this price is becomes clear from an interpretative comparison with Alfred Cortot, and even more with Clara Haskil. Clara Haskil, until her death in 1960, was almost a saint of the piano. Her Mozart interpretations were applauded almost without reservation. To me, her Schumann and Brahms playing seemed even more convincing, flowing and beautiful. The artist, marked by a physical ailment courageously borne, was – let it be said with all respect – locked in the prison of her infirmity. Utterly concentrated, almost turned away from the world, Clara Haskil presented in this way with high purity and art all those works of the classic and romantic repertoire which she could manage physically. Mozart's C minor concerto, some Brahms intermezzi, and this same Schumann concerto she played with ineffable transparency. When one hears the ending of the Schumann concerto in her interpretation, it suddenly becomes clear what is missing in Arrau: the darkness and weight of the insistent harmonies, the luminous animation of the passage-work, which goes far beyond mere liveliness. At the same time, Clara Haskil by no means played the piece affectedly; she did not 'celebrate' it. She achieved its fullness, she grasped its romantic bliss, its rhapsodic character. Suddenly one thought one could see why in the nineteenth century, thronged with virtuosi, Clara Schumann's interpretation of this concerto acquired nevertheless a legendary fame.

Can one say, therefore, that the tension, the care and the culture behind Claudio Arrau's interpretations are not only a merit but also a kind of inhibition, an aloofness tending to restraint? This would explain that final residue of neutrality, the coolness still sometimes created, for all the culture and power of expression, which always characterizes Arrau's playing when the artist relies neither on unfettered virtuoso self-display nor on 'intimacy'. Perhaps one can put it thus: Arrau's sense of style is far too great for him to make any and every piano piece the object of an outburst of pianistic temperament. In regard to the thundering cadenza, say, of the piano concerto by Grieg, timidity and restraint really would be superfluous, and here indeed Arrau shows clearly and captivatingly how splendidly he can, to put it crudely, 'let himself go'. He plays Liszt's Totentanz at a public concert more arrestingly, in a more turbulent, riotous and virtuoso manner than Byron Janis on records. The roaring and on-driving power of the passages is fascinating. He makes of this Totentanz, which he performs incidentally not in Siloti's arrangement but in Liszt's original version, a piece of sinister brilliance. At the beginning, Arrau here out-thunders even Tchaikovsky, while in the Tchaikovsky concerto itself he falls short of the ultimate in élan. Arrau's interpretation of Liszt's A major concerto almost attains the order of Richter's.

Yet in all those works in which the titanic gesture would be out of place, and in which titanism cannot always be replaced by equally extreme, fervent submersion -- in these Arrau is often a shade too restrained and neutral; in these he relies too much on finger technique, on culture, on taste. Where Beethoven's sonatas express clear control of line, austere espressivo and an affirmation of life 'on this side', if the term may be forgiven, Arrau's art does justice to him. The difficult Vivace alla Marcia of the late A major sonata, Op. 101, for instance, cannot be played in a more decisive, precise and sovereign manner than by Arrau. Anyone who has heard at a concert how most pianists agonize over this uncommonly tough piece, how far even a Kempff has to fall short of it, will admire without reserve Arrau's sense of style, his temperament and art of touch. This late Beethoven Vivace alla Marcia, furthermore, can easily pass over into fantastic near-Schumann, whereby it loses its seriousness and austere unapproachability, and becomes impoverished into an innocuous genre piece. It can also wither into a prim technical exercise for the fingers. Arrau catches the 'classic' fantasy of the piece.

Arrau is regarded as an outstanding Chopin player. The way in which he is able to master the studies, Op. 10, or the luminously clear concert allegro, Op. 46, with unshadowed bravura is impressive. But if one hears Rubinstein's interpretation of Chopin's wild B flat minor Prelude, Op. 28, No. 16, in which he dissociates himself from his sweet and typical 'Rubinstein tone', throws himself with tremendous verve into the waves of this Presto, and traces the angry lines much more sharply and distinctly than Arrau, then the conclusion is probably no longer premature that a certain brightness, a Latin clarity, if one likes to call it that, both characterizes and also limits Arrau's playing.

The finale of Chopin's B minor sonata, that overwhelming Presto which rhapsodically anticipates and surpasses Wagner's Ride of the Valkyries, Arrau also plays somewhat too coolly. Nobility can be a barrier: sometimes a pianist has to abandon himself in order to win.

Thus Arrau commits himself to Liszt with wonderful tension, masters Grieg without reserve, and shows his temperament wherever extroverted compositions seem to demand it. Yet the dark side of fantasy, the note that is high-strung and wild, is not for him. Instead, Arrau discloses a wonderful range, a bright diversity of nuance and colour, in the realm of the intimate. He finds in Beethoven's lyrical G major concerto a scope for variation, of soft and active piano, of shading of life and urgency, such as one would hardly have suspected any more in this concerto, which is devalued often enough into a popular draw or a sentimental melodrama. He avoids anything approaching radiant brilliance and even more any complacent virtuosity. And that most moving spot in almost every classical concerto, where the orchestra joins in again at the end of the cadenza and the soloist takes his leave, acquires under his hands a conquering lyrical truth. The G major concerto can be conceived and played in many other ways. In Arrau's understanding of the first and slow movements, he has achieved, if one can so put it, a subjective perfection.

Clifford Curzon and
Paul Baumgartner

Clifford Curzon is the only pianist of world class who could be described as a chamber musician elevated to soloist. Since the other great English pianist fell ill – Solomon (Cutner) – there is hardly any doubt among British music-lovers that he is Britain's most distinguished interpreter. Curzon was born in 1907, and studied in Berlin with Artur Schnabel. The artist became known in Germany, however, not for instance through his responsible interpretations of Schubert and Brahms, truly 'serving' them, but in connection with a law suit. It was Curzon who, after much coming and going, followed by the newspapers with delight and curiosity, was allowed to adopt the two children of the not-forgotten Maria Cebotari.

The term 'chamber musician' implies no kind of disparagement. It does not mean that Curzon is lacking in power or brilliance to cope with the great concertos and sonatas. It refers to the type. Curzon's excessive, sometimes almost crotchety rehearsal ethos is clearly not aiming at his own fame, at 'making sure' or at unassailable perfection, but relates solely and determinedly to the work. Curzon takes nothing easily. He belongs among the great pianists of our time because the pregnancy, restraint and true fullness of his playing give rise to performances of pure and noble beauty. Compared with Paul Baumgartner, the pianist, born at St Gall in 1903, a pupil of Eduard Erdmann, who likewise set himself the goal of extreme precision and honesty, Curzon really does play with far greater refinement. In spite of all the asceticism, he commands a lustre, a worldly spirituality, if the expression is permissible, which seems superior to the dry severity, rather, of Baumgartner. The performances of these two pianists enable one to see how great the differences can be between two relatively similar, mature pianists, full of respect and seriousness of approach, when one reaches the pianistic standard of the world élite in an unassuming and non-virtuoso manner – and the other just falls short.

Now of course Rubinstein, Kempff or Sviatoslav Richter also by no means avoid chamber-music work. Artur Rubinstein often plays in piano trios or violin sonatas by Beethoven and Brahms: Kempff has likewise applied himself to Beethoven's violin sonatas, and we know that Sviatoslav Richter not only plays piano quintets but also 'accompanies' his wife, who is a singer, Fischer-Dieskau, or the 'cellist Rostropovich. Yet when a Sviatoslav Richter accompanies, one hears a great soloist subordinating himself as it were in a chamber-musicianly way, but without ever renouncing the great soloist. There is a scintillatingly beautiful recording in which Richter performs the Brahms Piano Quintet with four first-class string-players from Moscow. Richter is the intellectual leader, the guiding personality. Even when he places only a gentle stress, it is more important than all the efforts of violin and 'cello. Clifford Curzon has recorded the same piece with the Budapest String Quartet. Curzon restrains himself without being cramped – and one becomes aware of how much of beauty and temperament the violin of Mr Roismann, too, is allowed to say and lament.

That a musician who voluntarily foregoes the soloist manner can still become a sought-after soloist says much, not only for the artistic understanding of the concert-going public, but also for the quite exceptional qualities of the musician. Curzon learnt from Artur Schnabel analytic acuity, respect for detail and the courage to avoid conventional effects. His anti-virtuoso attitude is in no way the outcome of necessity. Curzon can do what he wants. He is capable, for instance, of playing the dreaded octave trills from the first movement of Brahms's D minor concerto, where no god and no conception is of any avail, but where manual colours are bound to come out, at least as drummingly, as hard and evenly as Serkin or Arrau. But to him there is nothing in the concertante manner. And it is not in him.

Thus he does not heighten the Scherzo from the early F minor Sonata, Op. 5, by Johannes Brahms into something like a convulsively rhythmic dance, nor the solemn trio into a hymn-like chorale.

He preserves even in fortissimo an ethos of moderation, of restraint. The piano does not break up under Curzon's hands. Carefully, but without pedantry, the lines are traced. At the same time, Curzon's playing is free from any mannerism. In spite of all temptation, he will not phrase at all costs 'against the grain', as was sometimes done by Schnabel, who in the E flat concerto by Beethoven, for instance, broke off the majestic chords in the development abruptly and senselessly, in order to avoid all pomposity. Because Curzon always seems to be intent on transparent, clear and temperate playing, he is an exemplary interpreter of Mozart; and Schubert's impromptus, in which all musicality can be delightfully shown, take flight under his hands with pure tone. The variation impromptu in B flat loses itself in intimate magic. Curzon begins it innocuously. But he is able to carry out the individual variations so richly and naturally that the theme at the end is charged with enchanting seriousness and grand melancholy – if the expression may be forgiven.

Of course, in observing such chamber-musicianly moderation, there is also a limitation. Curzon keeps away not only from brooding darkness but also from virtuoso exultation. He has even tried to win back some of Liszt's works. He plays them as though they were absolute music. In this way the Liebestraum nocturne, marred a thousand times by coarse virtuoso hands, suddenly becomes once more a piece of masculine, nobly sensitive music. But the close of the B minor sonata fares less well when tamed to a chamber-music finale: a dash of delirium, of daemonic wizardry, indeed, to put it crudely, of 'hamming', belongs to the nature of the thing. Curzon plays a Liszt for despisers of Liszt. Arrau and Richter would drown all opposition with a brilliant pianistic muster – Curzon, pianistically far more sovereign than Kempff, would lead us to Liszt by stealth.

But not only the extroversion of Liszt – the introversion of late Brahms also sometimes seems beyond discreet, moderate good-breeding. Chamber-musicianly equability conceals the catastrophes, which even the extravagance of the pianissimo knows about in Brahms. If one listens one's way into the desolate enormities, say, which the later Brahms composed into the Adagio of the early B major trio, when he made the second version of this youthful work, one gets some idea of how far even a soft, suppressed crisis can refute the positiveness of the chamber-music tone, so blissfully self-assured.

Curzon demonstrates, on the other hand, Brahms's phlegmatic reserve. When he plays a late intermezzo, it befits him not to overstep the limits of the expression. A gentle melancholy, not too dismayed, not too subtle, avoids encroaching on 'the work itself'.

Such an anti-sentimental seriousness can raise Brahms's B flat piano concerto from the realm of tearful triviality back into the by no means cold air of austere classicism: that is why the B flat concerto is also one of those pieces which Curzon puts on his programme again and again. Over the torn intimacy of 'last' Brahms, he passes lightly, with that vigorous, somewhat robust old-gentleman's attitude which the aged Backhaus demonstrates in the sweet distress of Beethoven's Moonlight Sonata.

Thus chamber-musicianly restraint sometimes turns into conscious restriction. When one hears the beginning of Brahms's D minor concerto, as conceived by Curzon, with the help of the Concertgebouw Orchestra, it becomes only too clear that the soloist is unable to match the great tragic tone of the orchestra – or is unwilling to match it, which comes to the same thing. The piano answers privately, with almost self-forgetful sadness, softly, plaintively. Only very slowly does it grow together with the orchestra into a unity of expression. Curzon plays the beginning a little unconcernedly. This is neither a conscious contrast nor a correspondence. Curzon does not want to subdue the orchestra's statement pianistically. His restraint could be of great charm, a specific reaction to the tremendous gesture of the orchestra. Yet the chamber-musicianly reserve fails to become recognizable and comprehensible as contrast. For this the melodic line is still a shade too neutral. If one hears the same passage by Rudolf Serkin, everything at once sounds far more agitated: by no means faster or louder or more theatrical, but simply indeed more expressive, far more serious and more powerful. With Curzon the concertante manner is lacking, which is naturally bound to be perceptible precisely when a soloist wants to show restraint, reserve and discretion. For restraint can be recognized as a dynamic and interpretative quality only when the listener thinks he can sense what greatness and strength in the expressive dimension is available to the one who is restraining himself. Curzon's expressive decisions have nothing to do with pianistic problems, let alone weaknesses. They are the honourable outcome of a typical will.

If one measures the distinguished Swiss pianist Paul Baumgartner against Clifford Curzon, one can recognize the differences which open up between chamber-musicianly interpretation of pianistic world class and an honest, serious, well-considered, but more limited pianistic solidity. When Baumgartner performed all thirty-two Beethoven sonatas, together with the Diabelli Variations, at a public series of recitals, a reverence for Beethoven's text could be discerned which was naturally impressive at first, but then became after all problematic, because it simply paralysed all creative spontaneity. This pianist allowed himself and his listeners no moods, no indulging in emotion, so long as they were not actually imposed by the course of the music. He applied himself in this way, with great seriousness, to Beethoven's slow movements above all: again, however, not with the fervour of a poet, but with the calm conviction of an apostle, who quietly and in a well-considered manner repeats the Words of the Master, until their sacred character has seized both him and the others. This is abstemious, betrays a splendid mistrust of rhetorical feelings – and demands considerable knowledge of the text.

One is naturally very inclined to consider an antipathetic, objective mode of interpretation as 'modern' and appropriate. If one reads something of the sort characterized in writing, as here for instance, one probably finds it highly sympathetic. In listening, however, doubts nevertheless set in.

In his early sonatas (Op. 2, No. 2 and Op. 2, No. 3). Beethoven tucked away considerable pianistic feats. Barely twenty-five, he probably hoped for a career as pianist; he wanted to shine and give his rivals some technical nuts to crack. ('He is universally admired on account of his unique dexterity and the extraordinary difficulties which he overcomes with great skill', it was said after the sonatas had come out, as early as 1796.) The radiant elegance of these concert sonatas, however, remains dull, barren, dead – if, out of sheer respect for the notes of the text, all freshness, all verve, all delight in melodic and harmonic surprise is suppressed. Then passages that could be a miracle of sound and splendour, such as the modulation leading from F major through F minor to A flat major, C minor, etc., which befalls the second subject of the finale of the C major Sonata, Op. 2, No. 3, are suddenly merely obvious in their effect. It had to happen like that, of course; we know the piece. Rapture, great tone, luminosity: such words may seem alien to the notes, but are they to the music? In other words: Baumgartner's magnificent honesty draws attention to that contradiction, which is no more settled today than at any other time in the history of music. Even a Stravinsky, who is given to annoyance over the shameless 'liberties' of interpreters, conducts some things differently from the way he stipulated (the tempi of Petrushka, for instance). And Ansermet in his book of confessions has said how little one can rely, even with Stravinsky, merely on what is prescribed.

Paul Baumgartner, however, who tries to present Beethoven's sonatas in an anti-virtuoso, consciously objective manner, to serve them with chamber-musicianly discretion, has faith in the positivism of pure textual reproduction. He takes the recitative of the first movement of the D minor sonata out and out with the pedal, although the result is a bewildering effect of dissonance that puts Debussy in the (tonal) shade. It is true, the text prescribes this pedalling. In the finale of the Waldstein Sonata, too, with Baumgartner the theme disappears in the waves of a sustained pedal, which indifferently swallows all modulation: this too is in the text (Example 11).

But when changes of tempo are not in the text, as in the variations of Op. 26 and Op. 109, then Baumgartner declines to play them, however urgently they may suggest themselves musically.

This boundless confidence in the possibility of communicating, within the five lines of the stave, everything that has to be communicated is attractive. The manner of the self-assured Titans, thundering away inaccurately, free and unconcerned, is no longer really tolerable today.

Yet may one put so much trust in the text? Did Beethoven's pedal bring about the same powerful effect as the pedal of a modern concert grand?

Positivism has its limits. Although at the beginning of the finale of the Waldstein Sonata Baumgartner proudly and shockingly performs the text, at the end, in the Prestissimo octaves, he has to cheat, just as most other pianists do: he leaves out the left hand and plays the part for the right, as a precaution, with both hands. Since the keys of a modern grand piano are heavy to move – and unless one can play octaves like Horowitz – this is probably unavoidable, but also at the same time a concession to the spirit of the whole (i.e. of the Prestissimo) against the demands of the details. If everything really

Example 11

From: Beethoven, Waldstein Sonata, Op. 53, last movement.

If one takes Beethoven's pedal markings literally, the result here is a dissonant effect: D, E flat, E natural and F sound together. So in interpreting this passage one has to ask whether Beethoven really intended such an effect, or whether the pedal of a modern concert grand does not create a different resultant sound from the instrument of Beethoven's time. Baumgartner settles the problem with radical positivism.

101

could be said in notes, then there would be no need, of course, for the numerous 'espressivo' or 'dolce' indications, which by no means always signify a certain tone indeed, but a process. Baumgartner permits himself no tricks of cadence. His touch renounces 'beauty'. He sacrifices sensuality of sound in order to serve the stern god of accuracy, of insistent seriousness. His freshest performances are of the B flat Sonata, Op. 22, and the E flat Sonata, Op. 27, No. 1, because he does not let himself be lured by the relative obscurity of the two works into taking them less seriously, less tensely. Where things go along with a powerful stride, he is not afraid of the élan, but the grand magic of breathing freely and soaring away he resists with narrow literalness.

Clifford Curzon and Paul Baumgartner show that objectivity does not by any means have to be a 'modern objectivity', but can be just as binding for pianists born in the first decade of this century as for younger ones, and the very youngest. Curzon's chamber-musicianly discretion seemed to us, for all its splendid and intellectually refined brilliance, endangered sometimes by constriction and limitation. Baumgartner's positivism suffered from slight pedantry. Both pianists remind us, meanwhile, of the pathos that lies in the words 'fidelity to the text'.

Rudolf Serkin and Solomon

Rudolf Serkin looks as Gustav Mahler might have looked grown older. An unruly, turbulent passionateness links Serkin with Mahler – quite apart from the fact that both musicians come from Bohemia. Mahler was born in Kalischt in 1860; Serkin in Eger in 1903, the son of a Russian singer. When Serkin plays, his treatment of the pedal rises now and then into a rhythmic stamping. Sometimes he whips his hands from the keyboard as though it were charged with high tension current. He hums as he goes; he risks extremes without regard for casualties or wrong notes. Yet what he gives are not titanic caricatures of great music. His unhesitating physical and mental engagement is controlled by a lightning musical intelligence. When Serkin plays late Beethoven, he does not thunder out mock-heroics or wallow in the abysmalness of sentimental ritardandi. He demonstrates rather – as did Gustav Mahler, incidentally, who is supposed to have played the last Beethoven sonatas in particular so marvellously – that sonatas are 'dramas', mighty stage sets on which the musical spirit of the world can appear. Every crescendo becomes for him as though Prometheus himself had composed it. Elegance and light pointing are not for Serkin. Instead, under his hands the Appassionata becomes a popular draw, so that superior listeners find it 'too passionate' – though one might well argue, of course, about how passionate passion should really be.

Now it is true, this sonata, which is perhaps the most famous that was ever written in the history of piano music, i.e. the Appassionata in F minor, Op. 57, by Beethoven, has a difficulty that can neither be mastered technically nor even described in any obvious analytical way. If one hears this work, whose powerful and violent details no musical person can evade, over and over again, one begins to suspect why it is so extraordinarily hard to catch interpretatively. Perhaps our surmise may be put like this: the Appassionata contains just pure passion, unleashed passion. It is like a storm. The recapitulation reverberates with the enormities that came to pass in the development – a quivering, insistently repeated C in the bass joins in here, disconcertedly. The last movement then continues the passion in this outburst with still greater intensity. Yet in all this it appears to be a matter of a passion without a subject, as it were. The human voice, as it sounds so overwhelmingly in, say, the Moonlight Sonata, or in the dialogues of the D minor Sonata, Op. 31, No. 2, or in the flights of the Hammerklavier Sonata, is hardly to be heard any more in this F minor inferno. The second subject remains helpless, remains – like the slow movement – more of an episode.

These conjectures may be too lacking in respect and too vague. Yet must one not try to explain, somehow or other, why the Appassionata seems so interpretatively neutral, why it often sounds so pallid, so menacing, so non-human, and why pianists so grievously fail this sonata when they play it as though it were an Eroica for the piano?

When Serkin tackles Beethoven's late sonatas, the Hammerklavier Sonata or the sonatas Op. 109, 110, and 111, he summons up for his battle with the angel of these sonatas, besides his highly-charged and nervous intelligence, a capacity to give himself lyrically. Everything slow turns out delightfully – the explosions, however, have something feverish about them. Serkin, it has become ever clearer in recent years, is possessed by a manifest 'wildness of old age'. He plays ever faster, ever less conciliatorily, ever more powerfully. His records fail to give an accurate picture of Serkin's quality. On them, his playing sounds polished; it seems to be distinguished by the wisdom of old age rather than the wildness.

In his youth, Serkin belonged to the group round Schönberg. He first became known to the musical public in Germany when he recorded Brahms's sonatas for piano and violin with the violinist Adolf Busch. The records, made in 1932, convey an impression of pure harmony. Of the nervous, magnificent wildness of the later Serkin, hardly anything can be heard in them. When Busch and Serkin were playing Brahms with so much Germanic pensiveness, they could have had no idea how soon they would have to leave Germany. . . . Since

104

then, Serkin has become a world-famous teacher and pianist. The feverish hecticness with which he demands at a concert an extreme of effort, from himself and his listeners, sometimes gives rise to a slight restlessness at Serkin's concerts. Is he not expecting too much of himself? – one asks, when Serkin reaches the limits of technical possibility, when his magnificent irritability stands in the way of majestic calm. Yet this irritability – not entirely unlike the permanent irritability of Schönberg or Beethoven in their later years – continually brings to light something new. Even a Mozart andante Serkin plays more interestingly than the Mozart specialists. Suddenly the quietly rhapsodic middle movement of the G major concerto (K 453) takes on a flight that wanders into the fantastic. Now in Mozart, of course, the contrast between the lively irregularity of the smallest features and the convincing balance of the large sections is in any case the source of a tension-filled perfection. So an artist who 'hears' and 'stresses' such details in no way offends against the style. For Mozart's perfection lies, indeed, neither in the mechanical regularity of a musical box nor in sentimental gestures, but in the unrepeatable whole to which these contrasts are joined in his music. All the same, Serkin's abrupt, almost pert attack lends the major chords in the first movement of the C major concerto (K 503) by Mozart something hectic, completely unsettled. If one compares Serkin's recording with that of the highly talented Fou Ts'ong (who was born in Peking in 1928 – he is Menuhin's son-in-law), which is characterized by brilliance, serenity, freedom and sensitivity, one understands for the first time just how audaciously Serkin, twenty-five years older, goes at it.

The Diabelli Variations are Beethoven's last great work for the piano. If one hears them one after the other, one can, of course, take them in completely, and with a little concentration also follow the course of the music; but one naturally loses after all, with regard to the 33 variations, the capacity for ever-renewed astonishment at the solitary and icy power of these sound-figures. Let us pick out three variations: the eighth of the Diabelli Variations seems like a speedy reminiscence of the Arietta theme from the sonata Op. 111 – only more reflective, richer and more fervent. The ninth sounds like a resolute Scherzo, which Serkin, comparatively restrained, plays with burning logic; and the tenth variation makes great demands, not only on manual technique, but also on the shaping-capacity of the

105

player: it has to slip along at a light presto, and yet every second has to be clear and consequential. Rudolf Serkin makes of the variations musical character-studies in the true and proper, demanding, sense of the word. He coins figures; he does not just play the piano.

Incomparably more severe, icier and weightier still is the playing of Beethoven's late works by a pianist whose name is scarcely known in Germany. His full name is Solomon Cutner – but he calls himself just Solomon – and he has been ill for a number of years. His interpretations of the Hammerklavier Sonata, the Les Adieux Sonata and (though not among Beethoven's late works) the Moonlight Sonata have the power of the unfamiliar. Solomon, who was criticized in Germany as 'cold', interprets Beethoven in such a way that the works are not indeed in any way 'objective' in their effect, but are nevertheless more than just the painful or joyful declarations of a real person. Solomon's seriousness catches, even more than Backhaus, the transcendental Subject, the 'larger-than-life' of this music: the matchless austerity of his playing, which is never severe in the usual sense, but of a masterly refinement, has nothing to do with Romantic titanism, and yet it prevents any hobnobbing with the 'humanness' of a classicist.

Solomon's seriousness is more than pathos. It has a strict ardour, emanating from the matter alone, an incisive absence of sweetness, and a tremendous commitment to the explanation and meaning of each and every note. When Solomon plays Beethoven's sonata for Hammerklavier, Op. 106, a rushing, powerful but never hasty spirit animates this larger-than-life work. One is moved by the strict consequentiality of this playing in a more than sentimental sense. All a pianist's vanity has fallen away here, all mediocrity of feeling, of tempo. The development has greatness, because the progress of the music confirms every detail. The sonata is no succession of beautiful passages, but a succession *sui generis* – a glorious one. Solomon also became famous as a player of Brahms and Schubert. His recordings of two Schubert sonatas and of the Grieg and Schumann piano concertos are indeed perfect, but still not as compelling as Solomon's Beethoven. Solomon plays Schumann a shade too austerely, too pressingly, too anti-sentimentally, when he could fulfil in a relaxed way the romantic lure of the 'Verweile doch'. His pianistic energy, his austere severity, not in the least thundering or aiming at giganticism, which everyone to whom piano playing means anything must know and admire, still finds its great subject really only in the works of Beethoven and Brahms. The calm, weighty inwardness, so icily authentic, with which he can shade for instance the opening Adagio of the Lebe wohl Sonata (Les Adieux), Beethoven's Op. 81a, has no equal. One might hear how the French master-pianist Casadesus conceives the sad chords of the 'Lebe wohl': with him they are certainly full of tension and gentle life. Yet with Solomon this brief beginning gains in seriousness, anguish and naked urgency, without the addition of any loud or at all obtrusive effect. Perhaps Solomon then takes the melodies of the Allegro a shade too unsensually, too fleetingly. The coda, however, with the delightfully abstract suggestion of stamping horses, he again plays up into spiritual heights. Solomon's mastery is demonstrated most clearly and at its purest in his interpretation of Beethoven's late Sonata in A flat major, Op. 110, because in this undoubtedly very difficult work no kind of virtuosity can come to one's aid any more – to drown the problems of shaping (as is still possible in the roaring finale of the Les Adieux Sonata).

This A flat Sonata, Op. 110, is full of unobtrusive problems. It sometimes approaches that quite conscious 'classicism' to which late Beethoven occasionally aspires – for instance, in the rococoish minuet ending of the Diabelli Variations. Here, in the A flat sonata, the opening at once brings a return to Mozart. When the A flat melody sings out pure and radiantly innocent, to an innocuous sixteenth-note accompaniment (bars 5–12), it is like a Beethoven recollection of his own beginnings, overshadowed by Josef Haydn. (Not imitation, but conscious and at the same time alienating reflection.) The first movement contains a lyricism that is delightfully broken, without being in the least dubious or sounding undermined: its soft harmony encompasses great contrasts, but they are never coarse. The Allegro then is a typical late-Beethoven scherzo. The middle movement, however – consisting of Recitative and Arioso – alludes distantly to an opera-scene, and the Fugue finally does not, strangely enough, turn to the past in a traditional way, as might have been suggested after all by the fugue form, but anticipates, rather, the Romantic, concertante type of fugue. It is radiant, dramatic, and has a very pianistic ending. Mendelssohn and Schumann would have been glad to compose such a fugue. Instead, it was Beethoven, and the fact

107

that in spite of this the sonata remained unquestionably a whole is perhaps the greatest miracle of all.

Solomon plays the piece with shy, serious feeling. He offers an interpretation that is masterly through and through, and at the moment probably unsurpassed by any other pianist in the world. His art consists in keeping quite firmly to the rhythm, paying scrupulous attention to Beethoven's agogic markings, and phrasing the transitions most precisely and with the greatest sensitivity, without sacrificing the prevailing effect of the over-all line. But at the same time, he lets the rests, caesuras and bar-lines between the different features play their part, without in the least upsetting the rhythm. Neither the lyricism, the melodious feeling, the severity, nor the polyphony – *nothing* obtrudes, and yet everything is there.

In the middle of the first movement, the A flat major motif of the beginning is developed through modulations until the main motif, accompanied by thirty-second notes, reappears (Example 12).

Only when one compares Solomon's interpretation with Glenn Gould's sentimentality, which creates an almost wilful effect in such a context, does one begin to suspect wherein the secret of great Beethoven playing lies. Glenn Gould plays nothing badly or thoughtlessly. On the contrary: everything with him becomes an expression of feeling. He stresses the dotted eighth-note (i.e. the third note of the main motif) enthusiastically. He plays the sixteenth-note movement in the left hand like a psychological commentary on the melody. No note is like another; each particular top note is strongly brought out. Glenn Gould also strongly underlines the middle voices, for instance the F in the last four bars. Through this, his interpretation has something sentimentally unstable about it.

Solomon keeps calmly and severely to the rhythm. At the very beginning, when he has to play the crescendo to the high, twice-accented C, which suddenly appears in piano, he carries out the crescendo powerfully and yet makes the (surprisingly!) soft C the climax, by dropping it in convincingly. In the bars we have quoted, he pays strict attention to the pseudo-polyphony, but no counterpoint obtrudes, however beautiful it might sound. Between melody, accompaniment, and filling voices, insulating layers, as it were, are preserved, which enable everything to exist in austere and splendid clarity. The whole acquires in this way a sublime seriousness, not in

108

Example 12

From: Beethoven, Sonata in A flat major, Op. 110, first movement.

What seems like melody and filling accompaniment is with Solomon a hier-
archy of austere lines. Thus in bar 6 of our example, and still more in bars
12 to 15, a flowing polyphony comes into being.

109

the least artificial, but flowing. It sounds – compared with Gould – unromantic, but nevertheless far more mysterious than the sentimental curves of the younger man.

The world of music has lost much, because Solomon, on account of severe illness, may never again be able to make recordings or give concerts.

Sviatoslav Richter

Of Sviatoslav Richter, one would have to be able to write how he plays Schumann: fluently, fierily, in a mighty onward flow, and yet carefully shaded, without omissions or amateurish slovenliness. Yet if one were to present him as he presents himself at the piano, when with radiant verve he thunders out Prokofiev or Tchaikovsky's G major sonata, one would not really have 'caught' him. The rousing variability of his playing, the nervous tension, the strain and the agony that are present, and overcome, at Richter's public concerts would be missing from such a picture.

Richter is a 'late arrival'. The pianistic career of this artist, born in 1915 in Shitomir, began only late in life – when one recalls Richter's phenomenal talent – at an age when others have long since acquired a 'name' and a wealth of platform experience. Richter had wanted to be a conductor. When he finished his piano studies with Heinrich Neuhaus in Moscow, he was nearly thirty.

His world career also began late. He had to carry it through in face of vast, fabulous rumours, further intensified by culturo-political hysteria; indeed, in face of an aura almost impossible to live up to. The name Sviatoslav Richter already stood for something when nobody in Central Europe or in America had heard this pianist. Even his recordings were hardly known at first; all the time the Russian authorities refused to let Richter travel to countries beyond the Iron Curtain, his reputation grew. If one praised Emil Gilels, who was somewhat younger but became known in the West much earlier, for his brilliant playing, he would reply that while he was, of course, delighted with such praise, Sviatoslav Richter, the dark horse, played a thousand times better than he. Was this just mock modesty?

A living mystery is a good concert agent. The man-who-could-not-be-heard became a world star. Then a few phenomenal Richter records penetrated the Iron Curtain. They made the curiosity greater still. And Van Cliburn, who had taken part in the Tchaikovsky competition in Moscow in 1958, reported in bewilderment: 'It's the most powerful piano playing I've ever heard.'

When Sviatoslav Richter was finally allowed to travel to America and set about winning the West in New York, an old lady sat in the audience, breathing heavily. Richter had not seen her since the war, and had even been unable to see her before the concert, so as not to lose his mental equilibrium: it was his mother. Richter's father, that is to say, had been a German-descended musician in Russia and had been killed there in connection with his German descent and the war-time chaos. His mother had fled with Sviatoslav's uncle to Germany. There she had moved into a little apartment in the neighbourhood of Stuttgart and gradually learned of her son's world fame, though she had never dared write to him openly, for fear of putting him in danger. Now, after nineteen years, they met again.

Richter finds it appalling to be assailed by the demand that he must be the foremost pianist of the world, that he must be a prodigy. Richter suffers from his aura. He has to make débuts and convince new audiences at an age when other pianists have long since got all that behind them. At his début in Lucerne, Richter complained to friends that it meant a frightful additional strain to him to be continually appearing for the first time at fifty in front of audiences hysterical with expectation. To stand up to that one has to be younger. In 1960, Richter was forty-six. Records have preserved his New York début. On that occasion a verdict was given. Since then, every Richter concert is a sensation.

With a pianist whose career runs a normal course, biographical details would not be so important: whether and in what circumstances the 'break-through' ensued is of more anecdotal than musical interest. With Richter, his peculiar situation is part of the matter itself. He is not a pianist who calmly puts into practice what he has sorted out for himself, who sees everything through the spectacles of his personal style. His art, his frame of mind and his problems depend on his situation.

Richter began his début in Carnegie Hall with Beethoven's Sonata

Op. 2, No. 3, in C major, an early virtuoso work, very conscious of the classical tradition, and composed with incredible sureness of grasp. When one listens to the recording of this New York 'début', one is naturally still aware at first of the tremendous anxiety of the man who is said to have been unable either to eat or sleep during the last few days before this all-deciding concert. Richter plays fast, but not stiffly. In spite of powerful technical reserves, he does not thunder out the sixteenth-note octaves in an approach to Tchaikovsky. The second subject, still completely indebted to Haydn, sounds with Richter just a friendly shade more elastic than with Emil Gilels, say, who exaggerates the dynamic element. Richter plays early Beethoven with a clear, incisive touch, though in the outbursts perhaps a trifle too compactly.

Richter knows how to give his playing a flowing, indeed sweeping, character, without in the least blurring the details. When he sets about the pointed Scherzo in this C major sonata, together with the rushing, black-as-night Trio, he holds the two parts together by not exaggerating the tempo of the Scherzo, but by bringing out in the Trio a large-scale movement that gives the listener a feeling of almost compulsory, self-evident and unavoidable unity. The finale, too, has greatness and inevitability under his hands. Without any affectation, the forms are moulded in the musical flow. This technique of a developing articulation Richter has mastered irresistibly in early Beethoven: his playing contains the past, present and future of the sonata movement alongside each other.

The second piece on his New York programme was Beethoven's E major Sonata, Op. 14, No. 1. It is considered easy. Since the outer movements remain restrained, or at least do not sound majestic or eccentric, Beethoven placed in the middle, not a pensive adagio, but a sad, hovering allegretto. Richter makes a poem of this E minor movement by taking it a shade slower, more singingly and deliberately than is usual. An element of – one cannot avoid this characterizing adjective – Russian melancholy, of endlessly sad distance comes into the piece. It is perhaps no longer a classical Allegretto. All the same, Richter avoids all forcing. It is not the 'conception' here that decides success, but the art of touch.

Beethoven's A flat Sonata, Op. 26, Richter does with luminous bravura; it passes by like a spiritual apparition, not free from Lisztian nobility. Chopin, who once performed this A flat sonata at a salon concert, had to suffer the reproach of the Russian pianist and biographer of Beethoven, Wilhelm von Lenz, that he had played too softly. Chopin, so Lenz reports, played Beethoven's A minor Sonata beautifully, indeed, 'but not as beautifully as his own things, not grippingly . . . not like a novel intensified by variation on variation'. When Lenz reproved Chopin with this, Frédéric Chopin replied without any touchiness: 'I indicate; the listener himself must complete the picture.'

Such a tendency to discreet indication is not Richter's way with Beethoven. He declines to let himself be intimidated by 'classicism'. A harmonic progression Richter takes in an effective way, like a Lisztian rinforzando. If one looks carefully at the music, an appropriate marking can indeed be found. The climax and end of Richter's New York début was the Appassionata. The pianissimo beginning had magic; the outbursts came with turbulent power. The finale Richter began at a fantastic, completely exaggerated speed. He took it so fast that in the Presto ending he could hardly produce any more. The whole piece was one single accelerando. Certain pianistic effects, such as the doubling, say, of the right-hand C over three octaves, which Beethoven prescribed, came to life with dazzling brilliance. Hardly anyone can play it like that today. The two-part runs also rolled with furious and yet completely accurate élan. In the final Presto, one even heard a few crude blunders. Richter has also played the piece for recording in the studio; here everything is naturally correct – but compared to the way the finale of this début came off at the concert, the pure recording is nothing like as arresting.

No definite style, no definite tone, not even a definite propensity, seems to be typical of Richter's playing, but a very personal combination of intelligence, bravura technique, and sure instinct. Richter's playing has the purity and directness of the ecstatic. Its effect, for all the exaggeration, is never distorted, but natural and purposeful, in the gentle parts as in the powerful. When Richter goes to the piano, shy and strange, a torn giant to whom the universal attention and anticipated pleasure is a burden, one would not be inclined to think that this same man, so inhibited, so seemingly at a loss, was yet supposed to know the secret of the great pure storm and the deep calm.

Example 13

From: Tchaikovsky, Sonata in G major, Op. 37, first movement.

Some things here may be felt to be trivial, rhetorical and forced. With Richter, it sounds magnificent and self-evident. Neither the passages nor the leaps and the far-flung accompanying movement are isolated. The supreme principle here is not thematic work, but the urgency of vehement self-display.

One would be more inclined to take him for one of the nervous ones, a decadent, one of the refined and irresolute. But his interpretations often strike the ideal type, having the great drive to self-display, the delight in the virtuoso and the balladesque, and the capacity for unblemished spiritual depth. Seen thus, Richter is an 'old-fashioned' pianist. At the same time, he admires Hindemith, is interested in Schönberg, and made friends with Prokofiev.

Young pianists of a 'modern' disposition fight shy of playing out their temperament wildly and exuberantly, for they have not got that moderation within them, that tact for withdrawing gently and setting to afresh, which with Richter, besides the incorruptible strength of his touch and rhythmic impulse, prevents inartistic frenzy (usually, not always!). Strangely enough, moreover, Richter has made an attempt, precisely in Tchaikovsky's first concerto, in which Horowitz, Rubinstein and Gilels truly have no scruples about thundering and sparkling, to give the piece depth. The recording, by Richter and Karajan, is famous. To me, however, it seems too refined, too tame. The two stars try to see whether Tchaikovsky might not be capable of sounding just as noble and lyrical as Robert Schumann. But they merely rob the concerto of its pathos, of its élan, which sweeps all doubts away: and the highly cultivated, perfect recording still fails to sound quite as profound as Schumann; it sounds, rather, somewhat academic.

For Tchaikovsky's great G major Sonata, Op. 37, however, Richter finds the grand manner. He thunders. He plays this musically quite innocuous piece, which bursts with vigour and mediates happily between German Romanticism and Mussorgsky, with rip-roaring vehemence. So mastered, this music is not only tolerable, but intoxicating. There is no letting up with Richter. He plays out the lyrical episodes with sonority, but even the somewhat theatrical general pause in the Andante, three (!) fermata long, seems with him to be filled with vehemence and eager striving. The pianissimo modulations in the Scherzo have an excited onward drive. In the first movement, for all the delight in sweeping gesture, in rhetorical declamation, he still amalgamates the digressive melodic curves into a continuous, self-evident unity of development. He knows that in this early Tchaikovsky to stop is to go back, and he makes of the sonata a piano-symphony. The rubato melodic progression

116

from the Moderato e risoluto of the first movement has a resonant naturalness that can hardly be discerned in the pattern of notes (Example 13).

In the finale, Richter attains a vivace pathos such as is rare even with him. That ecstatic, radiant tempo which imperils Richter's interpretations of Schubert's allegros (for instance, in the first movement of Schubert's great D major sonata), just as it does the finale of the Appassionata, is here not only in place, but life-giving and captivating.

Because Richter has not tied himself, or let himself be tied, to any 'personal' style, one cannot associate him either with any particular composer. His extraordinarily large repertoire – only Arrau and Rubinstein can boast a similar fullness – is the outcome of this all-embracing curiosity and capacity for change. There is no Richter style, indeed not even a Richter tone. The brilliance, strength and dynamism of his touch are beyond all praise, but also beyond all limiting characterization: put negatively, this means that his touch, meanwhile, has no 'individuality' such as one can ascribe to the tone of a Kempff or Rubinstein. Yet this lack of individuality can be understood more as lack of a definite tone-colour than as lack of animation or 'personal' expression.

When Richter played Brahms's B flat concerto at Salzburg – Lorin Maazel conducted – the difference between the two artists was already astonishing after the opening bars. The horn took the opening triplet and closing third calmly and without significance: Richter gave the movement animation. Under his hands, the third became the symbol of an upward look, of a touching questioning, of a cry pressing for continuation and answer. Richter played the difficult work with ecstatic commitment of body and soul. He risked the hazards of the extreme far more impressively than in his recording of the Brahms concerto. The driving power, for instance, with which he thundered out the chords of the first great solo; the solitary calm with which he experienced, before the orchestra, how reserved and soft a crisis can often be with Brahms; the urgency with which he chiselled out of Brahms the tragedian Hebbel and almost drove him into near-Slavonic wildness: all this was without any dripping contemplativeness. It was the counter-type to Backhaus's wisdom and Rubinstein's pianistic radiance. It was exciting like Horowitz, but at the same time

117

without Toscanini's brio joy, so much as grave and full of sober expression.

He does not always go to extremes. He resists overloading Mendelssohn's charm. In the 'serious' D minor Variations, he stays in the realm of a noble conversational tone, and just because of this lifts the piece out of this realm. Richter feels that a Mendelssohn melody cannot be taken either with the antique solemnity of a Beethoven adagio or with the Jean-Paulish world-enchantment of Schumann poetry. With overwhelming tact, he leaves the music within a protective spiritual frame. Thanks to this stress of the mortal, the worldly and the openly brilliant in Mendelssohn, he rescues his immortality – in the same way that a Molière play has a more moving effect, indeed, when the actors play out a lively comedy within the framework of bright conversation than when they try to be exaggeratedly expressive.

Richter's feeling for élan, for sheer ecstasy, for ample melodies, stands him in good stead in his interpretations of Schumann. When he undertakes the horribly difficult Toccata, Op. 7, it becomes a storm of youth, enchanting, clear and without vacillation. But in contrast to many other virtuosi, who play even the ending of the Toccata grandly – as though glad to have it all behind them – Richter at the end allows deep Schumann shadows to fall across the piece. One thinks then of the bitter misgivings with which Schumann could once set to music Eichendorff's words, 'And there's a shuddering in the depths of my heart.' . . . The Fantasiestücke, Op. 12, and the piano concerto Richter also plays in the spirit of Schumann, though here the pianist sometimes relies too much on his strength and élan, in contrast to the delicate Schumann playing of Wilhelm Kempff, so differentiated, broken indeed almost to the point of alienation. Richter's most magnificent Schumann record seems to be of the Humoreske, Op. 20. It fascinates, not only through its obvious technical brilliance, but through richness of expression, lyrical life and convincingly intelligent 'storm'. Here, when Richter approaches the Polonaise rhythm – Schumann prescribes 'with some pomp' – a great moment of contemporary piano playing is reached.

In the course of recent years, Sviatoslav Richter seems to have got into a 'crisis'. He has allowed too many records to be got out of him. At concerts that were by no means always as uncommonly successful as his New York début, recordings have been made and sold as valid discs. Richter's direct brilliance, the absence of a personal piano style, is not very well suited to Chopin, it seems to me. The tension between brilliance and sentiment is often created here a little superficially. Chopin's first study, Op. 10, No. 1, is not only difficult, but great. The right hand unfolds in ample strides and powerful modulations over a slow-moving bass. The broken tenths sound wonderfully luminous. Richter once played this study unfeelingly for recording, concerned himself only with the bass, and let his right hand just run to and fro. One really hears only the left; everything else remains colourless and empty. Brutally flung down, the bass notes rumble away – the piece itself is almost, and the pianist Richter completely, 'incomprehensible'. How much austere music the study holds can be heard only when Arrau plays it: Chopin's noble third and pensive fourth Ballades are also not to be numbered up to now among Richter's really successful interpretations.

Yet Richter is an inquisitive pianist. Nothing would be more foolish than to seek to pin down his interpretations once and for all. For Ravel he has brilliance, for Debussy taste. And if he fails to satisfy the hysterical expectations of the public completely, then he need only fall back on Liszt, who is particularly in keeping with his temperament, and who, thanks to Richter's nobility, is freed from all triviality. In London, where the critics were at first almost too severe with him, Richter prevailed only when he played the two Liszt concertos. Under Richter's hands, Liszt's greatness sounds, not only not hollow, but threatening, dramatic, animated as much by lyrical sensitivity as by cynical sharpness.

Richter's teacher, Heinrich Neuhaus, had introduced his gifted pupil to Prokofiev. For the celebration of Prokofiev's fifty-fifth birthday, shortly after the end of the Second World War, Richter performed the composer's sixth, seventh and eighth sonatas. His playing was such that Prokofiev dedicated the ninth sonata to him. . . . Richter's interpretation of Prokofiev's D flat major piano concerto came to the west as one of the first Richter recordings and excited incredulous astonishment. Prokofiev brings him luck. Even today, when Richter records dominate the market in great abundance, he has not surpassed his performance of Prokofiev's eighth sonata either pianistically or intellectually. The calm cantabile of the slow movements, the brio of the fast: so much clarity and so much radiance

119

Example 14

From: Prokofiev, Eighth Sonata, Op. 84, first and third movements.

In this harmonically attractive section from the first movement of Prokofiev's eighth sonata, Richter stresses noticeably, but not frantically, the four notes of the upper voice in the left hand (over the sustained low octave) in the third bar of our example. Through this, a connection is created which the listener recalls, consciously, half-consciously or unconsciously, when he hears the very pregnant forte motif in the last movement. The note-repetition is taken up there and the characteristic falling second of the two eighth-notes follows.

seem to dwell in each note that the interpretation has earned a word that must be used sparingly if one is not to lose credibility: perfection. The relations are created as if of their own accord. Nothing remains 'complicated', hard to grasp or loquacious. Under the fluently-played descending modulation in the right hand, which dominates the first movement, Richter already brings out the inner voice of the left in such a lively way that the two eighth-notes falling to the last quarter of the bar anticipate, quite without forcing, the motif of the finale – whose characteristic element is, indeed, also the two eighth-notes falling, after a long quarter-note movement, on the last beat of the bar. It is immaterial whether Richter intended to draw attention to this connection or not: when a pianist plays like this, the music, if it only has sufficient inner consistency, becomes a resounding, living whole (Example 14).

It must occasion reflection that Richter has so far still not found access to the world of late Beethoven, although the sonatas Op. 90, 101 and 110 often appear on his programmes. In Beethoven's 'middle' sonatas – between Op. 26 and the Appassionata – Richter can develop most of the movements from a single impulse, and present them as an intelligent unity. This is not so with Beethoven's late work. Richter plays the late sonatas without the ascendancy of an architect. Beautifully though many of the details are presented, the sonata Op. 110 sounds as though it consisted of unconnected fragments of early Beethoven sonatas. The contrasts of late Beethoven are neither 'interpreted' nor is the unity that lies behind them explained. Instead, the Adagio sorrow sounds sentimentally unstable, and the abrupt alternation between slow and fast often becomes mannered.

Emil Gilels

In October 1961, Emil Gilels gave a public piano recital in Moscow, which has been preserved on two gramophone records – complete with coughs, applause and the occasional quite unimportant mistakes that crept in. These two discs are not only among the best that I know of Gilels's, but they reveal a mastery which hardly more than three virtuosi in the whole world can offer at a concert – here and there Emil Gilels plays more convincingly (seen as a whole) than even a Rubinstein or a Horowitz. On the basis of these records, which contain magnificently Schumann's F sharp minor sonata, Chopin's Funeral March Sonata and Liszt's B minor sonata, besides trifles by Bach-Siloti, Stravinsky and Ravel, one may venture the conclusion that Gilels is over-modest after all when he continually maintains that Sviatoslav Richter plays far better than he. The two are, at least, alike in stature, though not in kind.

Added to Gilels's charm, his vitality, healthiness and his fist, is an intellectual ascendancy, a dynamic and dramatic modernism that probably does in fact make him the foremost pianist of Russia. On that October evening in 1961, Emil Gilels began with Robert Schumann's F sharp minor sonata. But he had made a studio-recording of the same Sonata a few years earlier. The two discs of the recital appeared in Russia under the serial numbers 011277–80 – the single record with the F sharp minor sonata was pressed specially for the Brussels World Fair in 1958, hence three years previously. It has the numbers D4080–4081. So one can compare how one and the same artist plays the same piece on records and at a concert. The differences are perceptible, musically and psychologically – and they are astonishing.

At first, the studio-recording begins with the odds in its favour.

122

The artist is naturally not nervous, he has no need to acclimatize himself, and so he takes the slow introduction broadly and powerfully, as it was probably meant to be by Robert Schumann. At the concert, Gilels is more self-conscious and somewhat more cursory. Here he plays the same introduction a good deal faster, as though he were afraid of not capturing the audience.

After beginning the Schumann sonata so much faster at the recital than he had conceived it for the studio-recording, Gilels naturally senses the danger he was running of blurring the contrast between 'slow' and 'fast'. He either senses it consciously or, since he is an artist in the middle of a concert, where he cannot indeed simply start again and verify his long deliberations, instinctively. Thus one can actually hear in the recital recording how the great Gilels tries hard to cushion, as it were, the cursoriness of the beginning by all the deeper expression. Even the tension with which he then articulates the Allegro is greater than in the studio recording, where everything takes its regulated, beautiful course. And then, when slow parts come in to dim this Allegro, Gilels plays incomparably more eloquently, more committedly, at the recital than in the studio recording; like someone who with every exertion of his senses and his passion wants to bring to an end an adventure once begun, who senses the 'uniqueness' of the public concert in every vein. So it is that at the end of the first movement, not only has all nervousness long since fallen away, but in the fulfilment and happiness of having done true justice to Schumann after all, of having captured the audience completely, Gilels surpasses himself. At the end of the first movement he manages an overwhelming più lento. Here he is now suddenly appreciably slower at the public recital than in the balanced studio-recording.

This ineffably pure inspiration of Schumann's is not caught by Gilels in the studio version nearly so spontaneously, so imaginatively, with such relaxed and happy persuasiveness. In the record that he made a few years before the recital, the same passage sounds more self assured, but less moving. Beautiful, certainly – but nevertheless not played so compellingly, with such abandon of body and soul.

Feeling may indeed speak more freely at a concert in happy circumstances, supporters of records will say, but in place of this a studio recording is relieved of the uncertainty of concert accidents, and the artist can play out passages which at a concert are a struggle with the cussedness of things according to their purely musical essence. Yet even this is doubtful. If one listens to the Scherzo in this recital recording, an unfettered, a brilliant, virtuoso seems to be sitting at the piano. Gilels risks a much faster tempo here than in the studio recording! One realizes that he will risk everything. A couple of untidy moments bother him as little as they do us. The Schumann Scherzo, certainly a pretty, capricious, romantic piano piece, becomes an enchanting affirmation of a spirited feeling for life. Crystal clear in the left hand, the chords of the right fall like lightning; the difference between concert fire and studio calm seems astronomical.

In this comparison of concert recording and studio disc let us not forget that in 1961, when Emil Gilels also made his tour of Germany, incidentally, and gave unforgettable interpretations both of Mozart's great C major concerto and of Tchaikovsky's B flat minor concerto, he may well have been more advanced and mature, of course, as pianist and artist, than at the time when he made the studio recording of the same F sharp minor sonata. Yet this is not of such great consequence. The attraction of the concert recording, for which there is hardly any other word but 'lively', long since grown colourless, lies above all in the reaction of the artist, not only to the principle of his calling, but also to the audience and the attention gained. Only this reaction, this non-conceptual concept of wholeness, on the other hand, allows that spontaneity to arise which can hardly ever dwell in mere individual points, however well performed.

Emil Gilels, born in 1916, the brother of a violinist (his sister), related by marriage to Leonid Kogan, and married to a composer, comes of a Russian family of musicians. He represents in fairly pure form the modern type of Russian virtuoso. Still present is the blatant connection with the late-Romantic piano-Titans of the Liszt and Siloti school, intent on magnificence and virtuosity.

Even the younger Russian virtuosi make no attempt to play in the 'modern' manner, as a Friedrich Gulda or a Glenn Gould try to do. Of course, they are not innocently old-fashioned either. Behind them they have the eccentric and ironic world of a Prokofiev. Grandezza divided by Prokofiev's fantasy and pianistic charm: this, then, might be a formula for the preconditioning of Emil Gilels. While the virtuoso turbulence of Horowitz penetrates some works so arrestingly that his boundless art becomes as it were an interpretative divining-rod,

Gilels always forces at most only the tempo – and seldom the nerves. He is a healthy pianist, not a mannered one.

The word 'healthy' has come to sound a little contemptuous of late. It is no longer pure praise, as in the time of Goethe. One almost always associates lack of refinement, want of passion, spiritual poverty, with an artist who is said to be healthy. In order to wipe out even the last vestiges of such associations, it should be added that Gilels clearly struggles with great effort, not only for his touch – here he is the only living pianist who can be matched with Rubinstein – but also for his 'harmonious' interpretations. When one watches him play, this pianist always seems more furrowed and tormented than his playing sounds.

The thoroughly trained hand, the charm and the freshness of his playing are evident in Gilels's interpretations of Scarlatti. Here, everything is incisive clarity, sparkling lightness, an exemplary accuracy and precision of touch. The chords of the main theme of the C major sonata – Puccini-lovers may discern the origin of the sequences of fifths in La Bohème, and Puccini would certainly have nothing against being brought so literally into connection with the Italian tradition – Gilels takes without any shy or tedious fuss. One might think of a predatory animal at play, pleased with his paws, when one listens to him here. In the second part, things become a trifle melancholy. But Gilels, carried along by the magnificent verve of his playing, in no way forces the melancholy nuance; he portrays, not the primordial sounds of the Russian soul, but only a pianistic treasure. For this reason, he even underplays it a little. The whole lasts only 100 seconds: but many piano-infatuated mortals would have to practise for 100 years, and still not be able to play it quite as well as Emil Gilels.

Yet even this fantastic pianist has limitations – and it is certainly no accident that these limitations mostly come to light when he wants to master Beethoven, or a Schubert impromptu, or Brahms's B flat concerto. When the 'early' Gilels encounters an early Beethoven sonata, namely the C major Sonata, Op. 2, No. 3, composed with entirely virtuoso pretensions, charm is no help. The rococoish second subject, really childishly easy, has no swing; the passages and chords, faultlessly played, of course, come out in too stabbed a fashion, too explosively, too much as though they already knew about

Tchaikovsky. The music lacks inner tension: one feels how everything has been brought to bear from the outside with pianistic art and virtuoso temperament, but that the music has no life of its own, no breath. It merely thunders, betrays naïve delight in ability, is spirited. The early Gilels really seemed unequal to early Beethoven. He overdid him – and was himself the victim.

Many Russian pianists cultivate a far too dynamic, too childish Mozart. They are afraid of distorting and thickening Mozart in a late-Romantic manner – so they impose on themselves (and on Mozart!) a disciplined restraint, a sort of 'stylistic diet': they rely on mere rippling and on mild expression. They 'dissimulate', pretend to be cool. When Horowitz plays Mozart, one can detect – in the first movement, say, of the great F major sonata, K 332 – traces of this dissimulation: then sometimes, of course, the artificial pretence comes to an end, and an over-hard forte breaks through. Emil Gilels, too, seems to have felt earlier that Mozart was above all a school of fluency. He is beyond that now. Gilels, as is shown by his interpretation of the 'great' C major concerto, K 467, has discovered Mozart's expression for himself. Occasionally, indeed, there are rhythmic fluctuations; but the tone is luminous, cantabile, and of admirable regularity; the passages have life and venture a concertante animation. Mozart under Gilels's hands becomes a pianistic experience. The intimacy of Mozart's little D minor fantasia is less in Gilels's line – here he forces the contrasts. But the 'great' C major concerto, in any case comparatively extroverted, he plays with controlled abandon: only with the cadenza does the surprised listener notice what breaches of style the artist has cleverly avoided during the piece. German and French pianists today prefer a more fine-drawn, more crystalline Mozart. Gilels plays the concerto in the grand, after-dark, festive manner; colourfully and ardently, like Rubinstein. He by no means drags Mozart into forbidden Chopin territory, but offers an example of great piano playing, wholly defensible artistically, and pianistically captivating.

Emil Gilels's sensitive Mozart seems more imperilled in the forte passages than in the piano ones. Gilels's Mozart already contains, that is to say – as does his delightfully pointed performance of Haydn's D major concerto – the inimitable basic tension typical of all Gilels's interpretations: the contrast between a smiling, charming,

Example 15

From: Saint-Saëns, Second Piano Concerto, Op. 22, in G minor, second movement, *Allegro scherzando*.

This is certainly no very great music, but the notes have feeling, elegance, melody and sensuality of sound. Gilels prepares the rhythm of the accompaniment artfully (bar 4), and plays the seventh chord (bar 6, etc.) with irresistible charm of touch.

sincere and personal pianistic manner on the one hand, and on the other, rattling bravura. When Gilels plays say the Scherzo in the very virtuoso second piano concerto by Saint-Saëns, hardly known any more, his exuberant delight in the lightness, in the grace, results here in a humanizing of the dynamic element. Gilels plays the very salon-esque second subject without any triviality, with cantabile care. No piano can sound more beautiful (Example 15).

In the third Rachmaninoff concerto, too, Gilels replies not only with sovereignty, but with charm. He is one of the most illustrious virtuosi of our epoch; he lends a popular 'draw' nobility. He is not a driven man, like Horowitz, whose wildness sometimes strains, violates, the pieces and makes them more fascinating and important than they really are – as one can hear overpoweringly when Horowitz, in the finale, say, of the third Rachmaninoff concerto, piles up such an ecstasy that Rachmaninoff himself became one of the startled admirers of the diabolically gifted young man. Gilels is more balanced. His virtuosity seeks the beautiful, perfect presentation of Romantic literature; but it does not turn into a musical divining-rod, a relentless splitting of the atom, as with Horowitz. Instead, Gilels's playing also remains without that manneristic touch, that desperate convulsion striving always for the extreme, which allows Horowitz's interpretations to become so exciting, and sometimes aberrant. Even when Gilels plays an ironically pointed, sparkling Prokofiev, he refrains from going beyond the bounds either of the piano or of taste.

13.   Elly Ney

14.   Robert Casadesus

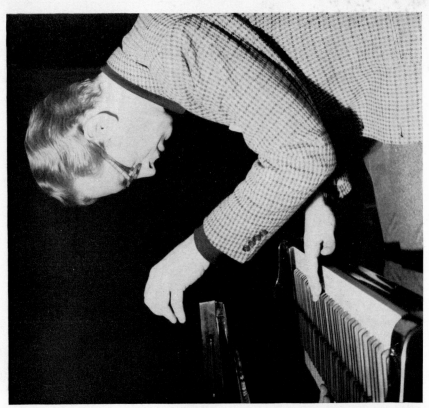

16. Geza Anda

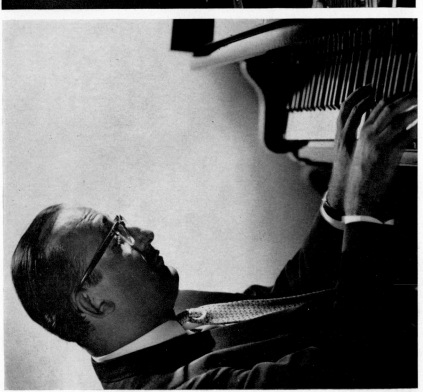

15. Friedrich Gulda

Arturo Benedetti Michelangeli and Robert Casadesus

In the wide world of pianists there is no artist who makes things so difficult for himself for the sake of sheer beauty as Arturo Benedetti Michelangeli. He is immensely scrupulous, mistrustful of his own achievement, and ardent in his desire to attain the greatest heights through decades of painstaking work, to venture nothing prematurely, to make the piano an instrument of pure tonal beauty. He has little to do with the robust type of artist who hurries easily from concert to concert, from platform to platform, sure of success, pleased and triumphantly healthy. Instead, however, the few interpretations that are known from him (Scarlatti, Mozart, Beethoven, Schumann, Chopin, Brahms, Ravel) represent pinnacles of piano playing in this century.

Arturo Benedetti Michelangeli was born in Brescia in 1920. He adapts himself with difficulty to the concert business, which depends above all on everything functioning smoothly. On the contrary. Michelangeli loses himself, not just for years, but decades, in a single piece, then unexpectedly gives a concert somewhere or other, and for that, by no means unexpectedly, cancels ten others. At the moment he is indeed planning once again a great many recordings, which he then wants to sell as favourably as possible. Yet that too should only be believed when the records are actually in one's hands. We should not be trying to speculate about what an Italian pianist is or is not doing if it were not for the fact that the few recordings that there are by Michelangeli, and the few concerts that one might have heard, point with overwhelming clarity to an outstanding talent. Michelangeli is mysterious because he is elusive.

In Michelangeli's playing, the brilliant and magnificent attack, as cultivated by the American and Russian virtuosi, and a, if one may so call it, European-conservative delight in the breathing diversity, indeed subtlety, of melody come together. Michelangeli combines Kempff's imagination and Horowitz's technique. Terrible though this sentence may sound, it is the highest praise one can bestow on a pianist – and the Italian has not yet by any means vindicated this sentence in the great works of piano literature. Yet the recordings that there are by him, and the concert experiences he has provided, suggest extravagant words. Thus Michelangeli not only plays the Scherzo in B flat minor, Op. 31, by Chopin with great virtuosity, which nevertheless refrains from all thundering, but he takes a subtle delight in gently fanning up the melody. The middle section full of chords, which comes to a gigantic crescendo, he begins quite coolly, like a Slavonic mystery. It is not the technical side that captivates, nor the abundance of nuance, but the unique proportions of the mixture. Rubinstein plays the piece far more like a ballade; Horowitz takes it with a somewhat mannered subtlety; Arrau tames it. Benedetti Michelangeli, on the other hand, does it the highest pianistic justice, without disrupting it, without abducting it from its French background to Moscow or New York. And in the course of years of intensive work, he has made his Scherzo interpretation richer still: now, from the passages of the middle section, further melodies emerge which are unknown to the recording.

Even in the dynamic piano concerto by Ravel, Michelangeli refuses to surrender to the mechanics. He is no victim of his own technique; he remains master of the piano, although the concert-grand occasionally turns into a percussion instrument. Physical strength is suddenly used here in order to consolidate the victory of the piano-playing subject over the almost irresistible explosion of the nearly mechanical object. One still feels the shaping, pointing, breathing Person even in this Ravel Presto; in a piece, that is to say, which degrades most other pianists into sewing-machine operators. An adventurous tension is thus created with Michelangeli, between a truly self-sufficient technique and a person, who declines to become the victim of his own capabilities.

When one hears Brahms's Paganini Variations played by Arturo Benedetti Michelangeli, one can understand that his appearance as a very young pianist was once an unparalleled musical sensation in Berlin. The work is the last great set of variations for piano that Brahms composed. It bears the Opus number 35 and is very rarely played in the concert-hall:[1] it is uncommonly difficult and almost impossible to realize in sound, even when the interpreter knows how to take the technical hurdles. Brahms's variations on the Paganini theme, also used for variations, incidentally, by numerous other composers, are in two books. Each book contains the original theme, from which one can conclude, perhaps that both books are not necessarily supposed to be performed one after the other. Michelangeli undertakes a few, undoubtedly permissible changes of order and leaves out three of the twenty-eight variations – by no means the most difficult. It is not the demonstration of brilliant technique that is really the astonishing thing, nor the stylistic tact, the liveliness of every voice, the appropriateness of every trill, every ritardando. A few other great pianists can do as much – though perhaps not so self-evidently and spiritedly. The interpretation overwhelms because it contains at the same time a drama, an almost clashing inner tension. Arturo Benedetti Michelangeli never forgets that it is a matter of a virtuoso piece, of Paganini studies, which Brahms wrote during his association with the famous virtuoso and Liszt-pupil Carl Tausig. It is a listening experience to follow how the variations move very gradually away from Paganini, and from the delight in fulfilling the virtuoso's duty. The pianist seems to forbid himself all cheap sentimentality, all emotional day-dreaming: again and again he holds on firmly to the gripping, dynamic element, to the study, and yet, by fulfilling the undertones, he slips slowly into dreaming. After a minute and a half, the theme and three variations have already rolled by, but some quite minute, austere bits of ritardando wariness have turned the piece, in spite of all the activity, into 'typical' Brahms. The slow variations, too, Michelangeli never reduces to perspiring manifestations of Germanic emotionalism. Yet there is no predominance of boring brightness; some things sound wonderfully shadowy. It is as though an artist wished to insist here on playing the Paganini Variations vigorously and austerely to the end, as if he had a dread of

[1] The author is naturally referring to conditions in Germany (ed.).

131

all-too-easy exhibitionism and sentimental kitsch. But then suddenly the deep darkness overcomes him after all, and the con grazia variation towards the end sounds almost numb. Michelangeli's Brahms interpretation is an example of pianistic mastery and a fascinating state of tension between clear dynamics and profound obscuration. Perhaps the artist was quite unaware that in his soul two principles were at war with each other as he played the Paganini Variations by Brahms.

Meanwhile, Michelangeli has also brought out that record on which, as rumour has it, he has worked for so many years: since the spring of 1965, Michelangeli's interpretation of Beethoven's sonata, Op. 111, has been available. Unfortunately, at the very highest pianistic level, the recording is a slight disappointment. And in fact probably because Michelangeli lets himself be governed too much solely by his feeling for sound, by his delight in pure, beautiful tones. He transfigures the contrasts, the abruptnesses and the stresses in a classical manner. It is true, there is probably no one who can play the chain of trills in the Arietta variations more ethereally than the Italian master-pianist. But in the first movement, does he not fall short of the disturbing Beethoven touch? His playing seems masterly in a sense that is here no longer adequate. It is too pleasing, almost decorative. Beethoven's early C major Sonata, Op. 2, No. 3, on the other hand, Michelangeli is able to interpret with intelligent tension.

Glenn Gould, who makes things difficult for himself by always exaggerating, exaggerates also in this first movement of Op. 111. But his wild tempo, which acts as though it had to overtake the spirit of the metronome markings prescribed by Beethoven for many late works, which are insanely fast and hence regarded by most musicians as aberrant – I recall merely the terrifically fast metronome markings for the Hammerklavier Sonata – Glenn Gould's crazy tempo is a conscious, provocative exaggeration. And the sforzato accents, which he even plays into the gentle second subject, are not arbitrary, but prescribed. Gould offers the complete contrast to all interpretations of Op. 111 known to me. He plays the piece even more incisively than Schnabel, more precipitately than Serkin, more austerely than Fischer, more explosively than Gulda, and more nervously than Kempff. Many German lovers of Beethoven will be able to listen only with angry laughter, although nothing in this exploded Allegro is botched.

Near Munich lives an old lady who feels, better than Michelangeli or Gould, how Beethoven needs to be played. She is pianistically – of course, of course – far inferior to both of them. Yet after 1945, when she was no longer fashionable, she went and played Op. 111 from out of a great, calm solitude that was infinitely more becoming to this artist than the heroic attitude. We refer to Elly Ney.[1] Electrola have brought out a record on which Miss Ney plays the sonata, Op. 111, twice: the first recording was made in 1936, the other in 1958, when Miss Ney was seventy-six. When one hears these recordings, one does not think of pianistic matters. What becomes important is the weight, the fervour, the calm pathos. Elly Ney's playing has nothing to do with the aims of the great virtuosi. In Op. 111 – the piece, that is to say, which she seems to me to master better than Beethoven's concertos or early and middle sonatas – she seeks to convert time, not into piano playing, but into expression, calmness and devotion. She succeeds. In the Allegro she may indeed fall short slightly in pianistic force: the calm of the Arietta is her kingdom. Whatever one may otherwise think about the dangers of pianistic high priestliness, one must bow before Elly Ney, because she can lift the end of Op. 111 to the heights of unforced feeling and play it out with admirable slowness. Anyone who has read the description of this sonata in *Dr Faustus* by Thomas Mann, or in Theodor W. Adorno's remarkable essay 'Style in late Beethoven', which first appeared in 1937, will remember that in both the talk is of the relationship between death and convention. Yet are the closing bars of Op. 111 really material which, as Adorno suggests, was set free by the Master's hand, touched by death? When Elly Ney plays this ending, it no longer has anything 'bleak' about it. At the same time, Miss Ney, even in the ninth decade of her life, by no means turns only to so-called 'world-forsaking' music. It is astonishing with what freshness this artist can still play, even today, the most powerful and radiant of all Beethoven's piano concertos, namely the E flat major. Technical problems are of no interest to her. But again and again she tries to bring out, even in the Emperor concerto, what dazzling pianists readily storm their way over: spiritual depth. In this concern for the

[1] Died 31 March, 1968 (ed.).

133

poetry, which is looking, not say for sentimental effects, but for the representation of pure, harmonious, so to speak 'wise' feeling, the continuity of the work, it is true, becomes lost. One hears it in pieces; between piano and orchestra there is hardly any dramatic correspondence any more, although Miss Ney restrains herself far more than other pianists whenever a wind instrument has a melody to play, and the pianist has only to accompany. Young pianists might learn all the same that expression, in the slow movement for instance, can be the very absence of sensitive self-display – and that the Rondo theme takes on an authentic, knotty character if one underlines, not say the E flat major rise of the theme, but far more its fall, running out with emphasis on the forte dominant.

The French master-pianist Robert Casadesus – he was born in 1899 – has by no means let himself be persuaded by his (relatively) advanced years into mumbling emotion or tearful nostalgia, let alone the noble, wisdom-of-old-age posture. He now demonstrates, like Serkin, the opposite of all that: namely, the wildness of old age, a quasi-Cartesian integrity always to begin with what is 'given', and to stick to it. The victim of this candid approach is called Mozart. Casadesus, whose *jeu perlé* was world-famous for decades, has freed himself from the trap which unimaginative managements had set for him by trying to make him a specialist in some few Mozart piano concertos. He now plays a rough, almost too aggressive Mozart, often forced in a virtuoso manner. Today, when he 'attacks' a Mozart sonata, a Mozart concerto, or a Haydn sonata, one might well wish back something of the elegance of which Casadesus was once master. The piano for him is no longer a place for the hard-to-learn toe-dance of ruthlessly trained fingers.

Strangely enough, although Mozart's piano compositions are, amongst other things, social music of the highest grade, their nevertheless intimate effect is endangered to an extraordinary degree in vast concert halls, whereas conversely even the most introverted confessions of Beethoven and Chopin before as many as 2,000 listeners suffer no damage to their intrinsic quality. Casadesus's interpretation sometimes bursts the Mozart frame; a Beethovenish intensity of sound appears. Suddenly one realizes that piano compositions are distorted by a vast audience, as though a silent Chaplin film were shown on cinemascope.

Casadesus seems to feel this. So he tries, for instance in the last movement of the F major sonata (K 332), to impress, to compel attention, with the utmost technical brilliance. This often results in hasty playing and cursoriness, even with him, normally so faultless. With Beethoven, Casadesus silences any such doubts. The Appassionata with him has a greatness, a shape and a fire that carry one along. And not in fact because Casadesus regards this bottomless piece from the outset merely as a playground for pianistic thundering. On the contrary, he starts at 'zero', plays the unisono of the beginning not yet as glowing lava, but just as pianissimo unisono, and declines to treat the A flat major second subject as a mysterious figure, like 'the appearance of the earth-spirit' – but always sticks close to the matter. He derives the tension entirely from the vast power of the musical evolution. With him, the development becomes the climax of the musical events, because he is not trying to illustrate musically considerations brought in from outside. Suddenly the audience stops coughing, turning round and dropping programmes. They feel the spirit of Beethoven passing over them.

Thus the programme of the pianist Casadesus at the moment is compactness. He begins – and in this lies the really dependable, unconfined, rudely healthy element in his playing – unconfinedly with what is pianistically possible, and then lets himself be drawn by the development into an often extreme situation temperamentally, which is not necessarily always the wildness of old age, moreover, but can also, of course, sometimes be a kind of unsuspected delicacy.

With him, and this is the outcome of such Cartesian consistency, nothing ever breaks apart. Details never obtrude; impressionistic touches never take up too much room. He plays Schumann's Symphonic Studies as though in one breath – and this really few can do. Their structure, their mixture of melancholy and grandezza, becomes the background for a romantic-heroic flight. With the velvet poetry of the work Casadesus does not concern himself: other pianists may pin Schumann down to a romantic Zwickau – he carries him off to a Spanish Paris. How wonderfully Gallic Schumann's piano works can turn out to be appears when Casadesus includes Waldszenen in his programme, a work that often sounds so guilelessly 'German'. One suddenly enters a forest of French Romanticism. 'The huntsman lying in wait' waits in style, loudly, and magnificently dressed. (The

135

'white hart' of German folk-song would certainly not have slept through *him*; faced with such a man, the animal would have decided on a detour at the outset.) Through this forest blows not only the fragrance of beech trees, but also a whiff of perfume, as though a gay Parisienne were hiding somewhere. Casadesus plays these genre scenes with a refinement that cannot be learned; he develops the forms, small and large, with elegant assurance, and rounds out the series of pieces into a work.

That impressionistic touches are lacking in Robert Casadesus's interpretations of Mozart, Beethoven and Schumann is a merit. But they are also lacking where everybody really does revel in transitions and breaks: namely in Debussy and Ravel. Casadesus commands such a power and liveliness of tone, so much grand-seigneurial tension and self-assurance, that he simply takes no part in the cult of tiny transitions, which in Debussy interpretation often enough leads to refined pampering. He stresses the masculinity, the logical constructivism, even of impressionistic music. When one hears how Claude Debussy interprets some of his own Preludes, on the LP records 'Famous Composers Playing their own Works, Telefunken HT 18 and HT 34,[1] one knows where Casadesus got his impulse from. When the composer plays them himself, Debussy's Preludes stand far more readily in the great piano tradition, far closer to Brahms and Beethoven, than one is allowed to suspect from the somewhat boring whole-tone twilight into which modern pedal-virtuosi so often plunge Debussy. From this – let it be said with a grain of salt – classical sub-soil, the bold harmonic innovations stand out all the more astonishingly. For when, as so often, Debussy's music is turned into an all too free-floating cloud of tones, the daring harmonies are indeed hardly striking any more. This sometimes causes his music to appear static and boring. Debussy himself clearly conceived it otherwise.

Casadesus plays the Preludes utterly compactly. Under his hands Les Collines d'Anacapri is a dramatic, witty piece. The piano expressif passage has a touch of Lisztian climactic joy. Over Des pas sur la neige lies a whiff of Winterreise tragedy. All this dispenses nevertheless with any coarseness. It has the authenticity, rather, of a music that is offered, not under the compulsion of a supposed style of the time, but

[1] In Britain, GMA 65 and 79; originally on Welte piano rolls (ed.).

136

Example 16

From: Ravel, Concerto for the Left Hand, cadenza.

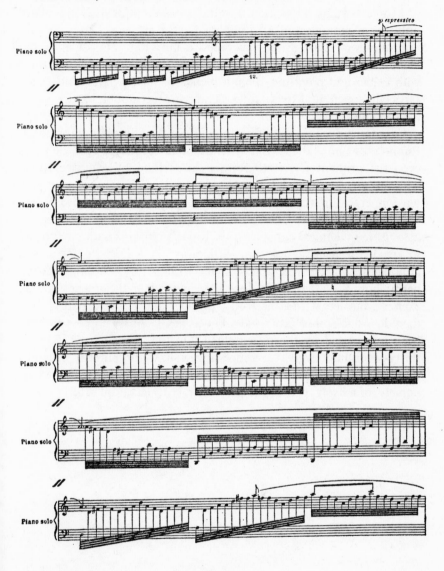

All this is played with the left hand only. Casadesus interprets the music strictly, marmoreally and imperturbably. He has no need to cheat or slip in ritardandi (say at the grace-note in bar 6 of our example).

137

as tonal sequence. That Casadesus is not alone in consolidating impressionistic music is demonstrated by the Debussy interpretations of Monique Haas. This artist puts into the animating of Debussy not only her technique, but also her unaffected art, which sets to with improvisatory élan. She sometimes brings him almost into the vicinity of Rameau and Couperin, whom she again dares to furnish with values and pointings. That a pianist of such a nature and art is especially open to Mozart and Schumann no doubt hardly needs mentioning.

Casadesus declines therefore to share in the stylistic conformities. Binding for him is the text, not the usual 'conception'. Thus he plays even the brilliant Concerto for the Left Hand by Maurice Ravel without any sentimental touches; instead, with perfect rhythmic tension, crackling regularity, and not so much delicacy as fire. When one hears how in the cadenza he draws the conclusion, from an astonishing technical capacity, that Ravel's music should be allowed to speak for itself calmly and brilliantly; how he puts across the appogiature with marble precision and without any ritardando (usual here); how for all that he does not emasculate the music into an exercise, but lets it breathe freely, proudly and imperturbably: only then does one realize into what a blind alley Debussy and Ravel have been interpreted by the over-refined. On the printed page, Ravel's thirty-second notes give an impression, indeed, of youthful garlands, of affected decoration. But they are more than that: the utterances, namely, of a lively, proud and masculine heart (Example 16).

Glenn Gould
and Friedrich Gulda

The two pianists whom we will try to characterize in what follows are younger by one or even two generations than most of the artists with whom we have been concerned up to now. In 1939, at the outbreak of the Second World War, Friedrich Gulda was nine years old and Glenn Gould seven. The other interpreters against whom we shall be setting Gulda and Gould, without any inappropriate concessions to their youth, were at that time already mature and experienced artists: one must not forget that Backhaus, Rubinstein and Kempff even date from the nineteenth century, and that Solomon, Arrau, Serkin, Horowitz, Curzon, Sviatoslav Richter and Emil Gilels still belong to the generation of those who were born before or during the time of the First World War. Compared with them, Gulda and Gould are youngsters of the 1930 and 1932 age-groups respectively. Their playing is attested not by decades of experience, but by another factor: both are brilliant pianists, but neither offers a copy of a great model. Their interpretations reflect true modernity: the expressive constructivism of the Vienna atonalists has not been without influence on Gould's intellectuality, nor the alluring spontaneity of the jazz age without lasting effect on Friedrich Gulda's improvisatory and dynamic élan.

Yet whenever one ventures such reflections and characterizations, in the background there is always the ghost of so-called historicism, by which we have no wish to let ourselves be paralysed. To belong to a certain generation, to be stamped by certain developments and styles, is a destiny, sometimes a misfortune, sometimes good fortune – but in no event a merit. So we have to make a double effort. We have to concern ourselves with everything that is typical of a time and a generation in the playing and in the artistic physiognomy of Gulda and Gould, but also to stay with that other question which one would gladly avoid like a coward: namely, how well do these pianists play, who meanwhile are nevertheless also over thirty? Are they able to penetrate masterpieces like Serkin or Rubinstein? Do they command the technique of Horowitz or Arrau? If this were not the case, one could certainly make no reproach of it for the two younger players – but one would still have to be allowed to establish the fact. Let the answer, which will be illustrated in what follows, be given at once: in both Gulda and Gould there is a spark of genius. Their best is undoubtedly to be set alongside the very best that the great pianists of our time can do. Gould sometimes commands an elegance and a transparency unattained by any other living pianist, even Rubinstein – and Gulda plays some of the great quasi-classical works, such as Beethoven's Waldstein Sonata, with unique animation and tension: of all the in any way accessible interpretations of this sonata, he still seems to me to surpass, not only Kempff's refined magic, but also Horowitz's perfection or Gieseking's relaxation.

Friedrich Gulda and Glenn Gould, the two most interesting pianists of the younger generation, are manifestly capable of standing up to even the highest demands. So all should be well. One should be able to breathe freely and be only too happy that after all, somewhere or other, someone thus always appears, to take over the bright torch of great art and carry it further. And yet, in thinking precisely of Gulda and Gould, nobody will console themselves with the beautiful idea that the resounding grand piano of our concert platform is thus now, as ever, in good hands. With the talent, clearly a curse has also been bequeathed. Or is it really supposed to be merely an accident that of all people the two best pianists of the younger generation are prone to the strangest eccentricities, that so much self-destructive extravagance was placed in their cradles?

What is condescendingly called a 'crisis of development' in anyone else has disquieting dimensions with Gould and Gulda. The jovial serenity of a Rubinstein, the sureness of a Backhaus, the reliability of the good average performer, who acquits himself satisfactorily at his recitals – of all this one perceives hardly a trace with Gulda and Gould. The guild of musicians, ever since the days of Orpheus, has probably been prone to mockery and malice, for everyone indeed who has to occupy himself wholeheartedly with the beautiful and the sublime understandably needs some compensation. Jokes of shocking indecency, plain rudeness and wounding unkindness restore the balance. Mozart's often coarse letters, Wagner's tasteless self-advertisement or Pfitzner's spite are the reverse side of honest dedication. In this guild of musicians dozens of malicious anecdotes circulate in which Gould's moody peculiarity or Gulda's way-out theorizings are mocked by their colleagues.

The one continually cancels concerts, hums uncontrollably as he records, walks on to the platform in gloves, and sprawls grotesquely at the piano. It is true, things are difficult for Gould. His constant coldness may be connected with a circulation deficiency. But his eccentricity goes beyond anything normal in this respect. . . . The other has got the idea that Beethoven is not music for our time, that even modern music is not music for our time, and that all pianists are to some extent deceiving themselves if they are content with Beethoven. Only in jazz music, so he believes, is spontaneous liberation to be attained.

It would be unfair to take all these reports with excessive seriousness, although they are only too readily confirmed when one speaks with Gulda or experiences Gould at a concert. Disquieting in all this is the fact, rather, that precisely the best are to some extent 'unreliable' and give their managers, as well as their public, cause for continual agitation. Some concert agents and music-lovers, because it is the most convenient thing to do, avoid this constant disturbance and stick to the good average performer. Gould and Gulda offer as much opportunity as one could wish for being 'right' about them, for reproaching them with this or that, or for holding something against them. In addition, they are not without arrogance. Yet if we make it easy for ourselves in this way to pin down, indeed nail, these 'difficult ones' to various excesses, and with that imagine we have disposed of them, we have capitulated too readily in face of the exceptional and have simply not grasped that nowadays the utmost achievement and capacity clearly has to be paid for with an inner strain or overstrain which is quite undreamt of by the good average performer. So let us not be confused by any silly caprice; let us protect Friedrich Gulda and Glenn Gould, if necessary, from their own escapades.

141

All this is valid, of course, only if there really is no doubt about the pianistic level, to use indefatigably this somewhat old-fashioned and finicky expression, only if really extraordinary talents are under discussion. And in this respect, too, Gulda and Gould are alike: the playing of both of them has indeed changed noticeably during the last ten years, even enormously in the case of Gould, but their pianistic class was present astonishingly from the outset. Gulda himself once said that at seventeen he could 'do' just as much as later – and in this he was not saying too much. Already at twenty he could do everything. Indeed, some of his friends think that Gulda played even better in 1950 than today. With Glenn Gould matters are no different. He really was only twenty-three when he coped with Bach's cruelly difficult Goldberg Variations. Many objections could perhaps be raised against the Bach of this recording. The technical perfection, the transparency and the flexibility of touch, Gould has never surpassed since – and has also probably never wanted to.

There is a word with which the enemies of the Toronto-born Glenn Gould seek to dispose of the young eccentric, when once again something absurd about the dress, the manner, the manias and hysterias of this pianist becomes known: they then call him a 'charlatan'. This is a detestable word, which only unthinking snobs could apply in a province that is far less open to the 'charlatan' than say acting, or directing or public speaking. With regard to the art of piano playing, the charlatan must be able to cope with the problems of a Bach fugue, a sixteenth-note passage or a late-Beethoven sonata to exactly the same degree as the non-charlatan – and it can be heard in practice whether he is able to or not. Naturally, some pianists try to feign 'depth', avoid technical problems and retire behind a fog of pedal and so-called 'conception'. But all this can be brought to the bar if an artist gives concerts and makes recordings without deceitful manipulations. Before Beethoven's semi-quavers all men are equal. To the solitary performer on the platform no kind of 'charlatanism' is then any help. I may be forgiven a not altogether appropriate comparison: 'charlatanism', at least with regard to pianistic skill, is just as laborious as say in a 100-metre race. There, if a 'charlatan' can manage 10·2 seconds, he is not a charlatan; although he may behave like one before or after the race.

Bach and Beethoven are the main points in Glenn Gould's repertoire, and during his European tour – which brought him deserved and overwhelming success – he also played mostly piano concertos by Bach and Beethoven. All the same, recordings show that this pianist has also come to terms with Mozart, Haydn, Brahms, Berg, Schönberg, Krenek, and even the monodrama Enoch Arden by Richard Strauss. He succeeds with Beethoven's early piano concertos more indisputably than with Beethoven's late works. Brahms becomes an El Dorado for Gould's intelligence and feeling for tone – but the uncontrolled genius pays little heed to Brahms's 'prescriptions' or even to the ritardandi in Beethoven's sonata, Op. 111, which are so important, completely necessary, and demanded by the composer. (These as it were gasping pauses for breath that divide up the tonal flow link the sonata Op. 111 with the first movement of the ninth symphony, whose precipitous ritardandi probably no conductor would dare to neglect. Glenn Gould, however, dares such things without further ado; he also occasionally turns a pianissimo into a forte. And for all who are well-disposed to him, it is certainly only a small consolation, but nevertheless still a consolation, that in all these provocations the young artist of such manifest intelligence clearly always has something in mind.) It is true, he is also far from making a principle of these 'liberties'. He does not go against what is laid down at any price – he sometimes follows prescriptions with slavish and captivating precision. This too he can do if he will.

If all these whims were really only whims, from which Glenn Gould could free himself without difficulty should he come round to it some time, there would be no need for us to chalk up his mistakes here in schoolmasterly fashion. But there is in Glenn Gould, not for instance the amusing refractoriness of a high-spirited genius who wants to provoke the Beckmessers of the world, but a demon: the demon of exaggeration. He exaggerates everything with great persuasiveness; not only the fast tempo and the slow renunciation, but also simplicity, spiritual depths, and indeed – paradoxical as it sounds – even unpretentiousness. In all this he always goes that step too far which marks him off indeed from the average, from the stale routine of the customary and the conventional, but which at the same time requires from him an extreme in art and skill: Glenn Gould's pianistic mastery is like a tight-rope act, because the artist imposes on himself again and ever again the task of making the 'too much' credible, of humanizing

143

the unusual and eccentric, of still controlling after all the wild and untamable. Anyone who was exasperated by the fantastic, mad tempi of the twenty-five-year-old will have shaken his head later over the absurd slowness of the thirty-one-year-old. Yet even in the furthest extreme, indeed there precisely, great pianistic and musical art was always revealed in spite of everything. Only once, perhaps because he is accompanying, does he remain restrained, without forcing: when he plays the piano part of Enoch Arden by Richard Strauss (hence when he partners the reader Claude Rains). Here, Gould's playing is 'merely' beautiful. Strauss's piano part sounds overwhelming: sweet, flowing, and light, never thick. For Gould's phrasing is so superior that no kind of triviality, striving for effect, or flimsiness can be heard. He rescues something unique, which is still Brahmsian and yet already contains Ariadne.

A few years ago, the world press reported that Glenn Gould and the famous conductor Leonard Bernstein had quarrelled in public. Before the start of Brahms's D minor piano concerto, Bernstein informed a bewildered audience that he was unable to identify himself with the interpretation that was about to follow, since Gould played everything much too softly and too slowly. Now it is luckily not all that often indeed that a conductor says so bluntly what he thinks of a soloist's interpretation – and so everyone had a good grin. Clearly, thought the connoisseurs, another madness of the ever mannered and peculiar Glenn Gould. But if one then hears the record on which Glenn Gould performs ten Brahms intermezzi, with noble fantasy of sound, tender distress, bottomless, indeed extravagant, but always well-formulated sensitivity, then one takes back the ridicule. Glenn Gould forces the inner depths – but in so doing he reveals nevertheless many glories that are undreamt of by the sober players. So one must know how to listen when in Brahms's A major Intermezzo, Op. 118, No. 2, by discreet emphasis, he not only plays the in any case obtrusive melody, but also brings the middle voice to life, which emerges in a wonderfully Brahmsian way and at the same time quotes the opening notes of the chorus 'Ich will euch trösten' from the German Requiem. Gould plays this with poetic art (Example 17).

The ease, say, with which Glenn Gould catches the musical conversational tone in Beethoven's second piano concerto, the B flat major, Op. 19, which arose incidentally before the first; the accuracy

Example 17

From: Brahms, Intermezzo, Op. 118, No. 2, in A major.

Where everything tends towards melancholy, restraint, and a veil of sweetness, as in the late-Brahms intermezzi, the pianist can yield to the temptation of the sentimental to a certain degree only – to the point where the melancholy has not yet become programmatic disruption. In his interpretation of the intermezzi, Glenn Gould goes to the very extreme of melancholy and refinement – all the same, he does not lay it on too thick. One never perceives the 'intention'. All the more artistic is the manner in which he picks out here the six upper notes in the left hand (bars 1 and 2 of our example, A sharp, C sharp, F sharp, E sharp, D sharp, C sharp) in such a way that they sound like a cantus firmus – and at the same time are a literal quotation of the beginning of the chorus from the fifth section of Brahms's German Requiem, 'Ich will euch trösten'.

and amiability with which the passages flow along, never merely for
the sake of their phenomenal technical neatness, but always in the
service of a progressive musical idea, with enchantingly bright and
irresistible eloquence: all this has Rubinstein's polish and Gilels's
precision, and relegates so many a first-class pianist to the region of
indifferent naïvety. For this early and unconfinedly virtuoso Beethoven, Gould chooses a tempo of breath-taking speed. However, no
wild chase develops out of the relatively chamber-musical dialogue.
The conversation is rippling, fast, but never breathless. No one in the
world, not even Casadesus, can play sixteenth-notes more evenly,
more freely, or more attractively. The piano comes in so lightly,
without the majestic posture of a powerful entrance. First and second
subjects are interwoven in unconstrained proximity. Glenn Gould's
phrasing is noble and without any solistic padding. Anyone who has a
feeling for the sound of a piano, for a tone-production that holds a
sovereign middle course between pure virtuosity and even purer
obviousness, finds his objections silenced by so much ability, so much
art.

This Allegro con brio of the B flat concerto by Beethoven, like
every true concerto movement, has a cadenza. The cadenza arose
from the final cadences; one spoke, for instance, of a 'Landino sixth',
which brought about the final note in a particularly apparent manner.
But it did not stop at that. In the classical instrumental concerto, it
came to the so-called 'suspended cadence'; that six-four chord on the
dominant after the sounding of which the soloist can extemporize,
alone and freely, until finally a resolving trill or a closing run calls in
the orchestra again. This may all sound superficial and perfunctory,
but even in Mozart's C minor Mass there is a written-out cadenza for
soprano and wind instruments. And in the fifth Brandenburg Concerto, J. S. Bach favours the harpsichord in detail.

Naturally, not all pianists and soloists have dared to extemporize.
So Beethoven wrote cadenzas for Mozart movements, Clara Schumann for Beethoven's concertos, and Brahms, too, composed
cadenzas for Beethoven's G major concerto. The question naturally
often presents itself thereby whether these cadenzas are still in keeping
with the 'style' of the concertos. When Glenn Gould, say, himself
composes a cadenza for Beethoven's C major concerto, there is a
yawning difference between Beethoven's and Gould's tonal idiom.

146

For the B flat concerto, a cadenza is likewise available, from Beethoven's hand. But this in itself is a problem. It does not really fit, that is to say, into the Viennese world of 1795 in which the B flat concerto arose. The late-Beethoven cadenza shows that so-called 'unity of style' between cadenza and concerto is not of absolute importance. When in about 1808 Beethoven wrote his cadenza for the early work, the spirit of his late work had already entered his production. So the wonderful cadenza sounds abrupt, solitary, punctuated, unconciliatory, harsh and wild. It grows far beyond the interior dimensions of the B flat concerto, for which it was written. Instead of Op. 19, it fits rather into the tonal world of the late A major sonata, Op. 101, whose second movement it recalls. Although Beethoven keeps very precisely to the themes of his early concerto, he makes something tremendously new out of them. With the cadenza it now proves useful to Glenn Gould that he has already planned the whole concerto on tempo, on brilliant riskiness and not just on innocuousness. He raises it to a stormy outburst, plays it in a balladesque manner, in a jagged great forte. When the orchestra then comes in again with the early concerto, two worlds collide: the styles of Beethoven's maturity and his youth. Gould's dramatic power forces the opposing elements formally together.

Friedrich Gulda, in his interpretation of the B flat concerto, naturally also plays this wonderful cadenza of Beethoven's. Gulda plays it with more restraint; he observes Beethoven's markings more carefully. Gould, for instance, let himself be led astray by his own verve into simply storming away over a dolce piano. Gulda more clearly sets to afresh, breathes more, and so does not quite achieve Gould's drama; just as Gulda in general performs this B flat concerto far more confidentially, more calmly and authentically, than Glenn Gould.

Gould makes things 'difficult' for himself. That Gould's pianistic perfection – to avoid flattening into commonplace trivial music – seeks out its own risk as it were, and yet is not destroyed by it, is shown by Gould's numerous, truly unorthodox Bach interpretations. Glenn Gould has not by any means chosen for himself only the virtuoso items, but plays also the two- and three-part Inventions, the Partitas, and The Well-tempered Clavier. Polyphony presents no difficulties whatsoever to this magnificent pianist; the independence and the freedom of his hands is astonishing, the art with which the parts are precisely held and shaded staggering. Yet it might not be so easy to find a German listener who would forgive Glenn Gould the Presto from Bach's well-known and much-loved Italian Concerto. When one hears this scorching Presto for the first time, one reacts with a plain 'impossible'. But the more one concerns oneself with the interpretation, the more distinctions one continually discovers in this piece. Gould creates a connection not only between little tonal features, but between whole periods and parts of a movement. He suppresses no detail. And although this Italian Concerto roars along in streamlined tempo Yankee fashion, the serenity composed by Bach, the amplitude and the dashing concertante splendour all come out.

The endless dispute about how Bach should be conceived and represented, no man can decide. The best way to deal with the stylistic dilemma is not to ask what a harpsichordist or a pianist is doing, but to listen mainly to what he brings to light. There is then no need to agonize over the laws of style, which are ever harder to codify, and which all amount to prohibitions, but instead the interpretation can be measured by the amplitude and unity of the work. Now this amplitude Gould, in spite of all his high-handedness, can manage. He treats the grand piano like an enhanced harpsichord; he forgoes no expressive effects, except perhaps too much pedal, which with Bach usually only befogs and intrudes, without clarifying or pointing. On the other hand – and this again is important for the spontaneous attraction of his Bach playing – Gould refuses to be diverted from investigating nuances on his own, from relishing harmonic shadings, from communicating in an enchanted and enchanting manner the self-evident flashes of genius in late Bach. Gould's playing only reaches a limit whenever he uses his phenomenal technique to bring out effects on the piano which can hardly be appreciated other than as purely mechanical, almost caricaturish effects – even if they were not so intended by the interpreter. The Goldberg Variations, played by Glenn Gould, demonstrate the richness and the aggressive freshness of his playing: a fascinating mixture, therefore, or constructivism, virtuosity and non-conformity. Sometimes our pianist pretends to be naïve, and the grace-notes carry on a veritable private concert with each other. In other variations Gould, without any doctrinaire doggedness, makes harmonic progressions so to speak elegantly clear; and the thirteenth variation offers some quite perfectly nuanced Bach playing.

148

Example 18

From: Berg, Piano Sonata, Op. 1.

To make clear the sequence-like relationship between bars 2–3 and 4–5, to bring out the difference between *ff* and *fff*, and yet never neglect the melodic lines of this climax, which is handled not polyphonically but 'pan-phonically': this is the art of Glenn Gould in his interpretation of Alban Berg's sonata. In this way the piece has at the same time a traditional air.

149

The fourteenth variation is a quick one; it oversteps the possibilities of the piano, not of Gould. Gould simply plays it too fast. In the famous twenty-fifth variation, an ineffably pensive piece in G minor, Gould's poetic power has to prove itself.

On how Glenn Gould plays this twenty-fifth of the Goldberg Variations endless speculation would be possible. A subjective element undoubtedly comes in here – not, say, a sentimental one. Subjective in the sense of Schiller means here more a stage of awareness, hence an absence of naïvety. This absence, in conjunction with deep lonely sorrow, could lead to the shattering of the variation, to its dissolving into surges and melancholies. This, it is true, is countered by the calmness with which Gould differentiates, the precision with which he holds firmly to lines. In playing Bach, he analyses him, just as the instrumentation that Anton von Webern gave to the Ricercare from Bach's Musical Offering was in fact an analysis. Modernity in Glenn Gould's playing of Bach can thus be recognized as a mixture of capacity for suffering, subjective feeling, and constructivism. This is not free from objections, but it is honest, personal and convincing.

Now if one already has to think of Anton von Webern during the interpretation of the twenty-fifth Goldberg Variation by Glenn Gould, it is not surprising that this pianist has also concerned himself directly with the works of the Vienna School. And when he plays the beginning of the sonata Op. 1 by Alban Berg, his sovereignty stands him in good stead: artistry of touch and intelligence make the piece compellingly melodious; it is a mixture of early Brahms and counterpoint. The climax of the Berg sonata, tamed by Gould, sounds like a combination of Wagner and Brahms (Example 18).

Glenn Gould, who plays Bach in a quasi-modern manner and who interprets the beginning of Alban Berg's piano sonata as though it were a matter of traditional music, has also occupied himself with late Beethoven. A record is available, curiously enriched with much singing and humming, which contains, along with an arrogant introduction from the pen of Glenn Gould, the last three sonatas, Op. 109, 110 and 111. Naturally, here too one comes upon many lyrical splendours. But when Glenn Gould at the beginning of Op. 109 combines the normal phrasing with his own original ideas, when he morosely fails the first movement of Op. 111, then such violences are really not outweighed by the occasional revelation of a magnificent feeling for sound and a driving pianistic sense of drama. When one hears the same works, however, from Friedrich Gulda, they suddenly have that great naturalness which Glenn Gould thinks he has to avoid, in order to be possessed of the exceptional.

Friedrich Gulda, certainly the most important of the younger Beethoven interpreters of our time, makes things difficult for himself and presents the piano world with a problem. In 1962, at the opening of the Berlin Festival, he played Beethoven's fourth piano concerto with Karl Böhm, whom he greatly admires. The performance was discreet, musical, sensitive, faultless, and perhaps too reserved. Then he cancelled a great world tour and all concerts. He had to be begged very hard to appear again a year later in Lucerne, at least as partner to the 'cellist Fournier. Asked why he had retired, Gulda, who wanted to become a jazz musician, replied that naturally he liked Beethoven and Schubert; that he had more to give up there than others, to whom their world in any case meant nothing any more. But, as Gulda said to me: 'The classicists have not got the problems of people today.' And: 'If I imprison myself in fifty piano recitals, I shan't be alive.' There is still much to discover in music. Of the sorrow hidden behind the modern façade, it is not Beethoven that speaks, but jazz. It is no life after all to travel from town to town, to sit about semi-occupied in hotels; for a concert is too strenuous for one to be able to do anything else with any determination before it, and yet on the other hand not stirring enough for one to have to be busy with it day and night. The modern world lives with jazz, not with the glorious dead.

I naturally asked Gulda whether it gave him no satisfaction to say something to people with a responsible Beethoven interpretation. He knew, after all, how much he did say to them in that way. No, he replied, it was more important to him to say something to people with what was their own. He would rather improvise than play – and even at his recording sessions for two Mozart concertos, to the horror of the sound engineers, he well and truly improvised the cadenzas, though in doing so blemishes were naturally bound to creep in. The question remained open whether Gulda was entirely convinced that jazz was not also 'manipulated', and whether – if it really had to be something contemporary – he ought not to risk an attempt at the modern composers.

Friedrich Gulda knows the danger he runs. He wants to avoid

being imprisoned by his outstanding talent in a way of life – namely, that of the travelling virtuoso constantly playing the classics – which he considers hateful and false. He only 'practised', so he says, between the ages of thirteen and sixteen. That was obviously enough, but only when one is as talented as Gulda. Now he is looking for 'reality'. And he believes that other artists, if only they were honest, must think exactly as he does.

This revolt does Gulda credit. He is not simply 'carrying on', self-satisfied and highly paid. Perhaps he is looking not only for life, for reality, but above all for the risk of life, which for him would no longer exist if he let himself be 'booked up' for years ahead and already knew today that seventy months hence he would be playing the Appassionata in San Francisco with great success, because he can do it so well. So, at Salzburg and Lucerne, too, he smiled only politely, strangely, and with resignation at the roar of applause for his interpretation of Beethoven. He is like a Hamlet who wants to play Ionesco at last.

Gulda's musicality is so self-evident that he himself, as it were, is quite unaware of it. Asked how he does it, he always says: 'Just let it go.' Thus the most prominent star of a series of excellent Viennese pianists – including, amongst many others, Badura-Skoda, Alfred Brendel, Ludwig Hoffmann, Jörg Demus and Ingrid Haebler – the most famous pupil of the pedagogue Seidlhofer, wants to break out into jazz. Probably many a music-lover thinks that if Gulda likes jazz better, one ought not to stop him. It discredits Gulda's love of Beethoven if he prefers jazz. Yet they only think that, before they have heard him. For luckily he has allowed himself to be talked into a double life. He is now a jazz pianist and an interpreter of so-called 'serious' music. He plays both, side by side, improvises runs into Mozart's little C major sonata, lets himself be lured occasionally into a Beethoven recital – and by no means convinces the jazz experts that he is a really first-class jazz pianist.

When Friedrich Gulda did after all give a Beethoven recital again, he silenced all who had been angry with him. He plays the most eloquent, the most natural, the most arresting and purest Beethoven of our decade. The manner and the accuracy with which he phrases not only the upper part but every detail of the accompaniment; the calm gesture with which he sets to afresh; the temperamental firm-

152

ness with which he comprehends and brings out what needs to be brought out as the musico-spiritual end-product: to him such matters are no problem at all. He speaks Beethoven's language – albeit sometimes without magic, without luminous cantilena and sixteenth-note brilliance. Whereas with many highly-gifted young pianists one must continually be surprised that although they represent some details admirably, others they let fall unmusically, Gulda's concentrated presence rivets the attention. The way in which, in the Adagio of the Moonlight Sonata, beginning calmly and without any forced emotion, he lets a melancholy tragedy grow out of the course of the notes themselves; how he has grasped that the piled-up thirty-second-note spot in the Presto agitato is the climax of the finale of the Moonlight Sonata, and that with the re-entry of the C sharp minor an elegaic air must hang over the tonal events: better than this it can hardly be played, and such a rendering only becomes 'self-evident' when Gulda has actually made it into the self-evident, expressive moment. Here most other pianists begin afresh and powerfully, as though nothing has happened. Gulda, meanwhile, has understood the finale of the C sharp minor sonata. With him, the initial fifth after the outburst creates an elegaic effect (Example 19).

Such concert impressions confirm what is evident, with difficulty from the available records, but all the more from the radio-recordings, that Friedrich Gulda, since he went over to jazz so decisively, is without that academic coldness which once surrounded his playing, so that his Beethoven could sound like 'Stravinskoven'. Now his Beethoven playing is truly arresting, truly exciting. Of course, it cannot go unnoticed that Gulda's technique seems to be a trifle less reliable than formerly. Nothing happens in the difficult passages. But he takes too little trouble over the 'easy' ones.

Gulda was ever a dynamic pianist. At the same time, he has not been afraid of the passions; he has come to grips with them, though he has always had to force himself to pathos. His playing has never sounded titanic, full of classic flourishes, showy. Gulda's animation goes beyond virtuosity and even beyond pianistic brilliance. While a Glenn Gould is prone to dangerous exaggeration, Gulda presents the music itself, so that it becomes highly expressive, significant and moving. This pianist has no need of subjectively exultant pathos. When one compares the fantastic assurance with which he plays two

153

Example 19

From: Beethoven, Moonlight Sonata, in C sharp minor, Op. 27, No. 2,
third movement.

The great climax of the piled-up thirty-second notes in the Presto agitato of
the Moonlight Sonata is not without repercussions on the quasi-psycholog-
ical continuation of the piece. Gulda, namely, takes the staccato-dot on the
C sharp (bar 6 of our example) literally; he thus conceives the entry ele-
gaically. Analogous is his interpretation of bar 10. Through this reaction
light is shed also on the power of what has gone before.

154

Beethoven finales, Presto and Prestissimo, one understands where Gulda's art begins. Beethoven's first piano sonata, the so-called 'little' F minor Sonata, Op. 2, No. 1, ends with a Prestissimo. Friedrich Gulda plays the piece so that it is indeed early, captivating Beethoven, but still not yet confessional music in the grand style. He plays into it the eighteenth century, when this sonata came into being. It is dedicated to Haydn after all, and still has a slight formality, such as we know in Bach's sons; but already alive in it is nevertheless the true Beethoven touch. The breathing accuracy with which Gulda accomplishes all this, with which he takes the staccato octaves, for instance, into the course of the sound, is a miracle. Gulda is never obtrusive with his staccatissimo and legatissimo. He has them available, but he lets Beethoven speak. More temperately and more captivatingly the piece cannot be played (Example 20).

If one compares the interpretation Gulda gives this early Beethoven Finale in F minor, Op. 2, No. 1, with the firm stride he summons up for the Presto of the Moonlight Sonata, with the intelligence that piles up and concludes the tonal drama, one must at least admire Gulda's sureness of style – and remind oneself, moreover, that he performs this finale of the Moonlight Sonata in a more unfettered way at a concert than in his recordings.

That Gulda is a jazz pianist can be perceived where one might least have thought it, namely in the Arietta finale of Op. 111, of all places. Gulda takes the dotted-note variation with 'bebop' ecstasy as it were. He does it no violence, but plays it exactly; yet with enthusiastic rhythm all the same. Beethoven might perhaps have smiled at it.

Strangely enough, Gulda is most in danger of mannerism with Mozart. He wants no sentimental Mozart, so he brings him at times, for instance in the finale of the B flat major sonata, close to a musical box: this trips along lightly like a ballet in sound, and hardly strikes a musical mean any more between stylization and pure rippling. Gulda succeeds all the more magnificently, however, with Mozart's slow movements. In fact there are moments when Gulda demonstrates as it were that he also commands the manner and the knacks of the piano Titans. By the simple means of a heavy up-beat he brings out a manifold pomp in the Funeral March from Beethoven's A flat sonata, Op. 26; he plays Schubert's C minor impromptu in melancholy solitude; and he gives the Burleske by Richard Strauss the charm of a waltz,

155

Example 20

From: Beethoven, Sonata in F minor, Op. 2, No. 1, fourth movement, Prestissimo.

The obvious temptation to conceive this unfettered youthful composition in the manner of Beethoven's confessional music Gulda avoids. He plays the pulsing octaves (third and fourth quarters of bars 7 and 8 in our example) in a restrained, springy, checking way. He takes the arpeggios, too, not all that dramatically yet, but leaves them a – scarcely 'provable' – baroque formality. In this way the piece stands between the periods: between Mannheim ecstasies, Beethoven flights, and the liberties of Bach's sons.

156

which transfigures and enriches the piece. At such moments one perceives how much enjoyment music can give Gulda, despite his severity. But all this, as also the vehemently mastered impressionists and the not quite so authentic Chopin, are still only preliminary stages to Gulda's encounters with late and classic Beethoven.

Geza Anda, Byron Janis,
Van Cliburn

The pianists Geza Anda, Byron Janis and Van Cliburn stand still deeper in the shadow of the Titans than Gulda and Gould; but they also seem instead to be less imperilled and extravagant than their colleagues. Geza Anda, of course, was already popular in Germany as a Tchaikovsky, Liszt and Mozart player when he was probably not yet up to comparison with the – at that time still distant – world élite. He made a few recordings a good ten years ago which are not on a par with his present level, although his brilliant talent was already evident at that time. . . . Byron Janis is the only pupil of Vladimir Horowitz who has become famous. Byron Janis's pianistic qualities and his programmes still allow, indeed, in spite of all efforts at dissociation, the more arresting model of Horowitz to be detected. . . . Van Cliburn, finally, is faced with the almost impossible task of catching up with his own world fame. The prize he won at a Moscow piano competition, which made him famous at one stroke; Khrushchev's kiss, whose propaganda value may have declined since the change of leadership in Moscow: all this brought the young artist all too far forward. Now he has an 'image'; he is expensive and much in demand. Contributing to this also was the almost unparalleled success of the recording Van Cliburn made of Tchaikovsky's B flat minor concerto, beautiful and lyrically sincere, but probably hardly unique or incomparable.

We are concerned, therefore, with artists who all three appear to be still on the way. But this 'on the way' holds a danger for talents who are not protected from fruitless errors by the sureness of genius: the danger in fact of a musical conventionalism. By this is meant the following: it is not at all times that the spirit or challenge of great works speaks directly to the developing artist. To take an analogy from conducting, there were years when Beethoven, for instance, appeared to say nothing to Georg Solti. Or when Geza Anda could obviously do nothing properly with Mozart. Now the danger is not, indeed, that such musicians then interpret Mozart or Beethoven emptily or without saying anything. This is naturally bad at the time, and must bring an attentive critic on to the scene. The danger, however, is not so much the gap itself as the temptation to fill it *somehow*. So many possible styles of Beethoven interpretation exist, of course, side by side. A young, intelligent musician naturally knows them all. Why should he not be expressive at someone else's expense, instead of displaying his own lack of expression? The calibre of a serious and independent musician can be judged also by the fact that he prefers to say nothing, rather than something that is not his own, or not genuine. All the time Solti had not yet arrived at Beethoven, his Beethoven remained poor: but for all that, he copied no one else; he did not paper over his own gaps with alien conceptions. He left himself the chance, as it were, of arriving at them himself. And then he did arrive at them, too. Matters were much the same with Geza Anda's readings of Mozart. Sometimes, although Clara Haskil had actually chosen him as her partner for Mozart's E flat double concerto, it was horribly apparent that Geza Anda, the brilliant player of Bartok and César Franck, was not equal to Mozart, despite his technical mastery of him. Much remained empty, virtuoso, haphazard. One was conscious of his anxiety in face of Mozart's genius. It is true, a pianist who attempts Mozart's piano sonatas, which in an absurd way are regarded as 'easy' and handed over to beginners at piano lessons, does have as it were nothing to get hold of. With the solo sonatas, too, the supporting, encouraging, filling orchestra is absent: here, with few notes, a piano player who is not really at home in Mozart's world is terribly alone. What should he do? If he has taste, he will not want to take Mozart over into the sentimental-romantic realm, nor to debase him to a rococo idol and leave him rippling in the lurch. He knows Mozart is no paltry imitation of Scarlatti, no tedious pupil of the 'Mannheim School', even when the notes happen to be the same. To make Mozart breathe is as difficult as to pluck shapes from the air. Every twist of Mozart seems to demand expression, love and devo-

159

tion: yet if it receives all this, what should be graceful and as though not of this world suddenly becomes thick and mannered.

But Geza Anda refused to let himself be disconcerted. Although he could play all three Bartok concertos one after the other in one evening, and reap ovations; although the young Hungarian was barely twenty years old when Furtwängler chose him as soloist in Berlin during the Second World War; and although Anda was able to bring off Liszt's E flat concerto triumphantly, he continued to concern himself with Mozart. Then, during intensive work with the Salzburg Mozart orchestra, Anda discovered his Mozart. And he will not rest until he has made him completely his own, until he has recorded all Mozart's piano concertos.

The Mozart that Anda has now gained for himself, and for us, is one of intimate sweetness, but of soloistic modesty. Naturally, not all his concerts, not all his records, succeed equally well, and certainly in ten years time Anda will play the A major concerto, K 488, more purely and with greater depth. Yet there is no need to look only to the future. Today Anda already plays, say, the B flat concerto, K 456, or the great C major concerto, K 467, or also the one in D minor, in a personal and beautiful manner. When once a firm stylistic basis has been gained, that is to say, a pianist suddenly has almost every liberty. He can then give any expressive fancy its head: it will still not become 'too much' and it will never become academically set.

Now it must be known, of course, that Anda conducts when he plays Mozart concertos. At a public concert this dual function often has disadvantages: the soloist who at the same time also conducts is never at rest; he has to give indications with his head or free hand and sacrifice some perfections of detail. It is true – and this one notices especially clearly on records – there is also an associated gain. When Anda both conducts and plays, he remains notably discreet as soloist. He does not come in with exaggerated emphasis, he pays far more attention to important wind voices, and he is pledged more strongly to the spirit of the whole than to the pianistic affect. All the passages that are performed in any case by the orchestra, Anda the conductor no longer takes so heavily on the piano, as nearly every soloist does, however, without thinking. Only where Mozart sets the piano in powerful motion does Anda too become flowing and brilliant: in return, he allows no little expressive nuance on the other hand to go unheeded. And where Casadesus prolongs some bass notes over-loudly, or, relying on his temperament, lets his sixteenth-notes of world-famous clarity roll too massively, Anda subordinates himself to the genius of the Mozartian motion.

Geza Anda combines convincingly the festive tone with that of chamber-music gallantry. It is astonishing the degree to which Anda has been able to free himself from Casadesus's Mozart of Hoffmann-like fantasy and grandezza, bursting with vigour and rippling self-assuredly, without falling into the opposite extreme of impersonal facility. At the same time, Anda's dynamic powers can still be very well observed even in his Mozart playing. However, as mentioned, Anda's feeling for style has set far too firmly meanwhile for any disturbing bits of unnaturalness to be able to creep in any more. Only Mozart's slow movements still sound a little neutral under his hands, because he fights shy of any romanticizing. Thus we are concerned with an artist who seemed destined to be an interpreter of late-Romantic, Russian and modern piano music, inclined to dynamic virtuosity, who at first followed this vocation, intoxicated with applause, and who now occupies himself with the musically very much more complicated problems of how to give perfect beauty of sound to Mozart, Beethoven and Schubert.

Naturally, delight in elegant, sparkling rhythmic impulse is a temp-tation for Geza Anda. Yet it is really touching how carefully Anda tries to resist this temptation. He plays Chopin's F major Study, Op. 25, No. 3, with a sonorous tone, but through his musicality refuses to let himself be deflected from the technical purpose of the study. All ritardandi he carries out with care, and the great forte passage in B major has resounding weight.

Byron Janis, for instance, takes this study much faster. Yet he really only lets his technique be heard, whereas Anda creates a tension between technical display and musical penetration. (Arrau conceals all its study-like features.) Musically, Janis behaves with appalling indifference. He only shows what he can do, by no means follows Chopin's markings, which it is true might be open to dispute, and with fast-working fingers turns a piece of music into an empty virtuoso number. Anda is clearly far superior to Byron Janis.

One cannot avoid wondering whether Anda's retreat to the German classics was not also connected perhaps with the fact that grand, dark,

late-Romantic demonism is not quite his mark. If one compares, for
instance, how Anda and Gilels manage the last movement of Tchaikovsky's Concerto, Gilels plays this music with far greater fascination. And even a work like the great Winter Wind study by Frédéric
Chopin, though it hardly counts as late-Romantic yet, seems to
make too great demands on Anda's shaping capacity. In this great
storm study the left hand plays a continual evocative melody,
while the right, with furious sixteenth-note triplets, is supposed to
create a stormy, precipitous and driving effect. At the same time
modulations arise which are both radiant and gloomy. Anda really
plays this great storm study in a way that is, to a decisive degree, too
controlled, too careful, too flat, although it is obvious that not
many pianists bring it off even like this. But even with the studies,
it is not just a matter of technique, but also of boldness in imagination,
of courage, and of not being afraid of possible wrong notes. Claudio
Arrau's tremendous tension and world-famous finger technique sweep
the work out of that relatively comfortable domain.

Thus Geza Anda abandons himself to Chopin's wildness just as
little as to Tchaikovsky's brutal lack of inhibition. All the more
seriously must one take Geza Anda's ever more resolute turning to
Schubert. The first movement of Franz Schubert's posthumous B flat
sonata is indeed less a technical problem than an almost insoluble
musical one. Even the theme consists indeed of that ambivalence, so
typical of Schubert, between pure song and pure natural sound. In
Schubert this ambivalence presents itself often enough in such a way
that the alternation between major and minor is not merely a point or
a development, but as it were the matter itself: thus a pale Winterreise
half-light spreads itself over the pure fullness and the pure sorrow of
this music. In the B flat sonata, this is symbolized by a very deep trill,
reverberating primordially, which concludes the melody diffusely,
has little connection with it, yet is part of it. Not, however, in the
sense of Beethoven's dialectic, but as an expression of the mysterious,
indescribable state of being in tune with nature. Anda has recognized
this conflicting association, which can be shown also in Schubert's
A minor string Quartet, Op. 29, or in the slow movement of the A
minor piano sonata, Op. 143. He gives the theme a captivating
melodic dignity and then spreads those half-light shadows over it
(Example 21).

Example 21

From: Schubert, Sonata in B flat, Op. posth., first movement.

In bar 8 of our example there is a trill which is not a logical antithesis or a consistent conclusion to what has gone before – but an expression of the erupting, magical state of being in tune with nature, typical of Schubert. In the thirty-second notes of bar 19, it seems to reverberate. Anda has recognized or sensed exactly the formal problem of this Schubert opening: here he lets a pale light fall on a pure melody.

163

Beautifully though Geza Anda plays the unutterably pure first movement of Schubert's B flat sonata, the temptation to martellato, to brilliance, is still not sufficiently avoided. In the pensive closing group of the exposition of the first movement, Anda carries out a staccato prescribed by Schubert as dispassionately as though it were a matter of a Haydn minuet. Suddenly all magic is gone, because the pianist has taken the place of the poet.

In the development of the B flat sonata, a throbbing D minor is reached. Then the song-theme of the beginning reappears. At first it cannot escape the desperately sad spell of the D minor, then it falls into an even stranger alienation, anticipating Hugo Wolf – and only by a detour via those piano-pianissimo trills do we again reach the pure melody. Geza Anda does not do enough shaping as yet. When, say, a desperately sad D minor overtakes Schubert's song-idea, this is not enough of an event with Anda. Anda's touch becomes flexible and reflective only later (Example 22).

Byron Janis, Horowitz's young American pupil, now in fact in his thirties, is already almost a legend. All the soothsayers of the piano-playing world are whispering amongst themselves that Janis is really the only American pianist of the rising generation who could perhaps match 'the' Russians – and it is no accident that even in Moscow recordings of Janis were made by American technicians. Janis has a comparatively limited repertoire. According to American magazines, before his concerts Janis inquires anxiously at weather bureaux if it is going to rain: when raindrops fall the piano sounds dull. Now it is perhaps no accident that precisely a pianist who takes the effects of a highly cultivated technique and the assumptions that go with it so seriously seemed to be pursued by particularly bad luck in the two concerts at which I came across him. In Baalbek, for instance, when Janis played Rachmaninoff's third concerto with captivating emphasis, before ancient columns, somewhat younger oil sheikhs and not so much younger American matrons, unusually bad acoustic conditions prevailed: one could hear the cries of desert animals and the sighing of the wind. And Rachmaninoff's third piano concerto seemed strangely dejected and insignificant as seventeen centuries, in the form of the smaller Temple of Bacchus, looked down upon the work. Yet Janis had nevertheless performed this third Rachmaninoff concerto at Baalbek with stupendous virtuosity, more transparently,

Example 22

From: Schubert, Sonata in B flat, Op. posth., first movement, development.

The melodic fate which the main theme undergoes (bars 15–17, 21–24), Anda plays perhaps a shade too unconcernedly, too unreflectively. One does not feel that the B flat figure has to go on a Winterreise, a winter journey, here.

more personally and more arrestingly than most other pianists of his generation could do it. Liszt's E flat concerto in Lucerne, on the other hand, was far less successful, not only on account of a broken string, but also because of the inadequate accompaniment. The Vienna Philharmonic under Zubin Mehta accompanied spinelessly. Liszt's E flat concerto, moreover, is no piano monologue, but a symphonic work, an orchestral piece with piano. But the tensions disintegrated; the concerto broke up into numbers. Some things Janis brought off with virtuosity; others were too weak, too much mere chord-work. The powerful attack was lacking. So, perhaps as a result of these two concert encounters, I now somewhat underrate this American pianist. But there is still no record of his either, as it seems to me, in which Janis amounts to more than Horowitz as an interpreter. Yet it is not fair to measure Janis only against Horowitz. The comparison with Van Cliburn he stands better. He is the more sinewy, the greater player. Unfortunately he confines himself too much just to Liszt and Rachmaninoff. His recording of Liszt's Totentanz for piano and orchestra shows with what fire young Janis plays. Janis reveals his best side, and he knows this only too well, in interpretations of Rachmaninoff. 'His' first Rachmaninoff concerto bears comparison with Sviatoslav Richter's recording.

Van Cliburn, Janis's six-years-younger American rival, conceives Rachmaninoff's third piano concerto more innocently and more beautifully than Janis, sometimes sweetly, shyly and almost mawkishly. Van Cliburn obviously endeavours to play as though a mixture of innocence, feeling and virtuosity can cope with all problems of interpretation.

It is impossible in connection with Van Cliburn not to speak of politics. Khrushchev's kiss we have already mentioned; it should be added that Van Cliburn played Beethoven, Brahms and Chopin at Johnson's ranch before the American President and a Federal German Chancellor. All the same, it must be conceded to the young virtuoso that even after that triumph in Moscow, after his successful Tchaikovsky records and his fantastic reception in New York, he has not stopped working. Today Cliburn has already played most of the great concertos in piano literature for recording.

Now if one were to judge Van Cliburn by the way he deals say with the Appassionata, one would be unjust. He has nothing to set against the impressive series of famous Appassionata interpretations. When one recalls, for instance, with what power a Casadesus makes the development of the first movement into its climax, what a storm a Sviatoslav Richter sets going in the finale, or what fullness an Edwin Fischer can draw from the slow movement, then Cliburn's Appassionata sounds innocuous. In the concert hall his tone is not big enough, his touch lacks roundness, and though many a turn of expression succeeds indeed in a sensitive-sentimental way, the self-evidence of great, convincing piano playing is not created.

Yet one probably underrates Cliburn when one measures him by the Appassionata. Liszt's B minor sonata, Tchaikovsky's B flat minor concerto, Prokofiev, MacDowell, Rachmaninoff: these are no doubt more in his line. He has sincerity for the emotional parts, bravura for the octaves, breath for the developments. In general, he is able to bewitch his admirers by playing that is both sure of its effects and yet shy. He is a human, sometimes slightly innocuous interpreter; his tone and his technique meet the demands of the gramophone record in a remarkable way. The distress and the brilliance of this pianist can be discerned when one hears him with Beethoven's G major concerto. He still has to struggle for the slow movement. In this famous dialogue between a fiercely threatening orchestra and a deeply grieving piano, Cliburn loses. He can neither command the tone of pure, refined sorrow, which is struck here by Wilhelm Kempff, nor is he able to transfigure the sorrow of the piano part into the calm sorrow of a folk-song, as is done by a Bruno Gelber. Beethoven's genius in this inconceivably short piece consists, after all, in the fact that the piano entries rise gently at first. Only when there is a sudden soft statement from the orchestra does the piano come in from above, falling. At the close there is a gleam of shrill fortissimo humour, as though all sentiment ought to be repressed as it were, which then, in the very last bars, speaks out magically after all. Cliburn is far from such realms of expression. How brilliant, fresh, unconstrained and arresting his playing can be, however, is shown by the Rondo finale.

Bruno L. Gelber
and Martha Argerich

It would be an imposition on the part of a music critic to characterize, with an apparent claim to finality, a pianist such as Maurizio Pollini, who is not yet even twenty-five years old, or a Bruno Leonard Gelber, who is likewise under thirty. For an artistic physiognomy, unless it is a matter of a really brilliant talent such as Glenn Gould or Friedrich Gulda – and even there a thorough characterization would certainly still have been impossible ten years ago – only comes into being, after all, in the course of time. On the basis of two or three concert impressions, however, of a few records and tapes, the disposition of a young artist can still not be determined so bindingly as it can be with a sixty- or seventy-year-old man, whose interpretations, it is true, are certainly not reducible to a common denominator either, for there are changes, of course, good or bad evenings, and developments in conception, but in whom the type nevertheless is perhaps more readily visible behind the actual musical manifestations. This alters the critical attitude. While the picture of such distinguished artists as Wilhelm Kempff or Artur Rubinstein, for instance, is more precisely fixed by drawing attention to what music is possibly not so much in the line of these two pianists – and nobody is equally at home with everything; this would be inhuman rather than superhuman – with such young pianists one should not at first ask so much about their limits as about their merits. The limits that may come to stamp the character more clearly perhaps than the strong points are impossible to take quite seriously all the time a pianist is in the middle of his development, of his musical puberty. It is damaging to fix a young artist by typing him. One must leave him freedom to develop. In our

168

look at young pianists not yet confirmed by a world career and a firm style there is, moreover, an accidental factor to be added. Strong points of some kind are common, of course, to every gifted young pianist. One knows indeed how often the careers of highly gifted 'prize-winners' have disappointed or even not taken place at all. It is to a particularly high degree a matter of taste to decide whether a person's merits are so compelling that he should already be reckoned among the great artists, or not yet. A reproductive obligation is only created after all precisely when someone has been fruitful in a characteristic way for more than one phase of his life.

The steadiest, most reliable and probably also the most serious among the youngest pianists seems to be Bruno Leonard Gelber. In 1960, when he was not even twenty and he made his début with Brahms's D minor concerto on a concert tour of Germany, his playing seemed almost like a miracle. The young man, who came to Europe from South America, is probably the greatest piano discovery since the appearance of Friedrich Gulda; a piano talent whose limits were not yet in sight at any rate in the D minor concerto by Brahms – God knows, no bravura piece with which it is easy to shine. If he keeps up what he so furiously promises, then the world will have one more pianist of the calibre of Gilels or Gieseking.

The D minor concerto can be played differently; it can be interpreted in a more reserved, more gloomy, more nebulous fashion. The young pianist brings into the work a southern brio, indeed now and then even a stretto character, which is by no means wholly absurd. Passages before which other pianists rightly quake, such as the octave development, say, in the first movement, he drives home with disarming pianistic verve; the octave trills ring out with icy, unwearying precision, and a spirited impulse animates and enhances the whole work.

Yet one would be mistaking the calibre of this young pianist if one implied that he was just one of those dazzlers who flock over from America in veritable droves, astonish us with their technique, which is almost always first-rate, have little to say musically, and can scarcely be told one from the other. The care with which Gelber phrases, the calm with which he plays out the second subject, the determination with which he dares to wander in the Adagio: all this, and of course his almost uncanny technical familiarity, raises him far above the level of ordinary good piano playing. It is true, some turns of phrase he takes too lightly, and other places, where the piano has only a virtuoso accompaniment, too loudly and too self-confidently, too powerfully – but still never thoughtlessly, perhaps, or unmeaningly. Gelber's weaknesses must not be concealed. He still sometimes lacks a flowing quality, in fact precisely in his soft cantilena. The grand piano is indeed a tricky instrument: how hard it is to wrest fullness from it, to avoid letting notes stand somewhat isolated and dying away, is borne out even by such a talent as this. Here one perceives for the first time what Rubinstein is able to do, when he animates the dull mechanism of the piano, as if it were a matter of course, into captivating and powerful sonority. Gelber, it is true, has already, within a few years, got a good bit further along the way to a singing cantilena. At twenty-two he interpreted Beethoven's G major piano concerto with rhythmic fire, great freshness and extraordinary grace, as though in fact a touch of youthful elegance transfigured his playing. With Gelber no note remains immaterial or merely brilliantly mechanical. In this way it emerges how much transfigured Mozart lies in the passage-work of the G major concerto. In the outbursts, Gelber is not to be held back, and a spirited, dextrous élan takes the place of restraint. In the cadenza Gelber exults almost too much, and in the last movement, too, he makes sure there is no lack of pepper. German pianists play it differently. Now with regard to the great dialogue in the Andante, Gelber plays his part, not as that sad voice answering a brutal orchestra, but far more as a beautiful, melancholy folk-song, which refuses to let itself be disturbed by the intervening strings. The pianist gives a highly independent interpretation, technically faultless, sometimes a shade too brilliant. One can say with certainty that in thirty years' time he will play the piece quite differently. But would it not be sad if a twenty-two-year-old pianist were trying to aim for a mature, old-man's style, instead of presenting the work in a manner corresponding to his age and actual state of mind and feeling?

The pianist Martha Argerich, born in Buenos Aires in 1941 and stupendously gifted, is a difficult case. Not, for instance, because her cigarette consumption is supposed to be considerable, nor because she sometimes plays brilliantly and sometimes without discipline – but far more because she is having to suffer for her start as a phenomenal child prodigy. What once came to her easily is becoming increasingly more difficult for her. Even at sixteen, seventeen and eighteen she enchanted her public. I still remember how she played Mozart's great C major concerto in 1959, with high-handed virtuoso attack, sprightly charm and astonishing facility. Certainly it was capricious, furious, unconsidered. But still with that fascinating, accomplished touch and pretension which nobody can acquire by 'working'.

Naturally she received prizes at that time. And what may have been far more important to her: a Walter Gieseking sung her praises, a Friedrich Gulda gave her lessons, and a Vladimir Horowitz expressed his astonishment at those remarkable records on which Miss Argerich played two great Chopin works with virtuoso charm, two Brahms rhapsodies still completely 'personally', and Prokofiev's dreaded Toccata with tremendous allure. After this start, Miss Argerich, whose playing began to show signs of confusion and lack of concentration, got into all manner of difficulties. After a long interval, she reappeared – though clearly still very indisposed – with Mozart's 'little' E flat concerto, K 449. During the moments that came off, one could see that she was still an exceptional pianist, that she still had 'world-class' possibilities. Sometimes she shaded with lively tonal imagination, sometimes she converted her technical freedom straight into rippling pianistic expression. Yet there lay over the concerto an often almost disquieting stiffness and irregularity. Nothing breathed. Rhythmic irregularities, impossible obscurities, were alarming. The artist played then as though in a passive trance, but not carried away so much as lifeless. Why, for instance, she always had to rush certain sixteenth-note replies, which the piano gives to the orchestra in the first movement, is incomprehensible, because it accomplished nothing. Why she chose a Mozart cadenza and then played it so thunderously, with such eccentric virtuosity, as though she had a wild Tausig arrangement in front of her, was equally puzzling. Determining a style by selection is no excuse after all for lack of style in execution! Many a light, tender word in the Andante, on the other hand, and also in the finale, Martha Argerich spoke with direct naturalness, almost as though against her own will. Yet shortly afterwards Martha Argerich played her way to a prize in Warsaw, against strong Russian competition. Perhaps she has come out of her crisis. Do all music-lovers know how much talent lies behind even the 'fluctua-

171

tions' of such a career? Martha Argerich not only has perfect pitch, which enables her to name even the most awkward dissonances without any trouble; she not only has an enormous memory, so that she hardly needs to mark in her fingering; not only, as her friends aver, an astonishing gift for parody, which enables her to interpret a piece at will in the style of many of the great pianists; but she can in a short time make completely her own works as different as a Beethoven sonata and a popular draw by Ravel. The piano world would indeed be truly richer if Martha Argerich were to find her way back to the necessary stability. To achieve this implies, of course, not only pianistic good fortune, but also a talent for living.

Chopin's studies, if one hears them played one after the other in the concert-hall, seem very short. They last on average hardly more than two minutes each. While the passages ripple rapidly by, a disinterested listener is hardly able to judge what a vast world of expressive possibilities the barely twenty-year-old Chopin conquered here for the piano. But these studies – quite apart from their musical majesty – are also among the hardest riddles that have ever been set for the hands of a pianist. Many adepts of the piano strive for years on end (and not always successfully) to resolve correctly the unshadowed marble clarity of the first study (Op. 10, No. 1), hence to play through without tiring or losing sharpness the broken triads that encompass the whole keyboard. The A minor study (Op. 10, No. 2), one of the most awkward chromatic ballades ever written, borders on the unplayable. What is expected here of the ring-finger of the right hand, sluggish in all mortals, is more than 'difficult'; it is torture for the pianist. Some piano-mad players have tried for decades to find the right technique, have practised doggedly and still got closer to inflammation of the tendons than to perfection. The E major study (Op. 10, No. 3), easier and slower, has meanwhile been adopted and profaned by the light-music industry. One can no longer hear its profoundly grieving melody without recalling the words 'so deep is the night', which thanks to thousands of involuntarily-heard radio programmes are firmly etched into the brain. In the study, Op. 10, No. 4, the young Chopin enters for the first time the realm of the demonically wild, the unfettered, made known by the later scherzos. What is demanded here in fire, strength (and accuracy) even the most talented can achieve only in months of work. The fifth study is known as the 'Black Keys Study', because the right hand uses only the black keys of the piano, apart from one exception, which makes the pedants grieve. It is also possible, incidentally, to strike this white F with the left hand, so that everything is once more in the best of order.

Thus it goes on, and thus each of the 12 Chopin studies of Op. 10 (there are 12 more in Op. 25 and a few posthumous ones) has its precise technical purpose, which was subordinated by an inventive genius of the piano to musical material of unfading originality. Only when one brings all this to mind does one grasp what a pianist is hazarding when he plays these studies on end at a concert. Not many do it. Neither does Stefan Askenase bring it off. It is true, he masters most of the technical difficulties, of course – he is after all among the best-known Chopin players of Europe – but this mastery still lacks the brilliance and complete sovereignty that are indispensable precisely in early Chopin. Op. 10, No. 1, becomes annoyingly vague towards the end; Op. 10, No. 2, comes over in an astonishingly relaxed way (not many can do that!), but in the course of the technical victory the composer's idea is forgotten; and the close of No. 4 is not an ecstasy, but only a rounding-off.

Askenase, that is to say, is a lyricist, a unique pianissimo player, dreamer and master of late Chopin. One has to hear how he plays the beginning of Chopin's last Ballade (Op. 52, in F minor) as a desolate folk-song, or how he reveals that pianissimo magic of the Mazurka in C major, Op. 24, for which the lanky blond artist must have worked hard and long. . . . The Chopin of the studies and ballades is not the ground on which Askenase holds his own. The sad waltzes are his line.

Askenase, and this is rare with Chopin players, is clearly not roused by brilliant piano movements, stormy polyphony, or even architectonic points, as they are so beautifully traced in the F sharp minor polonaise, the G minor ballade, or the first movement of the B minor sonata. He becomes eloquent meanwhile where many others have to cheat: in the seemingly monotonous repetitions of the C sharp minor waltz, or the not merely soothing but downright soporific Berceuse; during the dream-sections of the Largo from the B minor sonata and the euphonious liberties of the nocturnes.

In the highly dramatic polonaise in F sharp minor, Askenase's weak point is revealed: rhythmic lack of concentration and indecisive lyricizing. Askenase never enforces the polonaise rhythm, so magnificently prepared by Chopin; his limp left hand always remains a function of the right, and even the syncopated chords, which are indeed nothing else than a pure confirmation of the rhythmic structure, are more inclined to embarrass him. Instead, he picks out a few elegaic entries and gives them prominence, as though they were an end in themselves and not just an episode. Perhaps he wants to retract this markedly balladesque work a little. Yet instead of carrying

174

it out lyrically, he only presents it weakly, and without tension. Arbitrariness, however, is only justified if it is fruitful.

Chopin did not talk about 'endless melody' with the possessive pride of a Saxon. (He merely composed it.) Yet with the second subject of the first movement of the B minor Sonata, if one lets oneself be lured into loquacity, if one fails to underline the development with the greatest force (so that it becomes explicable why the recapitulation forgoes the main subject), then the movement falls apart into delightful details.

Adam Harasiewicz, awarded many prizes, praised by many critics, and born in 1932, still plays a remarkably unoriginal Chopin. Fluent, magnificent and eloquent, certainly, but at the same time as though at second hand. This can change, of course. He has a good technique, and apparently hates boredom; for he often intervenes in the course of the music, pointing and illuminating afresh. Unfortunately, he has as yet no proper relationship to Chopin the dramatist. Almost carelessly, he plays over the great, truly well-prepared climax of the A flat ballade; he lets the coda of the C sharp minor mazurka escape him, and makes of the second subject of the F minor fantasia, a miracle of sound, something merely innocuous and facile – quite as though Chopin really were what many take him to be: a *petit-maître*. Indeed, in the pianistically significant, piled-up places, Harasiewicz is able (unfortunately) to afford an increase of speed, whereby he degrades something impressive into emptiness. When Chopin's piano statement becomes richer, more radiant and urgent, such a heightening suggests after all that the musical form should be allowed to appear more clearly, more majestically, rather than simply become faster and turn a composed effect back into a pianistic cause.

So this highly gifted pianist frequently gets stuck in the obligatory. His playing and his gift have about them something flowing, round and charming. Sometimes, however, he decides to do things in earnest. Then, it is true, the technical reserves which this young master commands take his listeners' breath away. The study Op. 10, No. 1 is played by Sviatoslav Richter, even on records, worse than by this young pianist at a concert. The coda of the C sharp minor scherzo suddenly has a devastating force.

The suspicion may be expressed here, though only with reservations, that it is precisely the irresistible success that accompanies his

175

playing which may prevent this artist, who on top of everything is also extremely good-looking, from analysing and interpreting every work with equal seriousness. His fresh, fluent playing, the sureness of his octaves and the attractiveness of his pianistic eloquence at once make the public's heart go out to Harasiewicz. As a result, he runs the same risk as Van Cliburn. The more resounding his success, the harder it may become for him still to build into his playing that architect's sovereignty, without which, indeed, he can also get along so well. How remarkable that love of Chopin's inconsolable minor keys can go so well together with prodigally-endowed frivolity.

Vladimir Ashkenazy, who now lives in London, seems to me to be more independent and more gifted than the somewhat conventional Adam Harasiewicz. Rachmaninoff's third piano concerto gives Ashkenazy no difficulties at all, although its melancholic aspects are more in his line than the magnificence. The strength of lyrical intensification of which Ashkenazy is capable appears less in the Chopin ballades and the B minor sonata, whose outbursts the young pianist plays brilliantly, indeed, but nevertheless not yet committedly enough, than in the intimate sighs of Chopin's small works, which Ashkenazy performs compellingly.

It is probably a complete mistake to identify the composer of the B minor scherzo, the B flat minor sonata and the F major ballade too exclusively with the sphere of the salon and its perfume. The fact that it was always sought to play him off against Franz Liszt may have now caused Chopin to become an anti-Liszt; a composer of whom everyone thinks only in terms of sensitivity and never of fury, only of subjectivity and never of titanic delight in experimentation. But these prejudices can hardly be set right any more without creating new ones. Anyone who out of sheer antipathy to the vague notion 'salon' suppresses the fact that in reality all Chopin's works arose for the salon (without for that reason having to be salon *music*) is bringing another heroic myth into the world.

How does Halina Czerny-Stefanska play her Chopin? More luminously, more personally, more fully than most German pianists. Less accurately, less clearly, less steadily than the great American virtuosi. More fluently, more tragically than the French school. So that one listens and believes again, unreservedly, in Chopin's genius. Chopin's polonaises have been called 'festivals of tears'. Halina

Martha Argerich
(Acknowledgement: Deutsche Grammophon-Gesellschaft)

18. Adam Harasiewicz,

19. Shura Cherkassky

Czerny-Stefanska lets the tears freeze into the Funeral March and turns the festival into a volcano on which to dance. It is true, anyone who might think that in the C minor polonaise the A flat middle part, with its Schubertian progressions, would be slowed down into a drama of the soul would be mistaken. Here, where German pianists give way, the Polish woman presses on, and makes the polonaise sixteenth-notes springy and urgent. When Mme Czerny-Stefanska plays Chopin's E minor concerto, her every up-beat becomes a tender abyss; what the orchestra has boomed out first, she repeats a little slower and lost in dreams. In the first and second movements there are no passages any more, but only feeling. Chopin himself, whose too-gentle playing drew complaints from his contemporaries, appears to be sitting at the piano. In the finale, the pianist lacks strength and brilliance; those sixteenth-note triplets, which have to be played below a melody (by one hand!) – Rachmaninoff followed this up and developed it further – remain blurred; and the fortissimo risoluto, which Chopin after all prescribed over and over again, even if he himself was not fond of carrying it out perhaps, is lacking.

The Italian pianist Maurizio Pollini was born in Milan in 1942. He has meanwhile received so much praise from Rubinstein, and so many important prizes, and brought out one or two recordings of such brilliance, that he may be regarded as a world-famous 'secret tip'. But he obviously shares with Glenn Gould, Michelangeli, Horowitz and countless other pianists, an understandable and yet regrettable attribute: he is, in the sense used by the impresario, unreliable, and often cancels. He suffers from his nerves; he makes things difficult for others. That he may also have a difficult time himself means nothing to the people with their concert schedules.

As to Pollini's Chopin recordings, one has to get used to them. This young man plays Chopin, not by directing a tear-dimmed gaze to the heavens and giving voice to a personal lament, but by revealing the on-driving dynamism of the passages. Mme Czerny-Stefanska puts soul into every up-beat, warmth into every passage, sorrow into every sob. Pollini, on the other hand, does not make the mistake, say, of playing Chopin objectively or mechanically, which would indeed be simply wrong and stupid, but he does interpret him with fiery, urgent clarity. Certain passages which are full of double finger-ing and pianistic marvels he brings to glowing point. He plays them with rhythmic glitter; he dynamicizes Chopin; he takes no rest at well-established rubato spots, but falls to with youthful, dark impetuosity. His Chopin becomes, not superficial, but festive; not unlyrical, but forward-striving. Whether Pollini plays the great F sharp minor polonaise, the C sharp minor mazurka, or the E minor concerto, each time he brings it about that a music which so easily lures one into sentimentality suddenly seems to become aware of its own dignity and majesty. Friedrich Gulda also tried this. But under Gulda's hands Chopin's E minor concerto sounded like a weaker Beethoven; Chopin's roving imagination was stifled. Pollini gives voice to the genius of these notes. Only not, indeed, in the way one has been accustomed to up to now.

178

THE TOUCH FOR LISZT

Music critics and musicologists almost all have a respectful-acidulous attitude to Liszt's bravura. Liszt's rhapsodies have, as they say, a bad press. Anyone who plays the piano concertos, it is felt, wants to avoid exposing himself to mental demands; empty virtuosity can be displayed where serious musicality is superfluous. Even pianists who play Rachmaninoff and admire him are occasionally apologetic because they take delight in Liszt's Campanella. This uneasiness over Franz Liszt is undoubtedly connected with the tradition of the modern-German Liszt societies, which at the beginning of this century were the embodiment of progress against everything reactionary – and so today seem particularly outmoded. Now a diligent concert-goer, however, will make the following observation: with this Liszt whom enlightened artists hardly dare to put on their programmes any more, because the age of virtuosity is over (and also because they cannot play him), pianists who still smuggle him in at the end of the programme always have a resounding success. People are delighted to listen to well-performed Liszt, though perhaps with a guilty conscience; and the record catalogues in fact show an excessive supply of Liszt. A striking number of precisely the most talented young pianists have made Liszt recordings (for instance, Byron Janis, Ludwig Hoffmann, Alfred Brendel, Charles Rosen, John Ogdon; quite apart from Sviatoslav Richter, Rubinstein, and Gilels). There is, quite blatantly, a contradiction between the general consciousness of the musical world and the frank delight in Liszt.

Liszt, moreover, enables a pianist's manual capacity, his finger technique, his hands, his strength, his temperament, to be discerned with great clarity. When someone has played Liszt's B minor sonata, confusion, at least about the interpreter's pianistic equipment, can hardly exist any more.

Reference should be made here first to an artist who lives in Cologne and who up to now has got himself talked about far too little, although he commands an amazing pair of piano hands. His name is Ludwig Hoffmann. The burning ambition that animates most other career-mad pianists gives him no satisfaction. The fantastic manual talent which a kind pianistic fate has bestowed on him

179

Example 23
From: Liszt, Reminiscences de Don Juan.

From the way in which someone solves the pianistic problems of bars 1–3 and 10–11 of our example his finger technique and pianistic intelligence – with regard to Liszt's demands – can be judged.

180

becomes a temptation to him. It makes him arrogant that difficulties which cause other pianists laborious torments, for him seem to be non-existent. He forces, exaggerates, plays out his brilliance uninhibitedly. Yet these stylistic limitations cannot close our ears to the fact that Hoffmann plays Liszt's E flat concerto far more brilliantly, more speedily, more virilely, than, say, the famous Frenchman, Samson François, or the world-famous Byron Janis. If only there were someone to exorcise Hoffmann's exaggerations! Hence his tendency to stab out individual notes, to play out the passage effects all too adroitly, so that the boundary between entertainment and concert becomes blurred. Or his delight in unfettered wildness. Yet, on the positive side, it appears that there is no one, either in Germany or in France, who is in a position to surpass Hoffmann in brilliance.

The Lieder transcriptions and opera fantasies of Franz Liszt are not works that even an admirer of the Lisztian muse would wish to let stand unconditionally as profound, let alone great music. They are often merely ingenious pianistic jokes, the rousing homage of a great artist to the works of greater. Many of them have become intolerable. Yet the Rigoletto paraphrase, for instance, or the Don Juan fantasy, known as Reminiscences de Don Juan, is still played today at concerts and more frequently recorded. That the latter is to be heard more on records than at concerts is also connected, incidentally, with its difficulties. In his Don Juan fantasy, Liszt gave to his romantic admiration for the demonic world of Don Giovanni stormy, all too stormy, expression. At the beginning, the D minor theme from the Don Giovanni overture is dramatically introduced, then the piece offers several variations on 'Da mi il braccio, mia piccina', and in the last of these variations the commendatore theme roars in again with stormy élan. It is a piano fantasy in which the sparks fly. The tasteless and the brilliant are evenly balanced. Let us turn to the first great climax, which is supposed to be played 'tempestuoso', hence in a wild and stormy manner (Example 23).

The famous Shura Cherkassky plays this first great climax from Liszt's Don Juan fantasy with notable vehemence. Yet Ludwig Hoffmann can bring out far more convincingly not only the élan but also the musical structure of this cruelly difficult outburst. Right at the start, he does the lightning octaves, which here simulate a kind of three-part writing – the left hand plays Mozart's bass, while the right has to strike the string chords in the middle part and at the same time put in accents in the upper – far more clearly and recognizably. And at the close he is able to do the octave passages in the right hand so fast that one really recognizes the chords in the left, which provide the musical meaning, as belonging together. With Cherkassky one had to believe that here the left hand is merely entrusted with some kind of accompaniment.

So there can be no doubt that Ludwig Hoffmann simply has greater possibilities than the far more famous Cherkassky.

Charles Rosen, a many-sided, cultivated and comparatively young musician, made a name for himself through recordings of Schumann, Debussy, Ravel, Bartók, Stravinsky and Schönberg. He plays our Liszt passage a little slower, it is true, than Cherkassky and Ludwig Hoffmann, but also more carefully, pianistically less eccentrically, brilliantly or dominantly. He too, in contrast to Cherkassky, avoids all obscurity.

With Hoffmann, Liszt sounds disarmingly virtuoso, captivatingly brilliant and – as unfettered piano playing – perhaps a little lacking in seriousness. Even Liszt's effects need to be understood relatively. Charles Rosen, on the other hand, at least tries to keep the wild passages still within the realm of artistic beauty. Although he may not quite attain Ludwig Hoffmann's ecstasy, he too can cope with the piece in sovereign fashion. All the obscurities and embarrassments that can be heard with Shura Cherkassky during the passages are non-existent for him.

When Ludwig Hoffmann plays Beethoven's C minor variations, or still less his E flat concerto, pompously and without tension, he is not in his element. The finale of Tchaikovsky's B flat minor concerto is incomparably more in his line – and again, one would have to look around for a long time to find a pianist who can perform the piece so brilliantly. His tendency to exaggeration, to salon or bar-room effects, which out of sheer delight in success Hoffmann guards against all too little, also impairs some of his Liszt recordings, for instance of the Rigoletto paraphrase and the St Francis legends. All the same, Hoffmann's sureness is so great that he is capable of performing Liszt's E flat concerto, or these legends too, with exactly the same dangerous brilliance at a public concert as on records. What this pianist can do, what he has in him, can best be discerned perhaps,

Example 24

From: Stravinsky, Concerto for Piano and Wind, first movement.

Stravinsky's piano writing is merciless. Here, anyone who can keep a clear head and sure fingers, like Ludwig Hoffmann, has nothing technical to fear any more in the world of the black and white keys.

183

without any detraction, when Ludwig Hoffmann is tied down to Stravinsky. In Stravinsky's concerto for piano and wind, a piece in which expressionist fantasy and neo-classical uninhibitedness mingle in a fascinating way, every self-assured piano-Titan is reduced to a plodding robot. When Stravinsky's son Soulima subjects himself to this perilous opus of his father's, one has in effect a feeling of pure chord work. Now Ludwig Hoffmann plays this piano concerto by Stravinsky with an alarming perfection. And he even brings it about that a desolate, muffled sorrow lies over the percussion effects made by the piano. Here not a whiff of the salon can blow, no complacency unfold; here a pianist must obey, suffer or triumph, be an anvil or hammer. Hoffmann triumphs. All the more since the Greek conductor Miltiades Caridis proves to be a partner of equal calibre. The slow opening rhythm performed by the wind instruments is like a wicked parody on the theme of Chopin's Funeral March. And when the piano then adds its weight in Forte allegro, the mixture of sound, harsh wind-tone and rigid piano-tone, combined with the absence of any voluptuous sentimentality from strings, proves to be a compositional device of the highest order (Example 24).

Compared with Hoffmann, Charles Rosen plays a shade more severely, with greater sureness of style and more academically. In Schubert's posthumous A major sonata, Rosen has not enough delight yet in Schubert's melodious, natural happiness. The pianist brings out the formal relationships over-clearly here, yet the elementary gift for melody seems to be lacking. When, on the other hand, Rosen puts Debussy's études on the programme, or hazardous works by Ravel, then one hears how important and valuable pianistic solidity and pianistic intellectuality can be. The difficult movements, say, from Ravel's Gaspard de la Nuit or Le Tombeau de Couperin he masters brilliantly.

If one asks musical Englishmen who is among the great pianists in Britain following on Solomon and Curzon, almost all answer with the name John Ogdon. He is said to be an uncommonly clever and original pianist, who occupies himself with Bach's Art of Fugue, with Debussy and Schönberg, and who commands a magnificent technique and a great temperament. I have heard Ogdon with Beethoven's E flat concerto. Ogdon, after all, the Tchaikovsky prize-winner and thinker of the piano, is already considered prominent enough to crown a festival concert. But Ogdon's Beethoven was disappointing. The thrilling, soft, half-shadowy and secret elements he was able to reveal, yet Beethoven's onward stride was unsuited to him. He became inhibited, lost himself in heavenly piano turns of expression and made technical mistakes far below his level. The as it were improvised recitatives of the Adagio, full of painful restraint, were more in his line. After Beethoven something truly remarkable occurred. Ogdon said good-bye to all sterile concern for style and in the middle of the symphony concert, while the musicians looked at their instruments, gave Liszt's Don Juan fantasy as an encore. Here, suddenly, Ogdon seemed in his element. It turned out that he is a profoundly old-fashioned pianist, a virtuoso (to be a virtuoso, indeed, does not mean always to hit the right keys in difficult pieces – Ogdon was very far from doing that – but to take delight in falling to, to have the desire and the strength for the great appearance). Ogdon is full of this. When one examines some of the records which Ogdon has brought out up to now, this concert observation is confirmed. Ogdon, a powerful figure with a striking little black beard and thick intellectual glasses, has made a Liszt recording and furnished it with scholarly notes. The notes fail to divert attention from the fact that he is after all not yet coping with the B minor sonata as brilliantly as is usual from the foremost pianists of our time. When Ogdon devotes himself to Rachmaninoff, then his sensitivity and his old-fashioned delight in virtuosity show their worth. For all that, here too, as with Ogdon's Mozart and Chopin interpretations, a touch of the conventional lies over his playing. Rachmaninoff's famous G minor prelude, for instance, has still not quite got, with Ogdon, that captivating grandezza on which it depends. Like the great Polonaise passage in Schumann's Humoreske, Op. 20, which is supposed to be performed 'with a certain pomp', and whose passacaglia breadth is played overwhelmingly by Sviatoslav Richter, this G minor Prelude by Rachmaninoff also creates indeed the effect of a powerful accompanying rhythm. Hence like a harmonic model; of such vast dimensions that there can, as it were, be no melody capable of adding anything further to this accompaniment. The piece is like a pianistic promise: anyone who can think up such an accompaniment really has no need to write a melodic line for it. The promise must suffice. This point Ogdon fails to bring out adequately. He plays this Rachmaninoff as

185

Example 25

From: Rachmaninoff, Prelude in G minor, Op. 23, No. 5.

For this accompanying rhythm – Rachmaninoff suggests – there can really be no melody. So weightily, so dramatically, so imperiously does the piece begin that it will no longer conform to any melodic line on earth. John Ogdon fails to make a merit of the 'deficiency'. He plays the beginning with restraint, rather, as though the middle part – yearningly melodic – were the main thing, and not this beginning.

186

though the melodious middle part were the main thing, and not the bare accompanying rhythm of the beginning. What could be almost as exciting as Ravel's Bolero becomes under his hands a late-Romantic virtuoso piece, carefully shaded, calmly and roundly played (Example 25).

Great all-round pianists of the type of Rubinstein, Horowitz, Arrau or Kempff are usually better Chopin interpreters than the Chopin experts, under whose hands all the piano music of the world at once sounds Polish. Confinement to the work of one incomparably specific and typical artist clearly leads most often to an unmistakable affectation, to a mixture of sterility, rubato routine, and careless pedalling. These dangers probably exist with every specialization, although Beethoven players or pure Bach interpreters appear to be not quite so imperilled as the disciples of Chopin.

Liszt players, on the other hand – hence pianists who bother about no one at all but Liszt, and who consider everything else to be either naïve preparations for the Lisztian revolution or overbred reminiscences of Lisztian imitators – hardly exist. In general, specialization is fortunately going out of fashion. That Byron Janis would like more than anything to live only from Rachmaninoff concertos is in the meantime almost held against him.

Most pianists of the younger generation, hence those who are increasingly playing their way to the fore, consider exactly what they are doing. They are highly aware; they have been forced by the unjustly great difficulties that stand in the path of every pianist today into sharp self-criticism and careful planning of their careers. To this may be added a superficial characteristic, which is perhaps not purely superficial after all: many of them are notably erudite. One can hardly imagine a Wilhelm Backhaus or an Emil Gilels writing the text of his own record-sleeve, even if he wanted to or were in a position to. Glenn Gould, Julius Katchen, Charles Rosen, Paul Badura-Skoda and John Ogdon, on the other hand, are very much in a position to propound on theory. There are from all of them detailed, interesting, expertly-based remarks on piano works and theoretical problems. And Robert Alexander Bohnke, who plays the G minor concerto by Felix Mendelssohn-Bartholdy with a charm such as only a few pianists produce today, could draw up his own programme notes, or even the reviews of his concerts, just as well as any music critic or musicologist.

As against this, it seems almost strange how little, say, the brilliant technician Nikita Magaloff appears to suspect of where his strong points lie. Clearly, he considers himself to be a Beethoven player. And even more remarkably, he is clearly considered to be a Beethoven interpreter even by many conductors and concert organizers, although in fact nothing appears to be further from Magaloff's enviably well-balanced temperament than Beethoven's great rapture, Beethoven's passion.

Charlie Chaplin could undoubtedly learn the part of King Lear and play it faultlessly, even expressively. But he refrains from doing so. He knows he would be 'miscast', interesting certainly, but not good. That quasi-miscasting is also possible in the domain of instrumental music appears when Nikita Magaloff performs Beethoven's E flat piano concerto. Now 'miscasting' does not mean, indeed, that there is only one conception of Beethoven, namely the German, in face of which the French, Russians, Italians and Americans are from the outset at a disadvantage compatriotically as it were. One need only think of Oistrakh, or the Beethoven interpretations of the Budapest String Quartet, or of Solomon, to rule out such narrow-minded suppositions at once.

Yet Nikita Magaloff embodies – and one really cannot in my view get at Beethoven in this way – the type of unflurried, calmly smiling virtuoso. His Liszt interpretations are amazing, his bravura, accuracy, indeed his taste, beyond all dispute. All this can also be tested, of course, in Beethoven's magnificent last piano concerto. Magaloff plays the very difficult Rondo theme, for instance, a little bit faster than the others, and without misplaying thereby. But the comparatively 'easy' passages, the radiantly bold chord combinations in the first movement, he merely executes without fulfilling them. He fails to reveal the greatness of Beethoven's simplicity, the spiritual force of melodic ornaments. He plays with faultless technique and a somewhat dry tone, passage for passage, loud and soft, according to the markings. The octaves of the development are far too slow for him. He could do it much more thunderously and speedily.

Beethoven's G major concerto Magaloff also plays with fluent technique. The purest rippling can evoke astonishment. But listeners who wonder why all this still leaves them cold may simply not dare admit to themselves that this virtuoso seems to have no expressive relationship to Beethoven at all. Beethoven suddenly sounds like a salon piece by Hummel. The complete absence of an interpretative will is so monstrous that one believes in an intention, although one cannot quite follow it.

Also fluctuating between illuminating effect and palpable forcing are the interpretations of Monique de la Bruchollerie. The artist is capable of beginning a piano recital with Beethoven's A flat sonata, Op. 110, in such a way as to suggest that pianistic furore could sweep aside even the most delicate problems of style. The thunderous success with which Monique de la Bruchollerie plays year after year in German concert halls is a phenomenon that can hardly be explained only by quality, by the 'class' of this pianist. One could undoubtedly distil outstanding interpretations from her ecstatic performances if one could only leave out all the exaggerations, bits of fury and caprice. For Monique de la Bruchollerie can do much. Time and again it flashes out that she is a pianist of outstanding manual gifts, and in addition of high intelligence. But – and this makes the Bruchollerie phenomenon so interesting and so disquieting – she achieves her decisive successes, not in spite of, but clearly on account of her violent ways.

When she plays Mozart's most thoughtful piece, the C minor fantasia (K 475), one notes a concern for style in the pianist. Yet at the high-points she forgets it: the piece moves into the vicinity of César Franck and drowns in pedalling. Moments follow where she shades very beautifully; where she builds in semi-impressionistic effects.

And her success? It probably rests on this woman's undaunted gallantry. Circumspection is not for her, nor does she apportion her strength; instead, she becomes a valkyrie, the piano a charger, and away we go into battle with the octaves. This sort of thing carries one along. In Chopin's G minor ballade climaxes may be heard such as no one else achieves or trusts themselves to do.

If a great actor were to behave like Mme de la Bruchollerie, one would readily have at hand the appropriate term: 'hamming'. Now such 'hamming' is by no means contemptible, however; it captivates at any rate more than bleak concern for style. All the same, when Mme Bruchollerie plays Weber's Perpetuum Mobile as an encore at a really impossible speed – that is to say, hardly plays any more, but merely brings about somehow or other, with pedal, her last ounce of strength and the grotesque transformation of a C major scale, to be played out, into a thumb crescendo (in this way it goes indeed even faster and even louder!) – then it becomes pure circus. . . .

But Mme de la Bruchollerie is an idol, in the same way as Elly Ney or d'Albert may once have been. At the same time, her impetus, her strength, is not dedicated to self-display. Temperamentally though she plays, she does not stand on the stage like the sad eccentric, the clown of times past, with tragic face, hand on convulsive heart, and draw attention to inexpressible torments of the soul; her person remains as it were outside her temperament. The wildness is not ego-filled, but arrestingly-released brutality. Pure verve, such as our broken world, broken in every way and everywhere, hardly dares to produce any more, is recreated under the trenchant hands of Monique de la Bruchollerie. In this lies the secret of her success.

As against this, the pianist Erik Then-Bergh suffers rather from scrupulousness. Whenever he gives himself once again, torn and expressive, to Reger's piano concerto, which he plays so well, as far as this difficult, and in the last movement probably no longer manageable work can be mastered at all, one is forcibly reminded of the lady who heard Reger play, and said: 'He has such a brutal pianissimo.'

But Then-Bergh's art, technically not always completely reliable, is by no means dedicated only to Reger. He is even capable of 'surprising' with Beethoven's fourth piano concerto. This G major concerto is regarded indeed by all concert-goers and record-lovers as something to be taken for granted, as an assured cultural good, an elevating half-hour. One thinks one can assume that this piece, with its predominantly lyrical mood, stands in clear contrast to the Emperor-dramatics of the E flat concerto; from the first movement one expects nimble filigree, pastel shades, and one is equally delighted by the emotionally charged introductory bars of the piano as by the Andante dialogue between fierce orchestra and grieving soloist. It is considered as established that the pensive first movement, which seems to derive from the sphere of the violin concerto and the fourth symphony (although it contains the knock-of-fate motif in just the same way as the Appassionata and the fifth symphony), can only be mastered with lyrical variability.

When Erik Then-Bergh expounds this fourth piano concerto, it seems likely that an El Dorado of fine and finest pianissimo nuances is to be expected. Yet Then-Bergh achieves more than just a tastefully conventional reproduction of the piece, in any case so well known: he wrings from the first movement an unforced and moving new version. Then-Bergh takes the staccato dots of the main theme seriously, and avoids all romantic dimming. He declines to stick to the way everyone plays, say, the passages in thirds at the end of the first solo, with a charming and intimate gesture, but strikes up a concertante forte here. He delyricizes the whole G major complex – hence the main theme and its manifold variants – which with exaggerated sincerity is often too undynamic. Suddenly the numerous forte sforzato markings, which most other pianists never take literally, so as not to disrupt the basic lyrical character, make sense again.

Yet Then-Bergh charges with energy not only the solo sphere. This energy is communicated also to the extensive passage-work, right into the last ramification. The thirty-second-note and sixteenth-note triplets are never transitions that arrive sooner or later at the next theme, but they appear to be filled with metrical impulse. The artist then deals all the more freely with the quiet and lovely Dolce e con expressione bars, in whose gentle force the lyric happiness of the concerto is gathered. He interprets all the more freely also the sensitive beginning of the development, where he rightly blurs the syncopated entries of the passages in sixths and complies expressively with every harmonic turn. In this way the first movement of the concerto suddenly has once again greatness, structure and spiritual depth.

Naturally, a pianist who decides on this reading must make a few sacrifices. Then-Bergh ignores certain dolce markings of Beethoven's (bars 123 and 231, for instance). Here he lets himself be led astray by his temperamental urge to clarify or to play; here he forgoes the mystery.

In the playing of the pianist Julius Katchen,[1] it seems possible sometimes to detect a slight neutrality. Clearly, expression, 'reading', and technical capacity are not integrated yet into the specific language of a personality at the piano. When Katchen sets himself the Diabelli Variations, however, hence Beethoven's last great piano work (Op. 120), its power leads him and lures him into surrendering as it were, into giving himself up to the storm and mysticism of the piece – in so doing, moreover, he keeps exactly to Beethoven's dynamic markings. Katchen lets himself be carried away without losing his head.

[1] Died 1969 (ed.).

192

Yet in the first movement of Brahms's B flat concerto, in spite of all the technical skill, it remains an open question why Katchen chose precisely this difficult Brahms concerto. It is true, both the fortissimo outbursts as well as the mournfully lyrical passages are interpreted seriously by the pianist. He wants not only to master them but also to shape them. But he fails as yet to catch the background to the Brahmsian language. This can even be attributed perhaps to a technical detail: Katchen is no legato player; he has, rather, a light hand; he inclines to neutral non-legato. This gives rise now and then to a trivialization of the Brahmsian melos which is hard to describe. Even in the Scherzo, the A minor episode, with which the exposition ends, merely has charm, but no melancholy.

Ingrid Haebler, Alfred Brendel and Paul Badura-Skoda are young and thoughtful representatives of the great Viennese piano tradition. However one may regard them – and I admit that to me Badura-Skoda's interpretations often seem a shade too worthy, too nice, too little filled with vivacity and warmth of approach – all three have been able to inspire respect in the piano world. From the outset, interest has lain in their encounters with the literature – and not in the extent of their technical finesse. Perhaps one can put it this way: Alfred Brendel, Paul Badura-Skoda and Ingrid Haebler have convinced the 'experts' that with them the pianistic element is there, to be taken for granted, genuine and of service. Virtuoso *tours de force,* and that revealing bravura such as the great Russians and Americans sometimes command, seem to be not their affair. All the more clearly have they been able to carry the conviction that their playing reflects, as it were, the state of a generation's objective encounter with a problem.

When Badura-Skoda plays Chopin sonatas, an almost too modest sobriety prevails in the outer movements. Yet he masters the Scherzos of the B flat minor and B minor sonatas without inappropriate reserve. When he undertakes the most difficult work of all at a concert, namely the Hammerklavier Sonata, the assurance, indeed the ease, with which he achieves the dreaded fugue from Op. 106 is staggering. The vast movement suddenly sounds transparent, builds itself up logically. Not many pianists in the world can do this. And when he plays the introductory Adagio from the C sharp minor sonata speedily, evenly and imperturbably, listeners shimmer as under pale moonbeams. This miracle of sound over an apparently simple 'Alberti' bass (which only with Beethoven, indeed, has a different sound from all the others), which has been throttled endlessly by the hands of countless pianists and smeared with treacly oboe cantilena by chamber orchestras, Badura-Skoda shapes with great seriousness and intelligent taste. In the Presto he makes not a single mistake – the rhythm of the left hand, the hectic climaxes, everything is there; it convinces and conquers.

All the same, some reservations must be made. The most serious may be that this highly gifted artist has no unmistakable touch of his own. He is still playing keys, not notes. The great coda from the Adagio of the Hammerklavier Sonata remains colourless and unfulfilled. To be sure, Badura-Skoda risks pathos totally, but the music still fails to breathe enough with him. The rests are often slurred over or merely 'counted' – but they admit no fresh start; one does not feel the vast upsurge of the Beethoven soul. Perhaps the artist explains some things to himself too exactly. In the Fantasia, Op. 77, probably an authentic example of Beethovenish extemporizing, reflective runs, which wait and see as it were, are whisked often enough indeed over the keyboard, like nets with which the dreamer snatches at a sudden fancy. With Badura-Skoda the rests are so to speak counted through, and the improvisatory element is lost; he always seems to know all too precisely how it goes on. Yet although developments in Beethoven sometimes pass off a little too smoothly, too harmoniously, he is a remarkably disciplined artist. One would like to wish him still an increase in power, in severity and inner wrath.

Brendel's Beethoven and Liszt playing, and the interpretations of Mozart and Beethoven by Ingrid Haebler and Paul Badura-Skoda are, by virtue of the seriousness of these pianists, more than just good or bad concerts. Here something is being demonstrated. Ingrid Haebler, the young Viennese pianist, is still looking for the calm secret of the Schubert tone. Chopin cantilena, too, she sometimes fails to catch with sufficient determination, though she manages the harmonic fullness of the average Nocturne magnificently. All dissension disappears when Ingrid Haebler plays Mozart. Suddenly the tone conforms powerfully and pliantly to the Mozartian melody; suddenly it seems there can no longer be any difference of opinion about 'right' and 'wrong'. When Ingrid Haebler begins a Mozart adagio – and this is granted her ungrudgingly by the citizens of the piano world – one is at home.

Anyone who attempts to bring intellectual 'order' into the different types of current Beethoven interpretation comes up against obvious and much-used pairs of opposites, which are not so wrong as to be ruled out of their own accord, but also not so right as to be dependable. The 'subjective' can be set against the 'objective', the 'titanic' against the 'mechanical', and the 'expressive' against those that seem to leave the last word to the music. This scheme can probably accommodate an Edwin Fischer, but not a Wilhelm Backhaus, whose quiet composure seems to bring him close to the 'objective' type, while in his playing, nevertheless, the secret of a congeniality, a moved but never sentimental masculine restraint, finds expression. This scheme can accommodate the technically well-versed Andor Foldes, with his cool and almost dry playing, but not on the other hand a Friedrich Gulda, whose subcutaneous musicality saves him from all prosaic objectivity, although the pianist avoids titanic delight in self-display, to him untrustworthy, in almost too doctrinaire a fashion. This scheme can accommodate Furtwängler's pathos and Toscanini's brio, but not on the other hand Karajan's both perfect and yet Hölderlinishly serene pastorale, or Solomon's impressive, anti-Napoleonic, and yet high seriousness. This scheme can accommodate Hans Richter-Haaser's solid calm, his many-sidedness and restrained powers of expression.

Alfred Brendel, long since discovered by record-lovers, is still a secret tip. But hardly anyone who hears Alfred Brendel and Paul Badura-Skoda play Beethoven one after the other will deny that Brendel plays more intelligently, more interestingly, more modernly and more excitingly than Paul Badura-Skoda. Brendel fulfils something of the theory, usually employed merely as a figure of speech, according to which young artists reared on modern musical experience have a different relationship even to Beethoven than they would have had, as it were, without Schönberg. Brendel sometimes knows how to animate Beethoven's architecture magnificently. When he gives shape to three fortissimo chords one after the other in the Sonata Op. 31, No. 2; when he does justice to the details of the Allegro first movement with trenchant technique, and yet knows in an almost unparalleled way how to throw light and shade over large periods; when he makes the accents, say, in what is apparently such a 'social' sonata, Op. 2, No. 3, audible with all crassness (not merely as 'interesting' clashes, but as the main thing), then all this reveals a musical intelligence that reaches far beyond every other current Beethoven interpretation. Playing here is someone who has understood, who makes understandable, why a sonata movement has to go on.

We have now to deal with the fact that in Brendel these 'modern' components are joined by a strong dash of old-fashioned delight in thundering. His Beethoven forte is entirely of Lisztian dimensions. Liszt (himself a famous Beethoven interpreter, moreover, who was the first to put Op. 106 on his programme) strengthens as it were a young pianist's arm. The contradiction that arises in this way is both exciting and disturbing. For with Brendel two 'weaknesses' are added which endanger his Beethoven interpretations. First, an obvious tendency, possibly abating with the years, to be 'interesting'. He does too many things differently. In the trio of the Scherzo from Op. 2, No. 3, he plays almost only the bass, and reduces the right hand to a harmonious rustling. This is connected, perhaps, with the fact that his 'cantilena' is relatively weak. If intentional, it is mannerism. (Brendel should try some time to hear from the Gilels recording of this sonata all that lies in the trio.) Further and worse: wherever the music behaves naturally, it at once becomes colourless with Brendel. Problems are what attract him. Thus it is that beautiful gestures, say, such as the sentimental piano answer in the main theme of the first movement of the D minor sonata, remain without any weight, without any expression, and worst of all, that the slow movements are an obvious embarrassment to the pianist. For all the intelligence with which he contrasts the written-out Cadenza in Op. 2, No. 3, he badly fails with the tone of the E major Adagio (whose forte passages become downright outbursts). The first movement of Op. 54, too, has no calm, on-flowing eloquence, and the gentle Adagio from Op. 31, No. 2, whose first chord belongs entirely to the theme and is by no means a breaking-in of thunder, remains poor. In the E major sonata, Op. 109, of course, Brendel has to set himself the problem of the Adagio espressivo in full detail. Here one feels that he may yet be able to cope with it some time.

Brendel's Schubert playing – at a concert – is dubious. The outer movements of the posthumous C minor sonata are indeed held together by Brendel, but also ruined by the fact that he plays them too purposefully, too 'progressively'. The development, say, of the first movement, welling up from the depths like a natural sound, he takes as though it were striving towards something yet to come, as though it were not itself already the most sublime music. That such a musical person as Brendel should simply play away the melodious right hand with its intimate A flat major line (later D flat major), merely because he is more interested in the left, is incomprehensible and destroys the meaning of the passages. At the same time, Brendel is fully able to phrase Schubert's cantilena and rescue such a thankless movement as the Minuet. Yet it remains inconceivable why in the middle part of the finale, which modulates in a wide-swinging way from C sharp minor to E flat minor, he brings out only the rhythmic effects, as though all that mattered was not the chords, the transitions, the nuances and the merging melodies, but only the quick, trotting movement of the quasi-cavalry-march.

In Beethoven's virtuoso A major Sonata, Op. 2, No. 2 (as in Schubert), Brendel plays passages and arpeggios correctly, but without delight, without euphony, without sensuous happiness. Possibly this artist draws too sharp a distinction between an abstract conception of intellectuality and a slight contempt for 'sound-intoxication'. This is theoretically understandable, but in practice nonsensical, since the abstract essence of a piano sonata can only be made perceivable by means of a piano. There may be musical singers who have no voice. They are then indeed, for that very reason, not singers. The sixteenth-note triplets in the first movement of the A major Sonata should manifestly shine, after all; the passages in the last movement of the Appassionata should generate a pianistic F minor storm; and the changes of harmony in the Schubert sonata should be given time for their own sound. Anyone who denies himself all this, who is interested only in the grand design, the powerful accent, the occasional expression, has in his hand at the end a grand design indeed, but nevertheless also an empty one. And as listener one is not quite sure why one had to walk through a vast, well-ordered space when there was really nothing at all to see.

Brendel is a highly esteemed pianist in Europe. Unless he resolves to cultivate his technique with extreme care, so that it becomes a sonorous means to an end and not an indifferent shell for musical ideas, he will not be able to give fitting expression to all that he has to say as a pianist. The fact that many others play more obtusely, more indifferently and more uninterestingly than he should be no comfort to him.

Brendel's records correct these concert impressions only in part. The Waldstein Sonata remains dry; the Schubert-Liszt Wanderer Fantasy, it is true, he does magnificently. What Brendel does successfully stands high, not only above the average, but also above the level of what even first-class pianists can do. So let us wait without hysteria until this brilliant young artist is out of his 'crisis'. It is true, talk of crises always sounds impermissible, condescending and embarrassing. But all great, capable and responsible pianists are, in face of the demands of a work, not only executives but also co-authors. So Böll's observation, that an allusion to the crisis someone is going through conceals unconscious flattery, is true for them. Böll's words, 'To be an author and to be in a crisis are the same thing', probably apply also to all pianists who are young and questing.

DISCOGRAPHY

Author's Note from the Original German Edition

The records listed below have helped me to get to know the pianists characterized in this book and to analyse – to the best of my ability – their playing. Naturally, not all the available records of the pianists discussed are cited here. The list is supposed to be at the same time an anthology. All the records mentioned here are either particularly attractive and worth hearing, or particularly characteristic. Since it was impossible even just to touch upon all the 'important' recordings, say of Kempff, Rubinstein or Sviatoslav Richter in the text, the attentive reader should also encounter here titles which were not mentioned in the text for reasons of space. With the help of the musical examples and the records cited here, any interested reader can now follow critically how the author arrived at his 'verdict'.

It is true, the judgements and attempts at characterization which this book has ventured to make are based only partially on records. The impression conveyed by public concerts was for me in nearly every case more important in characterizing an artist.

To this must be added that – above all with Friedrich Gulda and Ludwig Hoffmann – I also took into account radio recordings, which are not usually accessible to private individuals. Precisely in the case of Friedrich Gulda, judged here – as many readers might find – in a notably 'positive' sense, it was not only Gulda's last concerts in Berlin, Lucerne and Salzburg that were decisive, but also his radio recordings of the Beethoven sonatas Op. 2, 26, 53 and 111. These recordings are far better than most of the widely-sold Beethoven records of other pianists. It is incomprehensible that the industry should withhold Gulda's Beethoven interpretations from us. Many a prejudice continues to exist – all because Gulda's commercially available records are not nearly as good as his radio recordings.

The author is infatuated with the piano and sufficiently curious to request readers to let him know, if they care to, of records of living pianists that seem especially successful and are not cited here. With the grotesquely confused state of the international record market, 'trouvailles' are always possible.

A book like this is always only a beginning, a provocation to contradiction or expansion. It would be a pleasure to the author to let the reader know, in an enlarged second edition, where he has been corrected.

Editor's Note

In adapting the record lists for British and American readers, in general no work originally listed by the author has been omitted, though many of these records are no longer current at the time of closing for press (the numbers where this is known to be the case are indicated*); many of the artists have, on the other hand, made newer recordings, or older recordings have been reissued, and where it has seemed desirable, certain additional material in these categories has been added and marked†.

Where the author originally quoted German or other numbers, the British (GB) and American (US) equivalents have been substituted though, in a few cases, the author's original numbers have been retained either in addition to or in place of the GB or US numbers where it seems likely that the information might assist readers to discover copies of non-current discs. In the case of modern Deutsche Grammophon (DG) numbers, these apply equally in Germany and other countries and may well continue available in Germany even where withdrawn elsewhere.

Although in his original lists the author gave titles and keys in the languages of the labels of the discs to which he had access, all titles and keys have for the present purpose been converted into English, except in the case of works well-known by a title or sub-title in a different language.

Owing to considerations of space, it has not been possible to add stereo numbers consistently throughout, but generally they are shown (sometimes in preference to mono) for all new material and for most new numbers added to existing listings. Stereo numbers can frequently be recognized by the 'S' in the prefix. The present tendency is for these numbers to supersede the mono versions.

All the lists are highly selective and many other recordings by most of the artists discussed exist or have existed.

Records listed as 'USSR' bear one number per side, and not one number per disc as is normal in other countries.

F.F.C.

Recordings for the chapter 'Artur Rubinstein'. Page 35 ff.

ARTUR RUBINSTEIN

Beethoven: Piano Concerto No. 1, C major, Op. 15
(†Boston Symphony, Leinsdorf)
US: RCA LM 3013
—(Symphony of the Air, Josef Krips)
US: RCA LM 2120* & in set
LSC 6702
GB: RCA RB 16041*

—Piano Concerto No. 2, B flat major, Op. 19
(†Symphony of the Air, J. Krips)
US: RCA LM 2121* & in set
LSC 6702
GB: RCA RB16042*

—Piano Concerto No. 3, C minor, Op. 37
(†Boston Symphony, Leinsdorf)
US: RCA LSC 2497
GB: RCA SB 6787

—(Symphony of the Air, J. Krips)
US: RCA LM 2122* & in set
LSC 6702
GB: RCA RB 16045*

—(NBC Symphony Orchestra, Arturo Toscanini)
US: RCA LCT 1009*

—Piano Concerto No. 4, G major, Op. 58
(†Boston Symphony, Leinsdorf)
US: RCA LSC 2848
GB: RCA RB 6787

—(Symphony of the Air, J. Krips)
US: RCA LM 2123* & in set
LSC 6702
GB: RCA RB 16044*

—Piano Concerto No. 5, E flat major, Op. 73
(†Boston Symphony, Leinsdorf)
US: RCA LSC 2733
GB: RCA SB 6598

—(Symphony of the Air, J. Krips)
US: RCA LM 2124* & in set
LSC 6702
GB: RCA RB 16045*

—†Sonata No. 23, F minor, Op. 57 (Appassionata)

—†Sonata No. 3, C major, Op. 2 No. 3
US: RCA LSC 2812
GB: RCA SB 6633

—†Sonata No. 8, C minor, Op. 13 (Pathétique)
—†Sonata No. 14, C sharp minor, Op. 27 No. 2 (Moonlight)
—†Sonata No. 26, E flat major, Op. 81a (Les Adieux)
US: RCA LSC 2654
GB: RCA SB 6537

—Violin Sonata No. 9, A major, Op. 47 (Kreutzer)

—Violin Sonata No. 5, F major, Op. 24 (Spring)
(Henryk Szeryng, violin; A. Rubinstein, piano)
US: RCA LM 2377
GB: RB 16209*

Brahms: Piano Concerto No. 1, D minor, Op. 15
(†Boston Symphony, Leinsdorf)
US: RCA LSC 2917
GB: RCA SB 6726

—(Chicago Symphony Orchestra, Fritz Reiner)
US: RCA LM 1831*

—Piano Concerto No. 2, B flat major, Op. 83
(Boston Symphony Orchestra, Charles Munch)
US: RCA LM 1728*

—(†RCA Symphony, Josef Krips)
US: RCA LSC 2296
GB: RCA SB 2069*

Chopin: Piano Concerto, E minor, Op. 11
(London Symphony Orchestra, Skrowaczewski)
US: RCA LSC/LM 2575
GB: RCA SB 2145/RB 16275*

—Piano Concerto, F minor, Op. 21
(NBC Symphony Orchestra, Steinberg)
US: RCA LM 1046*

—(†Philadelphia Orchestra, Ormandy)
(with Polish Fantasy, Op. 13)
US: RCA LSC 3055
GB: RCA SB 6797

—(†Symphony of the Air, Wallenstein)
US: RCA LSC 2265
GB: RCA SB 2067/RB 16183*

—Sonata, B flat minor, Op. 35

—Sonata, B minor, Op. 58
US: RCA LDS 2554
GB: RCA SB 2151/RB 16282*

—†Impromptus; Polonaises
US: RCA LSC 7037
GB: RCA RB/SB 6649 & 6640

—†Mazurkas (51), complete
US: RCA LSC 6177
GB: RB/SB 6702–4

—†Mazurkas, selected
US: RCA LM 2049

—†Nocturnes (19) complete
US: RCA LSC 7050
GB: RCA RB/SB 6731–2

—Scherzi
US: RCA LSC 2368
GB: RCA SB 2095/RB 16222*

—Preludes (24), complete
US: RCA LM 1163
GB: RB 16110

—†Waltzes (14), complete
US: RCA LSC 2726
GB: RCA SB/RB 6600

†Liszt: Piano Concerto No. 1, E flat major

Grieg: Piano Concerto, A minor, Op. 16
(RCA Symphony, A. Wallenstein)
US: RCA LM 2087*/LSC 2429
GB: RCA SB 2112/RB 16141*

†Falla: Nights in the Gardens of Spain
(San Francisco Symphony Orchestra)

Rachmaninoff: Rhapsody on a Theme of Paganini, Op. 46
(Chicago Symphony. Reiner)
US: RCA LSC 2430/LM 2087*
GB: RB 16141*/SB2144

Mozart: Concerto for Piano and Orchestra No. 23, A major K488

—Concerto for Piano and Orchestra No. 21, C major K467
(RCA Victor Symphony Orchestra, Alfred Wallenstein)
US: RCA LSC 2634
GB: RCA RB/SB 6532*

—†Concerto for Piano and Orchestra No. 17, G major K453
(RCA Victor Symphony, Wallenstein)
US: RCA LSC 2636
GB: RCA RB/SB 6578

†Concerto for Piano and Orchestra No. 20, D minor K466
(RCA Victor Symphony, Wallenstein)
US: RCA LSC 2635
GB: RCA RB/SB 6570*

—Concerto for Piano and Orchestra No. 24, C minor K491
—Rondo in A minor K511
(Symphony of the Air, Josef Krips
US: RCA LSC2461
GB: RCA SB 2117*/RB 16248*

†Liszt: Piano Sonata, B minor

†Schubert: Wanderer Fantasia
US: RCA LSC 2871
GB: RCA SB 6667

†Schumann: Piano Concerto, A minor, Op. 54
Noveletten
(Concerto with Chicago Symphony Orchestra, Giulini)
US: RCA LSC 2997
GB: RCA SB 6747

Rubinstein at Carnegie Hall
Debussy: La Cathédrale engloutie; Poissons d'or; Hommage à Rameau; Ondine.

Szymanowski: Four Mazurkas, Op. 50

Prokofiev: 12 Visions fugitives, from Op. 22

Villa-Lobos: Próle do Bébe
US: RCA LSC 2605
GB: RCA RB/SB 6504*

Recordings for the chapter 'Wilhelm Backhaus' Page 49 ff.

WILHELM BACKHAUS

Beethoven: Piano Concertos 1–5, complete
(Vienna Philharmonic, Hans Schmidt-Isserstedt)
Germany Decca LXT/SXL 20022/1–4
US: London set OSA 2401

—Concertos 1 and 2
GB: Decca LXT 5552/SXL 2178

—Concerto No. 3 (& Sonata Op. 27–2)
GB: Decca SXL 2190

—Concerto No. 4
GB: Decca LXT 5482/SXL 2010

—Concerto No. 5
GB: Decca LXT 5553/SXL 2179

—Sonata Op. 13 (Pathétique)
Sonata Op. 14 No. 1; Sonata Op. 28 (Pastoral)
GB: Decca LXT 2903

—Sonatas Op. 27 Nos. 1, 2 (Moonlight)
Sonatas Op. 49 Nos. 1, 2
GB: Decca LXT 2780

—Sonata Op. 53 (Waldstein)
Sonata Op. 57 (Appassionata)
GB: Decca LXT 5596/SXL 2241

—Sonata Op. 2 No. 1
Sonatas Op. 10 No. 1, 2, 3
GB: Decca LXT/SXL 6097
US: London 6389

—Sonatas Op. 14 No. 2, 54, 78
GB: Decca LXT 2931

—Sonata Op. 2, No. 2, A major
Sonata Op. 14, No. 2, G major
Sonata Op. 49, No. 1, G minor
†GB: Decca LXT/SXL 6359

—Sonata Op. 14, No. 1, E major
Sonata Op. 22, B flat major
Sonata Op. 49, No. 2, G major
†GB: Decca LXT/SXL 6358

—Sonata Op. 2, No. 1, F minor

—Sonata Op. 81a (Les Adieux)
Sonata Op. 90, E minor
GB: Decca LXT 2902
(US: London CS 6247, containing Opp. 71a, 28)

—†Sonata Op. 31, No. 1, G major
Sonata Op. 54, F major
Sonata Op. 90, E minor
GB: Decca SXL 6417

—†Sonata Op. 2, No. 3, C major
Sonata Op. 27, No. 1, E flat major
Sonata Op. 78, F sharp major
US: London CS 6638
GB: Decca SXL 6416

—Sonata Op. 101, A major
Sonata Op. 31, No. 2, D minor
Germany Decca BLK/SXL 21064
US: London CS 6365

—Sonata Op. 106 (Hammerklavier)
GB: Decca LXT 2777
US: London LL 602*

—Sonata Op. 109, E major
GB: Decca LXT 2535

—Sonata Op. 110, A flat major
Sonata Op. 111, C minor
†GB: Decca LXT 2939*
US: London LL 953*

—Sonata Op. 7, E flat major
Sonata Op. 79, G major
Sonata Op. 110, A flat major
GB: Decca LXT/SXL 6300
US: London CS 6535

—Thirty-Three Variations on a Waltz by Diabelli, Op. 120
GB: Decca LXT 6014*
US: London LL 1182*

Brahms: Piano Concerto in D minor, Op. 15
(Vienna Philharmonic, Karl Böhm)
GB: Decca LXT 5364*
US: London CM 9079*

—Concerto for Piano and Orchestra No. 2, B flat, Op. 83
(Vienna Philharmonic, Carl Schuricht)
GB: Decca LXT 5365*
US: London LL 628*

—†(Vienna Philharmonic Karl Böhm)
GB: Decca LXT/SXL 6322
US: London CS 6550

Chopin: Sonata, B flat minor, Op. 35
GB: LXT 2535
*William Backhaus plays Piano Music
from the Romantics*

Schubert: Valses Nobles, Op. 77;
Impromptu B flat major, Op. 142
No. 3
GB: Decca CEP 641/SEC 5051*

Mendelssohn: Rondo Capriccioso,
Op. 14; Three 'Songs Without
Words'
A major, Op. 62, No. 6; in G
major, Op. 62, No. 1; Op. 67, No. 4
GB: Decca CEP 640/SEC 5050*
(the GB issues are 45 rpm; on LP.,
Germany: Decca BLK 21053

Brahms: Ballade, G minor, Op. 118,
No. 3
Intermezzo, E flat, Op. 117, No. 1
Rhapsody, B minor, Op. 79, No. 1
Three Intermezzi: Op. 116, No. 6,
E flat
Op. 119, No. 2, E minor
Op. 119, No. 3, C major
GB: Decca LXT 5308*/SXL 2222*
US: London CM 9187; CS 6021*

Mozart: †Sonata, E flat major, K.282
—Sonata, G major, K. 283
—Sonata, C major, K. 330
—Sonata, F major, K. 332
—Rondo, A minor, K. 511
US: London CS 6534
GB: Decca SXL 6301

—Concerto No. 27, B flat major,
K. 595
(Vienna Philharmonic Orchestra
Böhm)
—Sonata, A major, K. 331
US: London STS 15062
GB: Decca SDD116

Haydn: †Sonata, No. 34, E minor
—Sonata, No. 48, C major
—Sonata, No. 52, E flat major
—Fantasia, C major

—Variations, F minor
US: London STS 15041
GB: Decca LXT 5457

**Recordings for the chapter 'Vladimir
Horowitz' Page 59 ff.**

VLADIMIR HOROWITZ

Beethoven: Piano Concerto No. 5,
E flat, Op. 73
(RCA Victor Symphony Orchestra,
Fritz Reiner)
GB: RCA RB 16114*
US: RCA LM 1718

—Sonata No. 14, C sharp minor,
Op. 27 No. 2 (Moonlight Sonata)
No. 21, C major, Op. 53 (Wald-
stein)
GB: RCA RB 16010*
US: RCA LM 2009

—Sonata, F minor, Op. 57 (Appas-
sionata)
—Sonata No. 7, D major, Op. 10,
No. 3.
GB: RCA RB 16230; SB 2102*
US: RCA LM/LSC 2366

Brahms: Concerto No. 2, B flat
major, Op. 83
(NBC Symphony Orchestra, Arturo
Toscanini)
France HMV FSLP 5001*
US: RCA Victor LCT 1025

Chopin: Andante Spianato and
Grande Polonaise brillante, E flat
major, Op. 22
—Nocturne No. 15, F minor Op. 55
No. 1
—Scherzo No. 1, B minor, Op. 20
GB: HMV BLP 1079*

—Scherzo No. 2, B flat minor, Op. 31
—Nocturne No. 3, B major, Op. 9,
No. 3
—Nocturne No. 4, F major, Op. 15,.
No. 1

204

—Nocturne No. 7, C sharp minor, Op. 27, No. 1
—Nocturne No. 2, E flat major, Op. 9, No. 2
—Barcarolle, F sharp minor, Op. 60
—Scherzo No. 3, C sharp minor, Op. 39

GB: RCA RB 16064*
US: RCA LM 2137

Clementi: Sonata, G minor, Op. 34, No. 2
Sonata, F minor, Op. 14, No. 3
Sonata, F sharp minor, Op. 26, No. 2

US: RCA LM 1902

Moussorgsky: Pictures from an Exhibition

GB: RCA 16194*
US: RCA LM 2357

Mendelssohn: Variations Sérieuses, Op. 54

US: RCA LVT 1043

Horowitz: Variations on Mendelssohn's Wedding March, after Liszt; Rakoczy March, after Liszt's Hungarian Rhapsody No. 15
Liszt: Funérailles; Valse Oubliée, No. 1; Sonetto del Petrarca 104

GB: HMV BLP 1048*
US: RCA LVT 1043

Rachmaninoff: Piano Concerto No. 3, D minor, Op. 30
(RCA Victor Symphony Orchestra, Fritz Reiner)

GB: HMV ALP 1017*
US: RCA LM 1178

Scarlatti: 12 Sonatas
US: Columbia ML 6058/MS 6658
GB: CBS SBRG 77274*

Tchaikovsky: Concerto No. 1, B flat minor, Op. 23
(NBC Symphony Orchestra, Arturo Toscanini)

US: RCA LM 2319
GB: RB 16190*

Schumann: Variations on a Theme by Clara Wieck (Third movement of the Piano Sonata in F minor, Op. 14)

Scarlatti: Sonata in E major
Chopin: Mazurka, B flat minor, Op. 24, No. 4
Polonaise No. 7, A flat major, Op. 61 (Polonaise-Fantasie)
Haydn: Sonata No. 52, E flat major
Brahms: Intermezzo No. 10, B flat minor, Op. 117, No. 2
Moszkowski: Etincelles
Scriabin: Prelude, D major, Op. 11, No. 5 – Prelude, C sharp minor, Op. 21
Sousa: Stars and Stripes Forever (arranged Horowitz)

GB: RCA RB 16019*
US: RCA LM 1957

Bach: Choral Prelude for Organ (arranged Busoni) 'Good Christians Rejoice'
Scarlatti: Andante mosso from Sonata in B minor – Presto from Sonata in G major
Beethoven: 32 variations in C minor
Chopin: Study, C sharp minor, Op. 10, No. 4
Study, G flat major, Op. 10, No. 5
Mazurka, F minor, Op. 7, No. 3
Mazurka, E minor, Op. 41, No. 2
Mazurka, C sharp minor, Op. 50, No. 3
Scherzo No. 4, E major, Op. 54
Debussy: Étude No. 11 'pour les arpèges composés'
Poulenc: Pastourelle – Toccata

GB: HMV COLH 300*
US: Angel COLH 300

Chopin: Sonata No. 2, B flat minor, Op 35
Barber: Piano Sonata
Rachmaninoff: Étude Tableau, C major, Op. 33, No. 2
Étude Tableau, E flat minor, Op. 39, No. 5
Schumann: Arabesque, Op. 18
Liszt: Hungarian Rhapsody No. 19 (trans. by Vladimir Horowitz)

GB: CBS SBRG 72067
US: Columbia KL 5771/KS 6371

Liszt: Sonata, B minor; Funérailles
Schumann: Toccata; Arabesque; Night Dreams; Presto appassionato
> GB: HMV COLH 72*
> US: Angel COLH 72

Czerny: Variations on La Ricordanza, Op. 33
Mozart: Sonata No. 12, F Major, K332
Clementi: Sonata, Op. 47, No. 2, B flat major (Rondo only)
Schumann: Sonata No. 3, F minor, Op. 14 (3rd movement only) Träumerei
Mendelssohn: Songs without words, Nos. 36, 41, 46
Chopin: Andante spianato ⎱ Op. 22
Grand Polonaise ⎰
> GB: RCA RB 6554

Scriabin: Sonata No. 9, F major, Op. 68
Barber: Sonata, Op. 26
Prokofiev: Sonata, No. 7, B flat major, Op. 83
Moszkowski: Étude, A flat major, Op. 72, No. 11
Saint-Saëns (arranged Liszt-Horowitz): Danse macabre
> GB: RCA RB 6555
(The above two records form 'The Horowitz collection' –
> USA: RCA set LM 7021)

Kabalevsky: Sonata No. 3, F major, Op. 46
Tchaikovsky: Dumka, Op. 59
D. Scarlatti: Sonata (capriccio) L. 375
Chopin: Mazurka No. 21, C sharp minor, Op. 30, No. 4
—Waltz, No. 7, C sharp minor, Op. 64, No. 2
Paganini-Liszt: Étude No. 2, E flat major
Debussy: Serenade for the doll
Demenyi-Horowitz: Danse excentrique.
Dohnanyi: Capriccio, F Minor, Op. 28, No. 6
> GB: RCA RB 6767
> US: RCA LM 2993

Beethoven: Sonata No. 8, C minor, Op. 31 (Pathétique)
Debussy: Three Preludes (Book 2) – Les Fées sont d'esquises danseuses – Bruyères – General Lavine
Chopin: Study, C Minor (Revolutionary), Op. 10, No. 12
Study, C sharp minor, Op. 25, No. 7
Scherzo, B minor, Op. 20
> GB: CBS SBRG 72180
> US: Columbia ML 5941/MS 6541

Chopin: Sonata No. 2, B flat minor, Op. 35
Ballade, G minor, Op. 23
Nocturne, F sharp major, Op. 15, No. 2
Liszt: Au bord d'une source
Hungarian Rhapsody No. 6, D flat major (Groves No. 94)
> GB: HMV ALP 1087*
> US: RCA LM 1235

Chopin: 7 Mazurkas
Schumann: Kinderszenen Op. 15
> GB: HMV ALP 1069*

Horowitz on Television

Chopin: Ballade No. 1, G minor
—Nocturne No. 15, F minor
—Polonaise No. 5, F sharp minor

D. Scarlatti: Sonatas, L33 and L335
Schumann: Arabesque, C major, Op. 18
Scriabin: Étude, D sharp minor, Op. 8, No. 12
Schumann: Träumerei
Horowitz: Variations on a theme from Carmen
> US: CBS MS 7106
> GB: CBS 72720

Horowitz at Carnegie Hall, May 9, 1965
> US: Columbia Set M2S 328

Bach-Busoni: Organ Toccata and Fugue, C major
Schumann: Fantasy, C major, Op. 17
> GB: CBS SBRG 72376

Scriabin: Sonata No. 9, F major, Op. 68
Poem, F sharp minor, Op. 32, No. 1
Chopin: Mazurka, C sharp minor, Op. 30, No. 4
Étude, F major, Op. 10, No. 8
Ballade, G minor, Op. 23
Debussy: Serenade for the doll (from 'Children's Corner Suite')
Scriabin: Étude, C sharp minor, Op. 2, No. 1
Moszkowski: Étude, A flat major, Op. 72, No. 11
Schumann: Träumerei (from Kinderszenen, Op. 15)
GB: CBS SBRG 72377
Scriabin: Sonata No. 10, Op. 70
Schumann: Blumenstück, D major, Op. 19
Debussy: L'Isle joyeuse
Chopin: Nocturne No. 19, E minor, Op. 72
Mazurka No. 25, B minor, Op. 33, No. 4
Liszt: Vallee d'Obermann
GB: CBS 72794
Mozart: Sonata No. 11, A major, K. 331
Haydn: Sonata No. 23, F major
(The above two records form 'Horowitz in Concert' –
US: CBS set M2S 757)

ALFRED CORTOT

Bach arr. Cortot: Aria, from Concerto 5, F minor, and works by Brahms, Chopin, Purcell, Schubert, Schumann.
GB: HMVALP 1197*
†Ravel: Sonatina
†Debussy: Preludes Nos. 5, 8, 11, 12
and works by Chopin, Schumann, Albeniz.
GB: HMV HQM 1182
A recording exists of player-piano rolls made by Cortot containing works by Saint-Saëns, Fauré, Albeniz, Liszt, Chopin and Schubert
GB: Decca ACL-R 173

Recordings for the chapter 'Wilhelm Kempff' Page 76 ff.

WILHELM KEMPFF

Beethoven: The Five Piano Concertos (Berlin Philharmonic, Ferdinand Leitner)
US: GB, Germany: DG SLPM 138770–3
(Also as separate discs SLPM 138774/7)

—The Complete Piano Sonatas
US, GB, Germany: DG SLPM 138935–45
—Nos. 8, 14, 23 also on SLPM 139300; Nos. 15, 21, 25 on SLPM 139301

—Older recordings, GB and Germany: (*inter alia*)
Nos. 1 and 2: DG LPM 18105*
Nos. 5 and 6: DG LPM 18106*
Nos. 15 and 16: DG LPM 18055*
Nos. 21 and 22: DG LPM 18089*

—Piano Sonata No. 29, B flat major, Op. 106 (Hammerklavier)
DG: LPM 18146*

—Piano Sonata No. 31, A flat major, Op. 110
Piano Sonata No. 32, C minor, Op. 111
DG: LPM 18045*

Brahms: Intermezzi, Op. 117
—Piano Pieces, Op. 118 and 119
DG: LPM 18093/SLPM 138903

Liszt: Piano Concerto No. 1, E flat major
—Piano Concerto No. 2, A flat major
(London Symphony Orchestra, Fistoulari)
GB: Decca Ace of Clubs ACL 58
US: Richmond 19023*

Mozart: Piano Concerto, E flat major, K. 271

207

—Piano Concerto, B flat major, K. 450
(Stuttgart Chamber Orchestra, K. Münchinger)
GB: Decca LXT 2861*
US: London LL 998*

—†Piano Concerto, A major, K. 488
Piano Concerto, C minor, K. 491
(Bamberg Symphony Orchestra, Leitner)
GB, US, Germany: DG SLPM 138645

—†Piano Concerto, C major, K 246
Piano Concerto, B flat major K 595
(Berlin Philharmonic, Leitner)
GB, US, Germany: DG SLPM 138812
(K 595 also on DG 135137, reverse not Kempff)

—Sonata, A major, K 331
—Sonata, A minor, K 310
—Fantasia, D minor, K 397
—Fantasia, C minor, K 475
GB, US, Germany: DG LPM 18707/SLPM 138707*

Schubert: Sonata, A minor, D 845
—†Sonata, G major, D 894
GB, US, Germany: DG SLPM 139104

—Sonata, C major, D 840
—Sonata, A major, D 664
—Allegretto, C minor, D 915
†GB, US, Germany: DG SLPM 139322

—Sonata, B flat major, D 960
—Scherzo, B flat major, D 593
†GB, US, Germany: DG SLPM 139323

Schumann: Symphonic Studies, Op. 13
—Kreisleriana, Op. 16
GB, Germany: Heliodor 478432*

—Papillons, Op. 2; Davidsbündlertänze, Op. 6
GB, Germany: DG SLPM 139316

Schumann: Fantasia, C major, Op. 17
Brahms: Variations and Fugue on a Theme of Handel, Op. 24
GB, Germany: DG LPM 18461*

Recordings for the chapter 'Claudio Arrau' Page 86 ff.

CLAUDIO ARRAU

Beethoven: †The Five Piano Concertos complete
(Amsterdam Concertgebouw, Haitink)
Germany: Philips set C71 AX 501
US: Philips set PHS 5–970
—separately:
No. 1 (with Sonata No. 6)
GB: Philips SAL 3712
US, Germany: Philips 839749 LY
No. 2 (with Sonata No. 1)
GB: Philips SAL 3714
Germany: Philips 839751 LY
No. 3
GB: Philips SAL 3735
Germany: Philips 835283 DXY
No. 4
GB: Philips SAL 3736
Germany: Philips 835284 LY
No. 5
GB: Philips SAL 3835
Germany: Philips 839600 LY
—older versions (Philharmonia, Galliera)
No. 1
GB: Columbia CX 1625*
US: Angel 35723*
No. 2
GB: Columbia CX 1696*
No. 3
GB: Columbia CX 1616*
US: Angel S 35724
No. 4
GB: Columbia CX 1333*
US: Angel 35300*
No. 5
GB: Columbia CX 1563*
US: Angel 35722

Brahms: Piano Concerto No. 1, D minor, Op. 15
(Philharmonia Orchestra, Carlo Maria Giulini)
GB: Columbia 33CX1739/SAX 2387
　　US: Angel 35892/S 35892

Chopin: Impromptu No. 4, C sharp minor, Op. 66
(Fantasie—Impromptu)
—Scherzo No. 1, B minor, Op. 20
—Scherzo No. 2, B flat minor, Op. 31
—Impromptu No. 2, F sharp major, Op. 36
—Barcarolle, F sharp major, Op. 60
—Ballade No. 1, G minor, Op. 23
　　Germany: DG LPEM 19237*
from GB: Brunswick AXTL 1043/4*
　　US: Decca Set DX 130*
—Études, Op. 10
—Allegro de Concert, Op. 46, A major
Études, Op. 25
　　GB: Columbia 33CX1443–4*
　　US: Angel 35413–4

Liszt: †Vallée d'Obermann
Sonetto 104 del Petrarca
Sonetto 123 del Petrarca
Les Jeux d'eaux à la Villa D'Este
Ballade No. 2, B Minor
Valse oubliée No. 1, F sharp major
　　GB: Philips SAL 3783
　　Europe: Philips 802906 LY

Tchaikovsky: Piano Concerto No. 1, B flat minor, Op. 23
(Philharmonia Orchestra, Alceo Galliera)
　　Germany: Electrola SHZE161
　　US: Seraphim S 60020

Grieg: Concerto, A minor, Op. 16
Schumann: Concerto, A minor, Op. 54
(The Philharmonia Orchestra, Alceo Galliera)
　　GB: Columbia 33CX 1531*
　　US: Angel 35561*
—(Amsterdam Concertgebouw, C. von Dohnanyi)
　　GB: Philips SAL 3452
　　US: Philips WSS 9122

ALFRED CORTOT

Schumann: Piano Concerto, A minor, Op. 54
Franck: Variations symphoniques
(London Philharmonic Orchestra, Sir Landon Ronald)
　　GB: HMV COLH 31*

CLARA HASKIL

Schumann: Piano Concerto, A minor, Op. 54
(Hague Philharmonic Orchestra, Willem van Otterloo)
GB: Philips GBR 6504*/GBL 5582*

WALTER GIESEKING

Schumann: Piano Concerto, A minor, Op. 54
(Philharmonia Orchestra, Herbert von Karajan)
　　GB: 33C 1033*
　　US: Angel 35321*

Recordings for the chapter 'Clifford Curzon and Paul Baumgartner' Page 95 ff.

CLIFFORD CURZON

Brahms: Piano Concerto No. 1, D minor, Op. 15
(London Symphony Orchestra, G. Szell)
　　GB: Decca LXT/SXL 6023
　　US: London CS 6329
†(Amsterdam Concertgebouw, van Beinum)
　　GB: Decca Ace of Clubs ACL277
　　US: London LL 850*
—Piano Concerto No. 2, B flat major, Op. 83
(Vienna Philharmonic, H. Knappertsbusch)
GB: Decca Ace of Clubs ACL 320
—Sonata, F minor, Op. 5
　　Germany: Eurodisc 70370 KK/
　　　　70371 KK*

o

209

—Sonata, F minor, Op. 5
Intermezzo, G major, Op. 119, No. 3
Intermezzo, E flat major, Op. 117, No. 1
    GB: Decca LXT/SXL 6041
    US: London CS 6341

—Quintet, F minor, Op. 34
(The Budapest String Quartet)
    US: Odyssey 321.60173

—Quartet, A major, Op. 26
(Budapest Quartet Members)
    US: Columbia   ML 4630*

Schubert: Impromptus Op. 142
    GB: Decca LXT 2781*
    US: London LL 720*

—†Piano Quintet, A Major, 'Trout'
(Vienna Octet Members)
GB: Decca Ace of Diamonds ADD/
                SDD 185
    US: London CS 6090

—†Piano Sonata, D major, Op. 53, D 850
Impromptus, Op. 142, Nos. 3 and 4
    GB: Decca LXT/SXL 6135
    US: London CS 6416

Liszt: Sonata, B minor
Liebestraum, No. 3
Valse Oubliée, No. 1
Gnomenreigen
Berceuse
    GB: Decca LXT SXL 6076
    US: London CS 6371

PAUL BAUMGARTNER

Beethoven: Diabelli Variations, Op. 120
    Germany: DG: LPM 18054*

Recordings for the chapter 'Rudolf Serkin and Solomon'. Page 103 ff.

RUDOLF SERKIN

Beethoven: Sonata No. 14, C sharp minor, Op. 27, No. 2, Moonlight)

—Sonata No. 8, C minor, Op. 13, (Pathétique)
—Sonata No. 23, F minor, Op. 57, (Appassionata)
    GB: CBS SBRG 72148
    US: Columbia MS 6481

—Diabelli Variations, Op. 120
    GB, Holland: Fontana 699024CL*
    US: Columbia ML 5246*

Brahms: Violin Sonata, A major, Op. 100, (Rudolf Serkin and Adolf Busch)
    Germany: Electrola COLH 41*

—Piano Concerto No. 1, D minor, Op. 15
(Philadelphia Orchestra, Eugene Ormandy)
    GB: CBS BRG 72017
    US: Columbia in set D3S–741

†(Cleveland Orchestra, Szell)
    GB: CBS SBRG 72718
    US: Columbia MS 7413

—Piano Concerto No. 2, B flat major, Op. 83.
(Philadelphia Orchestra, Eugene Ormandy)
    GB: CBS BRG 72003
    US: Columbia in set D3S–741

†(Cleveland Orchestra, Szell)
    GB: CBS SBRG 72557
    US: Columbia MS 6967

Mozart: Piano Concerto No. 17, G major, K 453
Piano Concerto No. 25, C major, K 503
(Columbia Symphony Orchestra, George Szell)
GB, Holland: Fontana 699011 CL*
    US: Columbia ML 5169*

Schubert: Moments Musicaux, Op. 94
—Sonata, C major (D 840)
    Holland: Fontana 699013 CL*

FOU TS'ONG

Mozart: Piano Concerto No. 25,
C major, K 503
—Piano Concerto No. 27, B flat
major, K 595
(Vienna State Opera Orchestra,
Desarzens)
US: Westminster XWN 18955*
Germany: Heliodor 478183*

—†Piano Concerto No. 9, E flat
major, K 271
Piano Concerto No. 12, A major,
K 414
(Vienna Radio Symphony, Brian
Priestman)
GB: Music for Pleasure SMFP 2105
US: Music Guild S 859

SOLOMON

Brahms: Piano Concerto No. 2, B flat
major, Op. 83
(Philharmonia Orchestra, Dobrowen)
GB: XLP 30093

†**Mozart:** Sonata, A major, K 331
†**Schubert:** Sonata, A major, D 664
†**Haydn:** Sonata No. 35, C major
GB: XLP 30053

Beethoven: Sonata, E flat major, Op.
27, No. 1
—Sonata, A flat major, Op. 110
GB: HMV ALP 1900*

—Sonata, C sharp minor, Op. 27,
No. 2 (Moonlight)
Sonata, E flat major, Op. 81a (Les
Adieux)
GB: HMV BLP 1051*

—Sonata, B flat major, Op. 106
(Hammerklavier)
GB: HMV XLP 30116

—†Sonata, C major, Op. 53 (Waldstein)
Schumann: Carnaval, Op. 9
GB: HMV HQM 1077

†**Beethoven:** Piano Concerto No. 1,
C major, Op. 15
Piano Concerto No. 2, B flat major,
Op. 19
(Philharmonia Orchestra, H. Menges)
GB: Music for Pleasure MFP 2067
US: Seraphim S 60016 (No. 1
only, with Sonata Op. 90)
Schubert: Sonata, A major, D.664
Sonata, A minor, D.784
GB: HMV ALP 1901*

Grieg: Piano Concerto, A minor
Schumann: Piano Concerto, A minor
(Philharmonia Orchestra, H.
Menges)
GB: HMV ALP 1643/ASD 272*
US: Pickwick S 4034

Recordings for the chapter 'Sviatoslav Richter'. Page 111 ff.

SVIATOSLAV RICHTER

Beethoven: Rondo for Piano and
Orchestra, B flat major, Op. posth.
—Piano Concerto No. 3, C minor,
Op. 37
(Vienna Symphony, Kurt Sanderling)
US, GB: DG LPM 18848*/
SLPM 138848

*'Sviatoslav Richter at Carnegie Hall',
October 19th 1960*

Beethoven: Programme

—Sonata No. 3 in C, Op. 2, No. 3
Sonata No. 9 in E, Op. 14, No. 1
Sonata No. 22 in F, Op. 54
Sonata No. 12, A flat, Op. 26
—Sonata No. 23, F minor, Op. 57
(Appassionata)
GB: CBS BRG 72022–3*
US: Columbia Set M2L 272*
—†Sonata No. 9, E major, Op. 14
No. 1
Sonata No. 10, G major, Op. 14,
No. 2
GB: Philips SFM 23015
US: Philips 900077

—†Sonata No. 11, B flat major, Op. 22
Sonata No. 19, G minor, Op. 49, No. 1
Sonata No. 20, G major, Op. 49, No. 2
GB: Philips SFM 23014
US: Philips 900076

—Sonata No. 23, F minor, Op. 57 (Appassionata)
Sonata No. 12, A flat major
GB, US: RCA VICS 1427

Brahms: Quintet for Piano, two Violins, Viola and Cello, F minor, Op. 34
(S. Richter – piano)
(R. Dubinsky – 1st violin)
(Ya. Alexandrov – 2nd violin)
(D. Shebalin – viola)
(V. Berlinsky – cello)
USSR, D 05576–05577

Liszt: Piano Concerto No. 1, E flat major
Piano Concerto No. 2, A major
(London Symphony Orchestra, Kyril Kondrashin)
GB: Philips ABL 3401/SABL 207
US: Philips 900000

Prokofiev: Piano Concerto No. 1, D flat major, Op. 10
(Czech Philharmonic Orchestra, Karel Ančerl)
GB, Czech: Supraphon SUA 10264
(Moscow Youth Orchestra, Kondrashin)
GB: Saga XID 5160
US: Period SPL 599*
(Moscow State Philharmonic, Kondrashin)
Germany: Eurodisc 74807 KK
US: Bruno BR 14042
USSR: D 09897–8

Rachmaninoff: Piano Concerto No. 1, F sharp minor
(Moscow Radio Symphony Orchestra, Kurt Sanderling)
Germany: Eurodisc 74807 KK
US: Bruno BR 14025
USSR: D 09897–8

Schubert: Sonata, A minor, Op. 42, D 845
—Impromptu, A flat major, Op. 90, No. 2
USSR D 04594–5
US: Monitor 2027
—Piano Sonata, D major, Op. 53, D 850
USSR D 03638–9
US: Monitor 2043

—†Sonata, A major, D 664
—†Wanderer Fantasia
GB: HMV ALP 2011/ASD 561
Germany: Electrola SME 80692
US: Angel S 36150

—Sonata, C major, D 840
4 Ländler (unspecified)
Moment Musical, F minor, D 780, No. 3
Allegretto, C minor, D 915
US: Monitor S 2057

Schumann: Humoreske, B flat major, Op. 20
—Aufschwung, from Fantasiestücke, Op. 12–2
Germany: Decca LW 50090*
—March No. 2, G minor (from 4 Marches, Op. 76)
Waldszenen, Op. 82
Six pieces from Fantasiestücke, Op. 12
Germany, GB: Heliodor 89528*
—Piano Concerto, A minor, Op. 54
(Warsaw Philharmonic, W. Rowicki)
—Intro. and Allegro Appassionato, Op. 92
(Warsaw Philharmonic, Wislocki)
—Novelette, F major, Op. 21, No. 1

—Toccata, C major, Op. 7
US, GB: DG LPM 18897/SLPM
138077

Prokofiev: Sonata No. 9, C Major,
Op. 103
USSR: ND 04448–9

Tchaikovsky: Sonata, G Major, Op.
37
USSR: D 04558–9
US: Monitor 2064 (both sonatas)

Chopin: Polonaise-Fantasie No. 7,
A flat major, Op. 61
Étude, C major, Op. 10, No. 1
Étude, C minor, Op. 10, No. 12
(Revolutionary)
Ballade No. 4, F minor, Op. 52

Debussy: Estampes
I. Pagodes
II. La Soirée dans Grenade
III. Jardins sous la pluie
Scriabin: Sonata No. 5, F sharp
major, Op. 53
US, GB: LPM 18849*/SLPM
138849*

Haydn: Sonata No. 44, G minor
Chopin: Ballade No. 3, A flat major,
Op. 47
Debussy: Preludes for Piano
(a) Voiles (No. 2)
(b) Le vent dans la plaine (No. 3)
(c) Les Collines d'Anacapri (No.
5)
Prokofiev: Sonata No. 8, B flat
major, Op. 84
US, GB: DG SLPM 138766/LPM
188766*
Extracts from the above two recitals
GB, Germany: DG 135044

†Bach: Das Wohltemperirte Klavier,
Nos. 1, 4, 5, 6
†Schubert: Allegretto, C minor, D 915
—Ländler, A Major, D 366
†Schumann: Abegg Variations, Op. 1
†Rachmaninoff: Prelude No. 24, D
flat major, Op. 32–12

†Prokofiev: Visions fugitives Op. 22,
Nos. 3, 6, 9
US, GB: DG SLPM 138950

Recordings for the chapter 'Emil
Gilels'. Page 122 ff.

EMIL GILELS

Beethoven: Concerto No. 5, E flat,
Op. 73 (Emperor)
(Philharmonia Orchestra, Leopold
Ludwig)
GB: Columbia 33CX1490/SAX
2252*
US: Angel S 35476
—†Concerto No. 4, G Major, Op. 58
(Philharmonia Orchestra, L. Lud-
wig)
GB: HMV SXLP 30086
US: Angel S 35511

Brahms: Piano Concerto No. 2, B flat
major, Op. 83
(Chicago Symphony Orchestra,
Fritz Reiner)
GB, US: RCA Victrola VICS 1026

Rachmaninoff: Piano Concerto No. 3,
D minor
(Paris Conservatoire Orchestra,
Cluytens)
GB: Columbia 33CX1323*
US: Angel 35230*

Tchaikovsky: Piano Concerto No. 1,
B minor, Op. 23
(Chicago Symphony Orchestra,
Fritz Reiner)
GB, US: RCA Victrola VIC/
VICS 1039

Medtner: Sonata, G minor, Op. 22
Beethoven: Sonata No. 3, C major,
Op. 2, No. 3
USSR D 02305–6
Haydn: Piano Concerto, D major
Mozart: Piano Concerto No. 21,
C major, K 467
(Moscow Chamber Orchestra, R.
Barshai)
USSR. D 05066–7

213

Debussy: Clair de lune
Ravel: Le Tombeau de Couperin
Mozart: Piano Sonata, C minor,
K 457
USSR: D 04046–7

Scarlatti: Sonatas,
B minor
G major
E major
A major
C major
Shostakovich: 3 Preludes and Fugues,
Op. 87
C major
D major
D minor
USSR: ND 02828–9

Mozart: Fantasia, D minor, K 397
Schumann: Arabesques, Op. 18
Schubert: Impromptu, F minor, Op.
142, No. 1
Weinberg: Sonata No. 4, Op. 56
USSR: D 07937–8

†Schubert: Moments musicaux D 780
†Schumann: Nachtstücke, Op. 23
GB: HMV ASD 2483
US: Angel S 40082

Recorded at Recital in Carnegie Hall,
New York, 2nd Feb. 1969
†Bach: Prelude and Fugue, D major
(arr. Busoni)
†Beethoven: Sonata No. 14, C sharp
minor, Op. 27, No. 2
32 Variations, C minor
†Medtner: Sonata Reminiscenza, A
minor, Op. 38, No. 1
GB: HMV ASD 2544

†Bach: Prelude (arr. Siloti)
†Chopin: Étude No. 14, F minor,
Op. 25, No. 2
Étude No. 26, A flat major, Op.
posth.
†Prokofiev: Love for three oranges –
March and scherzo

†Ravel: Jeux d'eaux
Pavane pour une infante défunte
Whole Recital – US: Angel set
SRBO 4110

Recording of a Recital in The Great
Hall of the Moscow Conservatoire,
Oct. 1961:
Chopin: Sonata, B flat minor
Liszt: Sonata, B minor
Schumann: Sonata, F sharp minor,
Op. 11 and works by Bach-Soloti,
Stravinsky and Ravel
USSR: D 011277–80

—Another recording of
Chopin: Sonata, B flat minor
with Shostakovich: Preludes and
Fugues, Op. 87 Nos. 1, 5, 24
GB: Columbia 33CX 1364*
US: Seraphim 60010

Recordings for the chapter 'Benedetti
Michelangeli and Robert Casadesus'.
Page 129 ff.

BENEDETTI MICHELANGELI

Galuppi: Sonata in C major
Scarlatti: Sonata, C minor, L 352
Sonata, C major, L 104
Sonata, A major, L 483
Beethoven: Sonata No. 32, C minor,
Op. 111
GB: Decca LXT/SXL 6181
US: London CS 6446

ELLY NEY

Beethoven: Sonata, No. 32, C minor,
Op. 111
(Two recordings from different
years)
Germany: Electrola E 83014*
(One recording only, Germany:
Somerset 591)

BENEDETTI MICHELANGELI

Ravel: Concerto, G major

214

Rachmaninoff: Concerto No. 4, G minor, Op. 40
(London Philharmonic Orchestra, Ettore Gracis)
GB: HMV ALP 1538/ASD 225
US: Angel S 35567

Brahms: Variations on a theme of Paganini, Op. 35

Bach: Chaconne from Sonata 4, D minor
Italy: VdP QBLP 1044

ROBERT CASADESUS

Beethoven: Sonata, C sharp minor, No. 2, Op. 27
GB: Philips ABE 10043*
US: in Columbia ML 5233*
with Sonatas 23, 24 26

Mozart: Piano Concerto, C minor, K 491
—†Piano Concerto, C major, K 467
(Cleveland Symphony Orchestra, G. Szell)
GB: CBS BRG/SBRG 72234*
US: Columbia MS 6695

Mozart: Sonata, B flat major, K 333

WILHELM KEMPFF

Schubert: Impromptu, G major, Op. 90, No. 3

CLAUDIO ARRAU

Schumann: Aufschwung Op. 12, No. 2
In der Nacht, Op. 12, No. 5

WILHELM BACKHAUS

Beethoven: Sonata No. 14, C sharp minor, Op. 27, No. 2

ALEXANDER BRAILOWSKY

Chopin: Polonaise No. 6, A flat major, Op. 53

BYRON JANIS

Liszt: Hungarian Rhapsody No. 6, D flat major
SPECIAL RECORD in aid of UNO World Refugee Fund

ROBERT CASADESUS

Ravel: Concerto for the left hand
Mozart: Concerto, E flat major for two Pianos, K 365
(Gaby and Robert Casadesus)
(Philadelphia Orchestra, Eugene Ormandy)
GB: CBS BRG/SBRG 72008*
US: Columbia MS 6274

Mozart: Concerto, F major, for three pianos and orchestra, K 242
Bach: Concerto, D minor, for three pianos and orchestra
(Robert, Gaby and Jean Casadesus) (Philadelphia Orchestra, Eugene Ormandy)
—Italian Concerto
GB: CBS BRG/SBRG 72150*
US: Columbia MS 6495
Bach: Concerto, C minor, 2 Pianos
Concerto, C major, 2 Pianos
(Philadelphia Orchestra, Ormandy)
US: Odyssey 321.60382

Debussy: Preludes (Vol. 1)
with Six épigraphes antiques, Piano 4 hands; and En blanc et noir, 2 pianos
(Robert and Gaby Casadesus)
GB, Holland: Philips A 01225L*
& ABL 3081*
US: Columbia ML 4977*

Bartok: Sonata for 2 Pianos and Percussion
Debussy: Duet music (as above)
(Robert and Gaby Casadesus)
GB: CBS BRG/SBRG 72233*
US: Columbia MS 6641
Saint-Saëns: Piano Concerto No. 4, Op. 44
Fauré: Ballade
(New York Philharmonic, L. Bernstein)
Fauré: 3 Preludes Op. 103, Nos. 1, 3 5
GB: CBS BRG/SBRG 72105*
US: Colombia MS 6377

215

MONIQUE HAAS

Debussy: Preludes, Vol. I
　　GB, US, Germany: DG LPM
　　　　　　　　　　18831*
Preludes, Vol. II
　　GB, US, Germany: DG LPM
　　　　　　　　　　18872*

Recordings for the chapter 'Glenn Gould and Friedrich Gulda'. Page 139 ff.

GLENN GOULD

Bach: Partita No. 3, A minor
—Partita No. 4, D major
—Toccata, E minor
　　US: Columbia MS 6498/ML 5898*

—Concerto, F major, (Italian)
—Partita, No. 1, B flat major
—Partita, No. 2, C minor
　　US: Columbia ML 5472/MS 6141

—Partita No. 5, G major
—Partita No. 6, E minor
　　　　GB: Philips ABL 3234*
　　　　US: Columbia ML 5186
(The 6 Partitas also in Columbia
　　　　　　set M2S 693)

—Inventions and Sinfonias
—No. 1, C major,
—No. 2, C minor,
—No. 5, E flat major,
—No. 14, B flat major,
—No. 11, G minor,
—No. 10, G major,
—No. 15, B minor,
—No. 7, E minor,
—No. 6, E major,
—No. 13, A minor,
—No. 12, A major,
—No. 3, D major,
—No. 4, D minor,
—No. 8, F major,
—No. 9, F minor
　　US: Columbia ML 6022/MS 6622
　　(and in set D 3S 754, with Partitas)
—The Goldberg Variations
　　　　　　GB: CBS 72692
　　　　US: Columbia MS 7096

Beethoven: Sonata No. 30, E major, Op. 109
—Sonata No. 31, A flat major, Op. 110
—Sonata No. 32, C Minor, Op. 111
　　US: Columbia ML 5130

—Sonata No. 5, C minor, Op. 10, No. 1
—Sonata No. 6, F major, Op. 10, No. 2
—Sonata No. 7, D major, Op. 10, No. 3
　　　GB: CBS BRG/SBRG 72357
　　　US: Columbia MS 6686

—†Sonata No. 8, C minor, Op. 13
—†Sonata No. 9, E major, Op. 14, No. 1
—†Sonata No. 10, G major, Op. 14, No. 2
　　　US: Columbia MS 6945

—†Sonata No. 8, C minor, Op. 13
—†Sonata No. 14, C sharp minor, Op. 27, No. 2
—†Sonata No. 23, F minor, Op. 57
　　　US: Columbia MS 7413
—Piano Concerto No. 3, C Minor, Op. 37
(Columbia Symphony Orchestra, L. Bernstein)
　　　US: Columbia ML 5418

Brahms: Intermezzi
—Intermezzo, E flat major, Op. 117, No. 1
—Intermezzo, B flat minor, Op. 117, No. 2
—Intermezzo, C sharp minor, Op. 117, No. 3
—Intermezzo, E flat minor, Op. 118, No. 6
—Intermezzo, E major, Op. 116, No. 4
—Intermezzo, A minor, Op. 76, No. 7
—Intermezzo, A major, Op. 76, No. 6
—Intermezzo, B minor, Op. 119, No. 1
—Intermezzo, A minor, Op. 118, No. 1

—Intermezzo, A major, Op. 118, No. 2
US: Columbia ML 5637/MS 6237

Beethoven: Piano Concerto No. 1, C major, Op. 15
Bach: Piano Concerto No. 5, F minor
(Columbia Symphony Orchestra, V. Golschmann)
US: Columbia ML 5208/MS 6017*

Beethoven: Piano Concerto No. 2, B flat major, Op. 19
†**Bach:** Concerto No. 1, D minor
(Columbia Symphony Orchestra, L. Bernstein)
US: Columbia ML 5211

†**Beethoven:** Piano Concerto No. 3, C minor, Op. 37
(Columbia Symphony Orchestra, L. Bernstein)
US: Columbia MS 6096*

†**Beethoven:** Piano Concerto No. 4, G major, Op. 58
(New York Philharmonic, Bernstein)
US: Columbia MS 6262*

†**Beethoven:** Piano Concerto No. 5, E flat major, Op. 73
(American Symphony, Stokowski)
US: Columbia MS 6888

R. Strauss: *Enoch Arden*
(Poem by Alfred Lord Tennyson)
(Glenn Gould, Pianist; Claude Rains, Reader)
US: Columbia ML 5741*

Berg: Sonata for Piano, Op. 1
Schoenberg: Three Piano pieces, Op. 11
Krenek: Sonata No. 3 for Piano, Op. 92
US: Columbia ML 5336*

†**Prokofiev:** Sonata No. 7, B flat major, Op. 83
†**Scriabin:** Sonata No. 3, F sharp major, Op. 23
GB: CBS 72776
US: Columbia MS 7173

†**Schoenberg:** Three Piano Pieces, Op. 11
(and Songs, accompanying H. Vanni, D. Gramm and E. Faull)
GB: CBS SBRG 72459

†**Schoenberg:** Piano Pieces, Op. 33a, 33b, 19, 25
GB: CBS SBRG 72460
US: (Together) Set M2S 736

†**Schoenberg:** Piano Concerto, Op. 42
(with Violin Concerto played by I. Baker)
(C.B.C. Symphony Orchestra, R. Craft)
GB: CBS SBRG 72642
US: Columbia MS 7039

FRIEDRICH GULDA

Mozart: Piano Concerto, G major, K 453
Beethoven: Piano Concerto No. 2, B flat major, Op. 19
(Friedrich Gulda and Orchestra, Paul Angerer)
US: Vanguard VRS 1080/2016*
Germany, Austria: Amadeo AVRS 130014

Mozart: Quintet, E flat major, K 452
Beethoven: Quintet, E flat major, Op. 16
(Piano and wind instruments)
(Vienna Philharmonic Wind Ensemble)
GB, US, Germany: DG LPM 18638/SLPM 138638

Mozart: Piano Concerto No. 14, E flat major, K 449
R. Strauss: Burleske, D minor
(London Symphony Orchestra, Anthony Collins)
GB: Decca LXT 5013*
US: London LL 1158*

†**Beethoven:** Complete Piano Sonatas
Europe: Amadeo ASY 906434-44
US: Musical Heritage Society OR B-116-126

Recordings for the chapter 'Geza Anda, Byron Janis, Van Cliburn'. Page 158 ff.

GEZA ANDA

Beethoven: Diabelli Variations Op. 120
    GB, US: DG LPM 18713/SLPM 138713

Brahms: Sonata, F minor, Op. 5
—Intermezzi, Op. 117, Nos. 1–3
    GB: Columbia 33CX 1624*
    US: Angel 35420*

Chopin: Études, Op. 25
—Ballade, G minor, Op. 23
    GB: Columbia 33CX 1459*

Liszt: Sonata, B minor
Mephisto Waltz No. 2
Étude de Concert No. 3, D flat major
La Campanella (arr. Busoni)
    GB: Columbia 33CX 1202*
    US: Angel 35127*

Mozart: Piano Concerto No. 6, B flat major, K 238
—Piano Concerto No. 22, E flat major, K 482
    GB, US: DG LPM 18824/SLPM 138824
—Piano Concerto, No. 17, G major, K 453
—Piano Concerto, No. 21, C major, K 467
    GB, US: DG LPM 18783/SLPM 138783
—Piano Concerto No. 16, D major, K 451
—Piano Concerto No. 23, A major, K 488
    GB, US: DG LPM 18870/SLPM 138870
—†Piano Concerto No. 8, C major, K 246
—†Piano Concerto No. 25, C major, K 503
    GB, US: DG SLPM 139384

—†Piano Concerto No. 12, A major, K 414
—†Piano Concerto No. 26, D major, K 537
    GB, US: DG SLPM 139113

—†Piano Concerto No. 13, C major, K 415
—†Piano Concerto No. 19, F major, K 459
    GB, US: DG SLPM 139319
—†Piano Concerto No. 14, E flat major, K 449
—†Piano Concerto No. 24, C minor, K 491
    GB, US: DG SLPM 139196
(Directing the Salzburg Mozarteum Camerata Accademica from the keyboard, in all the above concertos)

Schubert: Sonata, B flat major, Op. posth. D 960
GB, US: DG LPM 18880 SLPM 138880*

†**Schumann:** Davidsbündlertänze, Op. 6
Kreisleriana, Op. 16
    GB, US: DG SLPM 139199

†**Schumann:** Piano Concerto, A minor Op. 54
†**Grieg:** Piano Concerto, A minor, Op. 16
(Berlin Philharmonic, Kubelik)
    GB, US, Germany: DG SLPM 138888

BYRON JANIS

Tchaikovsky: Piano Concerto No. 1, B minor
(London Symphony, Menges)
Rachmaninoff: Piano Concerto No. 2, C minor, Op. 18
(Minneapolis Symphony, Antal Dorati)
    GB: Philips AL/SAL 3496*
    US: Mercury SR 90448
    Europe: Philips 838412 LY

Liszt: Totentanz
Rachmaninoff: Concerto No. 1, F
sharp minor
(Chicago Symphony Orchestra,
Fritz Reiner)
      GB: RCA RB 16071*
      US: RCA LSC 2541*
—Totentanz only
  GB, US: Victrola VIC/VICS 1205
—Concerto only
  GB, US: Victrola VIC/VICS 1101

Rachmaninoff: Concerto No. 3, D
minor
(London Symphony Orchestra,
Antal Dorati)
      GB: Mercury MMA 11162*
      US: Mercury SR 90283
(Boston Symphony, Charles
Munch)
      GB, US: RCA Victrola VICS
            1032*

†**Chopin:** Sonata No. 2, B flat minor,
Op. 35
—Impromptu No. 1, A flat major,
Op. 29
—Nocturne No. 8, D flat major,
Op. 27, No. 2
—Étude No. 5, G flat major, Op. 10,
No. 5
—Mazurka No. 45, A minor, Op. 67,
No. 4
—Scherzo No. 3, C sharp minor, Op.
39
      GB: RCA RB 16028*
      US: RCA LM 2091*

†**Liszt:** Piano Concerto No. 1, E flat
major
(Moscow Philharmonic, Kondrashin)
†**Liszt:** Piano Concerto No. 2, A
major
(Moscow Radio Orchestra, Rozh-
destvensky)
  GB: Philips Festivo SFM 23004

VAN CLIBURN

Brahms: Concerto No. 2, B flat
major, Op. 83
(Chicago Symphony Orchestra,
Fritz Reiner)
      GB: RCA RB/SB 6545*
      US: RCA LM/LSC 2581

†**Chopin:** Concerto No. 1, E minor,
Op. 11
(Philadelphia Orchestra, Orman-
dy)
      GB: RCA SB 6837
      US: RCA LSC 3147

Schumann: Piano Concerto, A minor,
Op. 54
(Chicago Symphony Orchestra,
Fritz Reiner)
      GB: RCA RA 13002/SRA 6001*
      US: RCA LM/LSC 2455

Prokofiev: Piano Concerto No. 3, C
major, Op. 26
MacDowell: Piano Concerto, D
minor, Op. 23
(Chicago Symphony Orchestra
Walter Hendl)
    US: RCA LM 2507*/LSC 2507

**Recordings for the chapter 'Bruno L.
Gelber and Martha Argerich'. Page
168 ff.**

MARTHA ARGERICH

Brahms: Rhapsodies Nos. 1 and 2,
Op. 79
Chopin: Scherzo No. 3, C sharp
minor, Op. 39
Barcarole, Op. 60
Liszt: Hungarian Rhapsody, No. 6
Prokofiev: Toccata Op. 11
Ravel: Jeux d'eau
    GB, US: DG SLPM 138672

†**Chopin:** Sonata, B minor, Op. 58
—Polonaise No. 6, A flat major, Op.
53
—Polonaise No. 7, A flat major, Op.
61

—Mazurkas Nos. 36, 37, 38. Op. 59,
Nos. 1–3
GB, US: DG SLPM 139317

†Chopin: Piano Concerto No. 1, E
minor, Op. 11
†Liszt: Piano Concerto No. 1, E flat
major
(London Symphony Orchestra, Abbado)
GB, US: DG SLPM 139383

†Chopin: Piano Concerto No. 1,
E minor, Op. 11
(Warsaw National Philharmonic,
Rowicki)
—Scherzo, C sharp minor, Op. 39
Mazurkas Op. 59, Nos. 1–3
Poland: Muza XL 0265

†Prokofiev: Piano Concerto No. 3,
C major, Op. 26
†Ravel: Piano Concerto, G major
(Berlin Philharmonic, Abbado)
GB, US: DG SLPM 139349

BRUNO LEONARD GELBER

†Beethoven: Piano Concerto No. 3,
C minor, Op. 37
—Piano Sonata, E flat major, Op. 81a
(Les Adieux)
GB: HMV SXLP 20107
—Concerto only, Germany: Electrola
SME 91667
—Sonatas, Op. 81a and Op. 28
Germany: Columbia SMC 80988
—Piano Concerto No. 5, E flat
major, Op. 73
(New Philharmonia Orchestra,
Leitner)
GB: HMV SXLP 20104
Germany: Columbia SMC 91610

†Brahms: Piano Concerto No. 1,
D minor, Op. 15
(Munich Philharmonic, Franz Paul
Decker)
GB: HMV HQM/HQS 1068
Germany: Columbia SMC91337

†Schumann: Carnaval, Op. 9
—Symphonic Studies, Op. 13
GB: HMV SXLP 20108
Germany: Electrola SME 81065

Recordings for the chapter 'In pursuit of Chopin'. Page 173 ff.

†STEFAN ASKENASE

Chopin: Concertos Nos. 1 and 2
—Krakoviak
—Polonaises Nos. 3 and 6
Germany, GB: DG 2705003

VLADIMIR ASHKENAZY

Chopin: Sonata No. 3, B minor, Op.
58
—Barcarolle, Op. 60
—Valse No. 2, A flat major, Op. 34,
No. 1
—Valse No. 6, D flat major, Op. 64,
No. 1
—Mazurka No. 35, C minor, Op. 56
No. 3
—Mazurka No. 36, A minor, Op. 59
No. 1
GB: Columbia 33CX 1621*
US: Angel 35648*

Chopin: †Études, Op. 10 and Op. 25
†Nocturne No. 3; Ballade No. 2;
and Liszt (in USSR only)
US, Germany: Bruno BR 14052
USSR: D 06307–10

†Chopin: Scherzi Nos. 1–4
—Prelude, C sharp minor, Op. 45
—Barcarolle, F sharp major, Op. 60
GB: Decca LXT/SXL 6334
US: London CS 6562

—Ballades Nos. 1–4
—Études Nos. 25—27
GB: Decca LXT/SXL 6143
US: London CS 6422

—†Concerto No. 2, F Minor, Op. 21
†Bach: Concerto No. 1, E minor
(London Symphony Orchestra,
Zinman)
GB: Decca SXL 6174
US: London CS 6440

220

†**Chopin:** Scherzo No. 4, E major, Op. 54
—Nocturne No. 17, B major, Op. 62 No. 1
†**Debussy:** L'isle joyeuse
†**Ravel:** Gaspard de la nuit
   GB: Decca SXL 6215
   US: London CS 6472

INGRID HAEBLER

Chopin: Nocturnes 1–20
   GB, US: Vox Set VUX 2007*
Schubert: Sonata, G major, Op. 78, D 894
—Sonata, A major, D 664
   GB: Philips SAL 3604
   Europe: Philips 835363 AY
—†Moments Musicaux, Op. 94 (D 780)
Deutsche Tänze, Op. 33 (D 783)
†**Schumann:** Kinderszenen, Op. 15
   GB: Philips SAL 3647
   Europe: Philips 802738LY

ADAM HARASIEWICZ

Chopin: Études, Op. 10 and Op. 25
   Europe: Fontana 698068 CL*
   US: Philips PHC 9115
—†Nocturnes 1–19
   GB: Fontana SFL 14019–20
   Europe: Philips 835218–9 AY

JULIAN VON KAROLYI

Chopin: Ballades 1–4
   GB, Germany: DG LP 16025*
—†Sonata No. 3, B minor, Op. 58
Bolero, C major, Op. 19
Mazurka No. 13, A minor, Op. 17, No. 4
Waltz No. 14, E minor
Andante spianato and Polonaise, Op. 22
   GB, Germany: DG SLPEM 136472*
   and Heliodor 89865

MAURIZIO POLLINI

Chopin: Polonaise No. 5, F sharp minor, Op. 44

—Mazurka No. 32, C sharp minor, Op. 50, No. 3
—Impromptu No. 3, G flat major, Op. 51
—Nocturne No. 3, C minor, Op. 48, No. 1

MICHEL BLOCK

—Prelude No. 17, A flat major
—Polonaise No. 6, A flat major, Op. 53
—Mazurkas Nos. 21, 35, 37
—Valse No. 2, A flat major, Op. 34, No. 1
   GB, Germany: Heliodor 89510*

MAURIZIO POLLINI

—†Polonaises Nos. 5 and 6
Nocturnes Nos. 4, 5, 7, 8
Ballade No. 1
   GB: HMV ASD 2577
—†Concerto No. 1, E minor, Op. 11 (Philharmonia Orchestra, Kletzki)
   GB: HMV ASD 370
   US: Seraphim S60066

Recordings for the chapter 'The Touch for Liszt'. Page 179 ff.

L. BERMAN

Liszt: Études d'execution transcendente
—Hungarian Rhapsody No. 3
—Rapsodie espagnole
   USSR: D 012511–14
Dupont: Fantasia and Fugue, C major
Jongen: Campeador
Debussy: Étude No. 6
Ravel: Ondine
Prokofiev: Toccata, Op. 11
   USSR: D 3252–3*
†**Scriabin:** Études, Op. 42
†**Ravel:** Jeux d'eau
†**Liszt:** Funérailles
—Hungarian Rhapsody No. 9
   USSR: D 08677–8

221

GYORGY CZIFFRA

Liszt: Polonaise No. 3, E major
—Sonetto del Petrarca No. 123
—Fantasie and Fugue on B.A.C.H.
—Étude de concert No. 3, Un sospiro
—Tarantella 'Venezia e Napoli'
—Étude de concert No. 2, La Leggierezza.
—Legend No. 2, 'Saint-Francois de Paule marchant sur les eaux'
   GB: Philips SAL 3465*
   US: Philips WS 9005
  Europe: Philips 835.191 LY

—†Mephisto Waltz
Valse oubliée No. 1
Rapsodie espagnole
Valse impromptu
Grand galop chromatique
Gnomenreigen
Paraphrase on Eugene Onegin
Années de Pélerinage III, No. 4
   GB: ALP 1534*
   US: Angel 35528*

WALTER GIESEKING

Liszt: Concerto No. 1, E flat major
(London Philharmonic Orchestra, Henry J. Wood)
GB: Columbia LX 181–2, 78 rpm.

LUDWIG HOFFMANN

Liszt: Six Paganini Studies
—Rigoletto Paraphrase
—Liebestraum No. 3
—Two Legends
 Germany: Telefunken TW 30219/
     30229*
  GB: Telefunken GMA 61*

CHARLES ROSEN

Liszt: Don Juan Fantasia
—Sonetto del Petrarca No. 104
—Hungarian Rhapsody No. 10
Bartók: Op. 18 and Op. 20
 GB: Columbia CX 1909/SAX 2551*
  US: Epic LC 3878/BC 1278*

†**Chopin:** Concerto No. 2, F minor, Op. 21

†**Liszt:** Concerto No. 1, E flat major
(New Philharmonia, J. Pritchard)
   GB: CBS 61094
   US: Epic BC 1320*

SHURA CHERKASSKY

Liszt: Don Juan Fantasia
Sonata, B minor
   GB: HMV ALP 1154*
—†Grand galop chromatique
Schubert: Sonata, A major, D 959
Schumann: Fantasiestücke, Op. 111
 GB: World Record Club T 58

LUDWIG HOFFMANN

Tchaikovsky: Piano Concerto No. 1, B minor, Op. 23
(London Philharmonic Orchestra, Gunnar Staern)
  GB: Marble Arch MAL 554*
  US: Stereo Fidelity 14900
(Philharmonia Hungarica, Caridis)
(and 2 Legends)
 †GB: Marble Arch MAL 715
  Germany: Somerset 612

JOHN OGDON: 'A Recital by John Ogdon.'

Bach: Prelude and Fugue No. 5, D major
Mozart: Fantasia, D minor, K 397
Beethoven: Andante favori, F major
Chopin: Scherzo No. 3, C sharp minor, Op. 39
—Mazurka No. 17, B flat minor, Op. 24, No. 1
Schumann: Nachtstück, F major, Op. 23, No. 4
Debussy: Clair de lune
—Danse de Puck
—La fille aux cheveux de lin
Liszt arr. Busoni: La Campanella
 GB: HMV ALP 1995*/ASD 546
Liszt:†Reminiscences de Don Juan
—Reminiscences de Boccanegra
—Csardas macabre
—En rêve
—Trauervorspiel and Trauermarsch

—Mephisto waltz No. 3
GB: HMV ASD 2283
US: Seraphim S 60088
(content varies)
—†La Campanella (arr. Busoni)
—Hungarian Rhapsody No. 15
—Polonaise No. 2
—Un suspiro
—Liebesträume Nos. 1 and 3
—Valse oubliée No. 1
—Funérailles
—Waldesrauschen
—Gnomenreigen
GB: HMV ASD 2416

—†Concerto No. 1, E flat major
(USSR State Symphony, Dubrovsky)
Ravel: Ondine
Busoni: Intermezzo
Liszt: Mephisto Waltz
Valse oubliée No. 1
USSR: D 010339-40
Liszt: Hungarian Fantasia
—Rapsodie Espagnole (arr. Busoni)
(The Philharmonia Orchestra,
John Pritchard)
—Sonata, B minor
GB: ALP 2051/ASD 600*

VARIOUS ARTISTS

—10 Hungarian Rhapsodies recorded
by Agnes Katona, Ernö Szegedi,
Gábor Gábos, István Antal, Lajos
Hernádi, Tibor Wehner
Hungary: Qualiton MMX 1101–
1106

**Recordings for the chapter 'Between
Intellectuality and Spontaneity'. Page
188 ff.**

CHARLES ROSEN

Debussy: Twelve Études
GB: Columbia CX 1849/SAX
2492*
US: Epic LC 3842/BC 1242*
Schubert: Sonata, A major, Op. Posth.
(D 959)

Mozart: Rondo, A minor, K 511
GB: Columbia CX 1857/SAX2502*
US: Epic LC 3855/BC 1255*
†**Bach:** Kunst der Fuge
Goldberg Variations
Musical offering (excerpts)
GB: CBS set 77309
US: Odyssey set 32360020

JULIUS KATCHEN

Schubert: Wanderer Fantasia, C
major, Op. 15
Schumann: Carnaval, Op. 9
GB: Decca LXT 5439

CHARLES ROSEN

Stravinsky: Serenade in A, for Piano
—Sonata for Piano (1924)
Schoenberg: Klavierstück, Op. 33a
—Klavierstück, Op. 33b
—Suite for Piano, Op. 25
GB: Columbia CX1836/SAX2480*
US: Epic LC 3792/BC 1140*

ALFRED BRENDEL

Beethoven: Sonata for Piano No. 23,
F minor, Op. 57 (Appassionata)
—Sonata for Piano No. 21, C major,
Op. 53 (Waldstein)
GB: Vox GBY/STGBY 12.650*

—†Sonatas 23, 8, 14 US: Vox 514270
—The complete Sonatas are also
available in US in
Vox sets SVBX 5417-20, and in
GB and Europe on Turnabout
individual discs
Schubert: Wanderer Fantasia for
piano solo
Schubert–Liszt: Wanderer Fantasia
for piano and orchestra
(Vienna Volksoper Orchestra,
Michael Gielen)
GB, US: Vox 511610
†**Schubert:** Wanderer Fantasia
8 Impromptus

223

6 Moments musicaux
Various other solo pieces
Sonata (Grand duo) C major, D 812
(with E. Crochet)
  GB, US: Turnabout TV 34141–4

—†Sonata, C major, D 840
—Sonata, C minor, D 958
—16 German dances, D 783
      GB: Vanguard VSL 11066
      US: Vanguard VSD 71157

HANS RICHTER-HAASER

Beethoven: Sonata, C major, Op. 53
(Waldstein)
—Sonata, A major, Op. 101
      Europe: Philips A 00368L*

—†Sonata, Op. 53 (Waldstein)
—†Sonata, F minor, Op. 57 (Appassionata)
—†Sonata, F sharp major, Op. 78
      GB: Philips GL 5683*

—†Sonatas, Op. 57, 13, 27 No. 2
      Europe: Philips A 02017L*

—Concerto, No. 5, E flat major, Op. 73 (Emperor)
(Philharmonia Orchestra, Istvan Kertesz)
Rondo, C major, Op. 51, No. 1
GB: Columbia CX 1775/SAX2422

LEON FLEISHER

Brahms: Variations and Fugue on a
Theme of Handel, Op. 24
—Waltzes Op. 39
      GB: Columbia CX 1839*
      US: Epic LC 3331*

PAUL BADURA-SKODA

Chopin: Sonata No. 2, B flat minor,
Op. 35
—Sonata No. 3, B minor, Op. 58
      US: Westminster XWN 18854
†Beethoven: Piano Sonatas, complete
      GB: Unicorn UNS 211, et seq

INGRID HAEBLER

Mozart: Sonata, E flat major, K 282
—Sonata, C major, K 330
—Sonata, D major, K 576
—Rondo, A minor, K 511
      GB: Philips AL 3531*
      Europe: Philips 835216 AY

—†Sonata, C major, K 279
Sonata, D major, K 284
Sonata, B flat major, K 333
      GB: Philips SAL 3666
      Europe: Philips 802827 LY
—The complete sonatas are available
in Europe
      Philips set C71 AX601

INDEX

227